国家文化产业资金支持媒体融合重大项目

高等职业教育教学改革特色教材·经济贸易类

ZUIXIN WAIMAO
DANZHENG SHIWU

莫运襟 崔蕾 主编

最新外贸单证实务

东北财经大学出版社
Dongbei University of Finance & Economics Press
大连

图书在版编目（CIP）数据

最新外贸单证实务 / 莫运襟，崔蕾主编．—大连 ：东北财经大学出版社，2021.12

（高等职业教育教学改革特色教材・经济贸易类）

ISBN 978-7-5654-4394-7

Ⅰ．最… Ⅱ．①莫… ②崔… Ⅲ．进出口贸易-原始凭证-高等职业教育-教材 Ⅳ．F740.44

中国版本图书馆 CIP 数据核字（2021）第 275500 号

东北财经大学出版社出版

（大连市黑石礁尖山街 217 号　邮政编码　116025）

网　址：http：//www.dufep.cn

读者信箱：dufep@dufe.edu.cn

大连天骄彩色印刷有限公司印刷　东北财经大学出版社发行

幅面尺寸：185mm×260mm　字数：334 千字　印张：12.25

2021 年 12 月第 1 版　2021 年 12 月第 1 次印刷

责任编辑：张晓鹏　宋雪凌　徐　群　责任校对：包丽华　石建华　孙　越

封面设计：冀贵收　版式设计：钟福建

定价：32.00 元

教学支持　售后服务　联系电话：（0411）84710309

如有印装质量问题，请联系营销部：（0411）84710711

富媒体智能型教材出版说明

“财经高等职业教育富媒体智能型教材开发系统工程”入选国家新闻出版署新闻出版改革发展项目库，并获得文化产业专项资金支持，是“国家文化产业资金支持媒体融合重大项目”。项目以“融通”“融合”“共建”“共享”为特色，是东北财经大学出版社积极落实国家推动传统媒体与新媒体融合发展的重要举措之一。

“财济书院”智能教学互动平台是该工程项目建设成果之一。该平台通过系统、合理的架构设计，将教学资源与教学应用集成于一体，具有教学内容多元呈现、课堂教学实时交互、测试考评个性设置、用户学情高效分析等核心功能，是高校开展信息化教学的有力支撑和应用保障。

富媒体智能型教材是该工程项目建设成果之二。该类教材是我社供给侧结构性改革探索性策划的创新型产品，是一种新形态立体化教材。富媒体智能型教材秉持严谨的教学设计思想和先进的教材设计理念，为财经职业教育教与学、课程与教材的融通奠定了基础，较好地避免了传统教学模式和单一纸质教材容易出现的“两张皮”现象，有助于教学质量的提高和教学效果的提升。

从教材资源的呈现形式来说，富媒体智能型教材实现了传统纸质教材与数字技术的融合，通过二维码建立链接，将VR、微课、视频、动画、音频、图文和试题库等富媒体资源丰富呈现给用户；从教材内容的选取整合来说，其实现了职业教育与产业发展的融合，不仅注重专业教学内容与职业能力培养的有效对接，而且很好地解决了部分专业课程学与训、训与评的难题；从教材的教学使用过程来说，其实现了线下自主与线上互动的融合，学生可以在有网络支持的任何地方自主完成预习、巩固、复习等，教师可以在教学中灵活使用随堂点名、作业布置及批改、自测及组卷考试、成绩统计分析等平台辅助教学工具。

富媒体智能型教材设计新颖，一书一码，使用便捷。使用富媒体智能型教材的师生首先下载“财济书院”App或者进入“财济书院”（www.idufep.com）平台完成注册，然后登录“财济书院”输入教材封四学习卡中的激活码建立或找到班级和课程对应教材，就可以开启个性化教与学之旅。

“重塑教学空间，回归教学本源！”“财济书院”平台不仅是出版社提供教学资源和服务的平台，更是出版社为作者和广大院校创设的一个自主选择和自主探究的教与学的空间，作者和广大院校师生既是这个空间的使用者和消费者，也是这个空间的创造者和建设者，在这里，出版社、作者、院校共建资源，共享回报，共创未来。

最后，感谢各位作者为支持项目建设所付出的辛劳和智慧，也欢迎广大院校在教学中积极使用富媒体智能型教材和“财济书院”平台，东北财经大学出版社愿意也必将陪伴广大职业教育工作者走向更加光明而美好的职教发展新阶段。

东北财经大学出版社

前　言

2021年10月12日，中共中央办公厅和国务院办公厅印发了《关于推动现代职业教育高质量发展的意见》，要求普遍开展项目教学、情境教学、模块化教学，培养能工巧匠、大国工匠，为全面建设社会主义现代化国家提供有力的人才和技能支撑。

外贸单证员是高等职业院校国际贸易及商务英语等相关涉外专业所对应的主要工作岗位。外贸单证制作是外贸单证员岗位的核心技能。本书根据外贸单证员岗位的技能要求，以外贸单证员的工作过程为主线，编排典型工作项目和任务，突出学、教、做一体化，强调知识、能力、素质三位一体，打破知识的系统性和连贯性，注重学生动手能力的培养。

本书有两大特色：一是针对外贸单证员工作岗位的工作过程编排典型项目，包括备证、分项制单、综合制单、审单和交单四个项目，顺序明确，条理清晰。二是突出学、教、做的授课环节，合理分配学生的课堂任务，充分调动学生在课堂上的主动性和积极性。每个任务安排有足够的训练，每个项目后面又安排项目训练以巩固所学知识和技能。此外，为配合课堂教学，我们设计制作了教师课件、配套习题（附有参考答案）、课程教学大纲，在书中附有大量的微课视频，以丰富教学手段，提高教学效果，并实现网上运行，充分发挥网络课程资源的作用。需要者可登录东北财经大学出版社“财济书院”（www.idufep.com）下载。

本书既可作为高等职业院校涉外专业外贸单证课程的实务和实训教材，也可作为社会人员学习外贸单证知识的参考书。

本书由莫运襟、崔蕾主编。其具体分工如下：莫运襟编写项目一和项目三的任务一；崔蕾编写项目二的任务一至任务三、项目三的任务二并负责微课录制；赵政旭编写项目二的任务四至任务六；刘海霞编写项目二的任务七、任务八；柳韬略编写项目二的任务九、任务十；吴竑编写项目二的任务十一；黄再平编写项目四的任务一；马志强编写项目四的任务二；马燕编写项目四的任务三。全书最后由莫运襟总纂定稿。

在本书的编写和出版过程中，我们得到了东北财经大学出版社、广州城建职业学院、汕头职业技术学院、广州工程技术职业学院、广西梧州加利进出口贸易有限公司、广州先达国际货运代理公司、中山市益富贸易有限公司等单位的领导、教师、朋友的鼎力支持，在此一并表示深深的感谢！

由于编者水平有限，书中难免有疏漏之处，恳请专家和使用本书的读者多多提出宝贵意见，以便我们进一步修改和完善！

编　者

2021年10月18日

于广州

目 录

项目一 备 证 ……1

能力目标 ……1

知识目标 ……1

思政目标 ……1

项目引例 ……1

任务一 认知外贸单证 ……2

任务二 催证 ……4

任务三 审证 ……7

任务四 改证 ……22

任务五 展证 ……28

综合训练 ……29

项目二 分项制单 ……35

能力目标 ……35

知识目标 ……35

思政目标 ……35

项目引例 ……35

任务一 商业发票 ……36

任务二 包装单 ……46

任务三 订舱单与提单 ……53

任务四 装船通知 ……68

任务五 保险单 ……71

任务六 一般原产地证 ……77

任务七 普惠制原产地证 ……88

任务八 东盟产地证 ……103

任务九 受益人证明 ……117

任务十 船东证明 ……124

任务十一 汇票 ……125

综合训练 ……135

项目三 综合制单 ……139

能力目标 ……139

知识目标 ……139

思政目标 ……139

项目引例 ……139
任务一 信用证项下的综合制单 ……140
任务二 托收和汇付项下综合制单 ……151
综合训练 ……153
项目四 审单和交单 ……172
能力目标 ……172
知识目标 ……172
思政目标 ……172
项目引例 ……172
任务一 审单 ……173
任务二 单据装订 ……174
任务三 交单 ……177
综合训练 ……181
参考文献 ……188

项目一
备 证

能力目标

1. 能用单证基本理论知识指导单证学习和制作；
2. 能用传真、邮件、电话等方式催促客户开出信用证；
3. 能根据贸易合同和国际贸易惯例对国外开来的信用证进行审核；
4. 能根据信用证的审核结果，决定是否修改信用证；
5. 能书写改证及展证函。

知识目标

1. 外贸单证基础理论知识；
2. 催证含义、必要性、途径以及催证函写作；
3. 审核信用证的方法和技巧；
4. 改证与否的依据和理由；
5. 改证及展证函写作。

思政目标

通过对外贸单证基础知识的学习，开启外贸单证岗位的职业认知，培养学生树立正确的人生观和价值观，逐步具备良好的职业素养和职业精神；通过备证的学习和实操，增强学生的职业意识和法律意识。

项目引例

备证失误导致损失

2021年5月，广州A进出口公司与日本B贸易公司订立合同，向后者出售有机化肥1 000吨。合同规定，2021年5月30日前B公司开出信用证，A公司6月3日前装船。5月28日买方开来信用证，有效期至6月10日。由于装船时间太短，故A公司请B公司将装船期延至6月15日，并将信用证有效期延至6月25日，B公司表示同意，但未通知开证行。6月15日货物装船后，A公司到银行议付时，银行以超过有效期为由拒绝付款，从而给A公司造成巨大损失。

引例评析：信用证的使用应遵循《UCP 600》的规定，即信用证一经开出就独立于买卖合同。银行只受信用证条款的约束，而不受买卖合同的约束。虽然合同上的装船期和有效期已改，但信用证条款未改，所以银行只能按照原信用证的有效期处理。本案例告诉我们，贸易双方在签约、履约的过程中，一定要遵守相关的惯例、公约与规则，只有如此，贸易才能顺利进行，社会才能和谐发展。

任务一　认知外贸单证

情境导入

谭雅梅同学是广西梧州某学院2019级国际贸易实务专业的毕业生。她不仅人长得清秀漂亮，活泼可爱，而且学习也很好，大二时就过了CET6，国际贸易基础知识也很牢固。最近她在某外资企业找到了一份外贸单证员的工作，十分高兴，整天又说又笑。她的同学们也着实替她高兴了一番。高兴过后，有人纳闷：什么是外贸单证？

第一步　教师教

微课1-1

外贸单证的含义和种类

一、外贸单证的含义

外贸单证是对外贸易所涉及的单据和证单的总称。

单据指进出口商自己制作签发的各种书面凭据，如发票、包装单、装船通知、受益人证明、寄单证明等。

证单是政府部门或外单位签发的各种证书或单据。如商检部门签发的各种检验证书；商务部门签发的进出口许可证、批文等；运输部门签发的船东证明、提（运）单；邮政部门签发的邮政收据等。

二、外贸单证种类

按照不同的划分标准，外贸单证有不同的分类。

1.从形式上划分

（1）要式单证

要式单证指外单位制作签发、有固定格式、不能由进出口商自己设计、制作和签发的单证，如提单、原产地证书、普惠制产地证书、商检证书、进出口许可证等。

（2）非要式单证

非要式单证指由进出口商自己设计、制作和签发的没有固定格式的单证，如发票、包装单、装运通知、受益人证明等。

2.从本质上划分

（1）基本单证

在各种外贸单据中，商业发票处于核心地位，起关键作用，是基本单证。商业发票指单位或个人在购销商品，提供或接受劳务、服务以及从事其他经营活动时，提供给对方的收付款的书面证明，是财务收支的法定凭证，是会计核算的原始依据，也是审计机关、税务机关执法检查的重要依据。

（2）附属单证

附属单证也称辅助单证，指除商业发票外的其他单证，如提单、包装单、装船通知、保险单、受益人证明、品质证书、数量证书、原产地证书、普惠制产地证书等。在各种外贸单据中，附属单证处于非核心地位，起辅助从属作用。

3.从功能上划分

（1）议付单证

议付单证是为办理议付手续而制作或办理的单证，如发票、提单、包装单、装船通知、保险单、受益人证明、品质证书、数量证书、原产地证书、普惠制产地证书等。议付单证是本教材重点分析、讨论和学习的核心内容。

（2）非议付单证

非议付单证是指不是为了办理议付手续而制作或办理的单证，如订舱单、进出口许可证等。本教材对非议付单证不作深入讨论。

4.从范围上划分

（1）广义的外贸单证

广义的外贸单证是指所有涉及进出口业务的单证，包括出口和进口两个方面。

（2）狭义的外贸单证

狭义的外贸单证仅指出口业务的结汇单证。它是本教材重点讨论和学习的内容。

三、外贸单证制作要求

1.正确无误

正确无误是外贸单证制作的首要要求。只有单证正确，才能保证安全收汇。

（1）错误性质划分

外贸单证的错误，可分为轻微错误和重大错误两类。前者指非关键内容的错误，如标点符号、英文字母等错打或漏打；后者是指关键内容的错误，如货物名称、规格、价格、总值、抬头、落款等错误。

对于轻微单证错误，在市场前景看好、买方又真正需要货物的情况下，一般通过开证行扣除不符点处理费来解决而非拒付货款。一个不符点的处理费用一般是50～60美元或其他等值货币金额。对于重大单证错误，单纯扣钱不能解决问题，很有可能被开证银行拒付货款。不管是轻微错误还是重大错误，都会给出口商的安全收汇带来或大或小的风险，都应尽量避免。

（2）正确性判断依据

单证的正确性判断依据一是“三个一致”，即单证一致、单约一致、单单一致。在信用证结算方式下，要做到单证与信用证规定一致、单证与单证之间一致；在汇付和托收结算方式下，要做到单证与进出口合同规定一致、单证与单证之间一致。这里的“一致”是指单证的表面一致。二是单证必须符合有关国际贸易惯例和进出口国有关法律、法规的要求。这里所说的国际贸易惯例主要指国际商会的《跟单信用证统一惯例》、《托收统一规则》和《国际贸易术语解释通则》。

2.完整无缺

在保证单证正确无误的前提下，还应该做到单证完整无缺。其包括：

（1）内容完整。它指单证内容完整，没有遗漏缺失，信用证或合同规定要显示的内容，一项不少都显示出来。

（2）种类齐全。它指单证种类完整齐全，信用证或合同需要多少种单证，就提供多少种单证，种类上不缺不漏。

（3）份数足够。它指每种单证所需的份数足够，信用证或合同需要多少份单证，要全部提供，正本或副本份数都不能缺少。

3.及时有效

（1）及时制单。在信用证付款方式下，在信用证规定的交单期内，要及时办理和制作好所需的各种有效单证。在汇付和托收方式下，虽没有规定具体交单期限，出口商也要尽早制作好所需的各种单证，以便尽早回笼货款。

（2）及时交单。出口商要将办理或制作好的单证及时提交给议付银行。错过了交单期，会给安全收汇带来风险。及时制单和交单还是讲求经济效益、减少费用支出、降低收汇风险、善于理财的体现。

（3）单证有效。它是指提交给议付银行的单证要真实有效，不能非法伪造、变造外单位的单证。

4.简明扼要

简明扼要是对外贸单证的基本要求。外贸单证上的内容要尽量做到简明扼要，不拖泥带水。无关大体、可有可无的内容要坚决去掉；一定要显示的重要内容要坚决地显示出来，不多不少、恰到好处。例如，不必在包装单上显示货物单价、总值和合同日期，不必在商业发票上用英文大写表示货物数量等。

5.美观大方

美观大方也是对外贸单证制作的要求。其要求制作出来的单据美观、大方、有艺术感，特别是对于非要式单据，表格的设计、字体的选用、字号的大小、行距和字距的选择，尽量做到大方美观，周周正正，切忌歪歪扭扭，潦草马虎。

第二步　学生学

（1）在信用证结算方式下，外贸单证制作依据是：外贸合同、信用证、商品原始资料、《跟单信用证统一惯例》以及国内相关法律、法规。

（2）在汇付和托收结算方式下，外贸单证制作依据是：外贸合同、装船指令、商品原始资料、《托收统一惯例》以及国家相关法律和法规。

商品原始资料指生产企业或出口商仓库或后勤人员提供的交货单、货物出库/厂装箱单、磅码单，主要包括具体出口货物数量、重量、体积、批号、生产日期、有效期限、色彩搭配、规格搭配、货存地点等内容。

第三步　学生做　思考与回答

（1）你如何理解外贸单证？

（2）你认为个人性格跟学好外贸单证有关系吗？

（3）开学伊始，你准备如何学习“外贸单证实务”这门课程？

任务二　催　证

情境导入

广西梧州市神光进出口有限公司2021年4月广交会期间与加拿大Firebird Trading Co.,

Ltd. 签订了一份150吨软锰粉出口合同。由于市场前景暗淡，直到同年6月初，客户还未按照合同规定开出信用证。这可怎么办？出口部副经理岑月婷让实习单证员谭雅梅向客户发函催证。

第一步 学生学

一、催证的定义

催证指卖方运用电话、电传、邮件等方式，催促买方按照合同的规定开立信用证。在实际对外贸易工作中，人们常说三句话：信用证不来不备货，修改书不来不装船，单据不合格不交单。在当今市场经济条件下，一般情况下，备证应先于备货。因为在买方市场条件下，先备证后备货总比相反操作风险小得多。

二、催证的方法

卖方可以电话、电传、邮件等方式直接催促买方办理开证手续，还可以请驻外的中资机构甚至请当地的客户或朋友协助代为催证。

三、催证的必要性

既然签订了贸易合同，双方按照合同办就行了，卖方为什么要催证呢？自古商场如战场。国际市场上的竞争十分激烈。在国际贸易中，经过千辛万苦的洽谈签订合同后，最好的情况是，买方能按照合同条款要求，准时开出信用证。但由于国际市价下跌、客户资金短缺、客户见异思迁、不可抗力等原因，买方经常不按时开出信用证、拖延开证甚至故意放弃业已达成的交易。在这种情况下，卖方就要催促客户按照合同的规定开出信用证，特别是在合同规定卖方在收到信用证后××天装运的情况下，只要买方一天不开来信用证，卖方就一天不能备货、检验、配船、报关、出口装运货物。因为溢短装条款的缘故，如果信用证不来，货物数量、单价、包装、运期等都不能最终确定，可以说一切都还是未知数。更有甚者，如果市价下跌得厉害，买方的亏损已成定局，硬要继续执行合同，买方的亏损会更大，买方就有可能“破罐破摔”，干脆不要货也不开证了，就等卖方提出违约索赔，赔偿款的损失还小些。此时，所签订的贸易合同还有多大实际意义呢？

第二步 教师教

一、催证原则

“先礼后兵”是催证的基本原则。

1.礼

催证时，一般先用委婉客气的语言强调卖方做了很多工作，并说明生产或备货情况，投入了多少人力、财力、物力，请求对方支持和配合，迅速开来信用证；强调双方贸易关系的重要性，劝买方立足未来，不要因为当前的困难终止了彼此的贸易关系；暗示将来合作前景是多么光明等，以此吸引、鼓动客户开出信用证。

2.兵

如果经过多次催促，客户还是未开来信用证，仍故意拖延甚至逃避开证的话，卖方就可适当使用严厉的措辞，直言相告对方不按时开证就是违反合同，要承担违约责任，卖方将采取包括诉诸法律等措施来应对。

一般情况下，经过这样先礼后兵的催促后，客户都会开来信用证。但当国际市价剧烈下跌时，有的客户宁愿承担违约责任也不愿意开证，使得卖方很被动。

二、催证函写作示范

1.简略式

To：Firebird Trading Co.，Ltd.（Canada）

Fm：Guangxi Wuzhou Shenguang Import & Export Co.，Ltd.

Date：April 10，2021

Attn：Smith Aims

Dear Sirs，

Re：150 M/T Manganese Dioxide Powder

Goods are ready for shipment. Till now we haven't received any L/C from you. Please rush to open L/C as soon as possible so that we can handle procedures accordingly.

Yours Truly，

Miss Tan Yamei

2.一般式

To：Paragon Import & Export Co.，Ltd.（America）

Fm：Guangxi Wuzhou Garments & Textiles Import & Export Group Company

Date：May 20，2021

Attn：Mr.Kaxi Wood

Dear Sirs，

Re：Sales Contract No.TW189

With reference to 4 500 dozen Man Shirts under Sales Confirmation No.TW189，we wish to draw your attention to the fact that date of delivery is approaching，but up to the present we have not received any letter of credit from you. Please do your utmost to expedite its establishment so that we may execute the contract within the prescribed time of shipment.

In order to avoid unnecessary subsequent amendments of your letter of credit，please see to it that the stipulations of your letter of credit should be in exact accordance with the terms and conditions of the contract.We look forward to receiving your favorable response at an early date.

Yours faithfully，

Mo Yunjin

（Sales Manager）

第三步　学生做　情境催证

（1）将学生分组，分别模拟扮演买方和卖方，在多媒体教室运用互联网，就20公吨核桃仁出口加拿大，卖方向买方书写一份英文催证函，陈述种种理由，要求买方立即开证；买方收到邮件后回复同意不日开证。

（2）广西梧州新大地进出口公司2021年3月16日与印度Seven Star Trading Company签订一份200吨石墨出口合同；合同号：ST210316；交货期是2021年5月和6月；付款条件是即期信用证。到2021年5月底，印度客户还未开来信用证。请催证。

（3）新加坡Paragon Import & Export Co.,Ltd.于2021年2月20日与广东省福林进出口公司签订了200公吨的锡锭进口合同，规定用即期信用证付款，2021年3、4、5月份交货。但直到4月中旬，新加坡客户的信用证还未来到。请以出口部经理的身份向客户写一份催证函。

任务三　审　证

情境导入

2021年6月15日下午，广西梧州市神光进出口有限公司派实习单证员谭雅梅前往梧州中国银行，在交纳了300元通知费后，领回加拿大Firebird Trading Co.，Ltd. 通过其银行开来的一份信用证。当天，她对照销售合同等资料，认真细致地审查国外开来的信用证。

第一步　学生学

一、审证的含义

审证是指对国外进口人通过银行开来的信用证进行全面审查。凡我方接受的信用证，必须符合我国的对外政策，有利于对外贸易的开展，有利于安全收汇。

二、审证的必要性

信用证的内容应该与合同条款一致。在实际工作中，由于种种原因，如工作疏忽、电文传递错误、贸易习惯不同、市场行情变化或进口商故意用开证的主动权加列不利于卖方的条款等，信用证中所列条款往往与合同规定不符，给卖方履行合同、安全收汇带来隐患。对此，通知行及出口商必须提高警惕，共同做好对国外来证的审核。

三、审证依据

1.进出口合同

合同是信用证的基础，信用证是依据合同开立的。信用证中的条款应该与合同的规定相一致；否则，卖方有权要求买方修改信用证条款，直到符合合同规定为止。

2.《跟单信用证统一惯例》

此惯例虽非国际公约，亦非国际成文法，对信用证当事人不具有法律约束力，但该惯例在国际上已被大多数国家和地区的银行公会承认和采用，具有普遍性，世界上的大部分银行开出的信用证都声明接受它的约束，在实际业务中应依照办理。

3.业务实际情况

对于合同中没有规定又无法根据《跟单信用证统一惯例》来确定是否可以接受的条款，可以根据业务实际情况来确定，主要包括信用证条款对安全收汇的影响程度、进出口法律和法规的规定、买卖双方的贸易习惯等。

第二步　教师教

一、审证步骤

审计步骤如图1-1所示。

第一步：　熟悉贸易合同各条款的内容

↓

第二步：对照合同条款，按照可操作原则，逐一审查信用证条款

↓

第三步：将合同与信用证对比，核实信用证有无错误和漏开条款

↓

第四步：　列出信用证中与合同不符的条款

图1-1　审证步骤

二、审证主体与责任

审核信用证是通知行与出口人的共同责任，但各有侧重。通知行重点审核开证行的政治背景、资信能力、付款责任、索汇路线及信用证的真伪等。出口人则着重审核信用证的内容与买卖合同是否一致，哪些条款能履行，哪些条款不能履行。审核信用证的内容包括审核信用证的种类、货物名称、规格、包装、唛头、数量、合同号、单价、金额、装运期、有效期时间与地点、溢短装条款、佣金、折扣以及特殊条款和限制性条款等。

出口人审证时必须全面、细致地核对证中的文字（包括打印的、手写的、缮打的、盖章的、正面、反面）以及面函、附件，避免发生遗漏。对信用证电开本和证实书也应全面核对。对于模棱两可的字句、模糊不清的字体，均应向国外进口方提出问询并进行确认。

（一）银行审证

1.从政策上审核

按照《跟单信用证统一惯例》(《UCP600》)的规定，通知行有合理审慎地审查信用证的义务。通知行要审查来证的各项内容是否符合我国的方针政策，是否有歧视性内容（如有，则需根据不同情况向开证行交涉）；来证国家（或货运目的港）是否属于我国不与之往来的国家（或港口）。来证国家必须是与我国有经济来往的国家或地区，应拒绝接受与我国无来往关系的国家与地区的来证。同时，审查来证是否带有诬蔑、歧视性的内容或不友好的词句，如有意制造两个中国、沿用旧国名和涉台、涉港、涉疆的不当言论等；如有，则用黄色或红色笔圈出提醒受益人修改。

2.对开证行的审核

为了保证安全收汇，要对开证行所在国家的政治和经济状况，开证行的资信、经营作风等进行审查。对于资信欠佳的银行，应酌情采取适当的保全措施。通知行还要审查来证的密押（Test Key）。审证时，通知行通常会在对出口人不利的条款上用红笔做标记以提醒出口人。

3.对开证行付款责任的审核

信用证中要有开证行保证付款的文句。

4.检查信用证的通知方式是否安全、可靠

根据《UCP600》的有关规定，通知行应对所通知信用证的表面真实性负责。信用证是通过受益人所在国家或地区的通知/保兑行通知给受益人的，因而比较安全。

5.寄单方式和索汇路线

信用证中应规定议付行使用什么方式寄单，按照什么路线将单据寄出。

（二）出口人审证

SWIFT是“环球银行金融电信协会”的英文缩写，它是银行同业间的国际合作组织，成立于1973年。目前，全球大多数国家的大部分银行都已是SWIFT会员。大多数银行开出的信用证都是用SWIFT电文开出的，主要格式有MT700、MT701（开证）和MT707格式（改证）。对于MT700和MT701格式的信用证，其开始部分和结尾部分的内容多为电传机在发送和接收信息时自动生成，与单据制作基本无关，审证时可以不用审核这两部分。有人把这做法叫作“掐头去尾”，即头和尾不用理睬。

一般来说，信用证条款“27：SEQUENCE OF TOTAL：1/1”前面的内容和条款“78：

INSTR TO PAYG/ACCPTG/NEGOTG BANK”后面的内容，受益人审证时可以掐掉不审，直接审核其他内容。

1.信用证金额与货币

审核信用证金额是否正确。信用证金额是否与合同金额一致，大、小写金额是否一致。如信用证中有溢短装条款，则货物数量和信用证金额必须同时具有伸缩度才能有效；否则，只允许货物数量有伸缩或只允许信用证金额有伸缩，就相当于否定了金额或数量的伸缩度。

信用证使用的货币应与合同规定的计价和支付货币一致。如发现二者不一致，视情况拒绝接受或在证内规定合理的折算时间，一般应按实际付款日或议付日的兑换率折算。

2.有关货物条款

审核货物是否允许分批装运和是否允许转运。此外，主要是对商品的品质、规格、数量、包装等依次进行审核，如发现信用证中的内容与合同规定不一致，不应轻易接受，原则上要求改证。

来证中有关分批和转船的规定，原则上应与合同相符。要注意来证对分批和转船有无特殊限制和要求，以及这些规定是否恰当。根据《UCP600》的规定，如果信用证未规定是否可以分批装运和转运，该批货物是可以分批装运和转运的。

3.装运期、有效期时间和地点、交单期

信用证的装运期必须与合同的规定相同；超出信用证规定装运期的运输单据将构成不符，银行有权拒付。此外，卖方审证时应注意以下问题：

（1）卖方能否在信用证规定的装运期内备妥有关货物，并按期装运；装运期与交单期的相距时间是否太短。

（2）信用证的交单期是否过短，卖方能否在短期内制单、交单。信用证的交单期一般规定在装运期限后7～15天，以方便卖方制单和交单。如果信用证未规定交单期，应理解为自提单日起21天止的期间为信用证的交单期，但不能超过信用证的有效期。

（3）如果信用证规定“双到期”，即信用证规定装运期与有效期为同一天，可根据货、港、船的具体情况来确定是否接受。如果货、港、船无问题，可以提前装运而不影响按时交单议付，即可接受“双到期”的规定，否则必须要求对方改证。

（4）信用证的到期地点通常要求规定在受益人所在国内，以便受益人控制提交单据的时间；一般不接受在国外到期，因为受益人无法控制邮程，可能会出现误期风险和国外政治罢工风险。如果信用证中的议付到期地点不在本国而在国外，那么受益人必须承担到指定地点交单的费用或邮寄单据的风险。对于到期地点在国外的信用证，一般应提请对方修改。

4.开证申请人、受益人

开证申请人的名称和地址应仔细审核，以防错发错运。受益人的名称和地址也需正确无误，以免影响收汇。由于这些信息在议付单据中出现的频率较高，需要仔细审核，以免制单和寄单时发生错误。这些名称与地址前后要一致，否则会造成出口方履约困难，影响收汇。

5.单据条款

这主要是对来证中要求的单据种类、份数、填制方法、签发人进行审核。要严格审核来证索要的单据是否可以提供，由谁提供，是否需支付费用，这些费用应由谁负担。如发现有不正常规定或我方难以办到的条款，应要求对方修改或删除。

6.运输条款

出口人要仔细审查来证的装运条款，特别是关于转船、分批及运输路线的规定。提单上的被通知人所在地如果是我国不与之进行贸易往来的国家或证内规定发货人为外商和侨商，一般都不能接受；非协定贸易国家来证而货去协定贸易国家不能接受；信用证内指定船公司、船名、转船地点、接转船名、船龄、船级、船籍一般不接受，但可先与有关部门联系，如能办到也可接受；来证明确规定船舶需于某月某日抵达某目的港，否则不接受。

来证的唛头需与合同中规定的唛头一致，如有变化，在备货时必须注意，防止错刷。如信用证规定唛头的位置不定，必须仔细查找，切勿疏忽，以免因未发现唛头而贻误工作或造成损失。

7.保险条款

注意保险条款的适用性，险别、投保加成率是否与合同相符。损失赔付地点应规定具体，不应笼统写“在国外”；如目的地无我方保险公司代理者，可订明在北京。在买方投保的情况下，如来证要求受益人在装船后通知其指定国外保险公司予以投保，可以接受。如果来证注明要国外保险公司出具收到我方装船通知的承诺（Acknowledgement）并作为议付单据，我方不能接受。这属于软条款，会影响出口人按时收汇并可能引起其他不良后果。

8.其他条款

信用证空白处、边缘处加注的字句等往往是信用证内容的重要补充或修改，审证时也应多加注意。要注意正确理解缩略语，以免造成履约及议付差错。例如“ASAP”是“as soon as possible”缩写；“EPM”是“European Main Ports”的缩写等。

审证时，除上述内容外，还可能出现超出合同规定的附加或特殊条款，如要求在目的港后加上“指定码头”“自由通道”“自由港”等字样。如发现这种超出合同规定的附加或特殊条款，一般不应轻易接受；如对我方无太大影响，也可酌情接受一部分。

三、审证难点

1.软条款

出口人要注意那些看起来简单、做起来其实很难甚至引人上当的条款。例如，美国开来的一份信用证要求广西梧州某进出口公司出口某批货物时提供开证人驻中国香港的办事处出具的验货证明作为议付单据之一。这种软条款看起来可以接受，做起来却很难。对于这类条款，出口人一定要求对方改证以保证安全收汇，不要碍于脸面或害怕麻烦。

审证时，要检查信用证中有无陷阱或缺陷，如1/3正本提单寄送开证人的条款、将客户检验证明作为议付单据的条款等；检查信用证中有无矛盾之处，如运输方式是航空运输却要求提供海运提单；检查有关信用证是否受《UCP600》的约束。

2.特约事项

所谓特约事项（Special Instructions），是指信用证或装船指令中要求出口人特别注意要做到的事项，一般是要求在所有单据上显示什么号码或其他内容。这些号码或内容在进口人办理进口报关手续、外汇申领手续等时要经常用到。所有单据都显示这些号码或内容，进口人就很容易找到。有的信用证有特约事项，有的信用证则没有。

例如：某信用证条款的“47A：ADDITIONAL CONDITIONS”中有如下规定：All documents must bear this credit number.

四、教师审证示范

1.根据情境，对照合同、信用证通知书等资料，审查国外开来的信用证

微课 1-2

审证

2021年6月15日下午，广西梧州市神光进出口有限公司收到了梧州中国银行的信用证通知书，公司派实习单证员谭雅梅前往梧州中国银行，在交纳了300元通知费后，领回了加拿大FIREBIRD TRADING CO.，LTD.通过其银行开来的一份信用证，当天就对照销售确认书，审查了国外开来的信用证。

中国银行
BANK OF CHINA

BANK OF CHINA，WUZHOU BRANCH
1，XINXING YI ROAD
TELEX：488008888

信 用 证 通 知 书
NOTIFICATION OF DOCUMENTARY CREDIT

日期：2021-06-15

TO 致： GUANGXI WUZHOU SENGONG I/E CO.,LTD.		WHEN CORRESPONDING PLEASE QUOTE OUR REF.NO.201098	
ISSUING BANK 开证行 NORTHEAST AMERICA BANK OF CANADA		TRANSMITTED/TRANSFER TO US THROUGH 转递行/转让行 REF.NO. 偿付行	
L/C NO. 信用证号 2021FTCL06-1401	L/C DATED 开证日期 2021-06-14	L/C TTL AMT 总金额 USD657 000.00	EXPIRY PLACE 有效地 LOCAL
EXPIRY DATE 有效期 2021-07-30	TENOR 期限 SIGHT	CHARGE 未付费用 RMB00.00	CHARGE BY 费用承担人
RECEIVED VIA 修改方式 SWIFT	AVAILABLE 修改是否生效 VALID	TEST/SIGN 修改印压是否相符 YES	CONFIRM 我行是否保兑修改 NO

DEAR SIR，迳启者：

WE HAVE PLEASURE IN ADVISING YOU THAT WE HAVE RECEIVED FROM THE NORTHEAST AMERICA BANK OF CANADA A (N) LETTER OF CREDIT, CONTENTS OF WHICH ARE AS PER ATTACHED SHEET (S). THIS ADVICE AND THE ATTACHED SHEET (S) MUST ACCOMPANY THE RELATIVE DOCUMENTS PRESENTED FOR NOGOTIATION.

兹通知贵司，我行收自上述银行信用证一份，现随附通知，贵司交单时，需将本通知及信用证一并提示。

REMARKS 备注：

(×)此通知不构成我行对此信用证之保兑及其他责任。

(　)此证系简电证实书。

(　)此证印鉴、密押未核符，我行已对外查询待复。

(　)此证项下费用由贵司承担。

(　)此证尚未生效。

THIS L/C CONSISTS OF 2 SHEET (S), INCLUDING THE COVERING LETTER AND ATTACHMENTS.（本证连同面函及附件共2张）IF YOU FIND ANY TERMS AND CONDITIONS IN THE L/C WHICH YOU ARE UNABLE TO COMPLY WITH AND/OR ANY ERROR (S), IT

IS SUGGESTED THAT YOU CONTACT APPLICANT DIRECTLY FOR NECESSARY AMENDMENT (S) SO AS TO AVOID ANY DIFFICULTIES WHICH MAY ARISE WHEN DOCUMENTS ARE PRESENTED.（如本证有无法办到的条款和/或错误，请径与开证人联系，进行必要的修改以排除交单时可能发生的问题）

THIS L/C IS ADVISED SUBJECT TO ICC PUBLICATION NO.600.（本信用证之通知系遵循国际商会《跟单信用证统一惯例》第600号出版物办理）

YOURS FAITHFULLY,
FOR BANK OF CHINA

合同如下：

SALES CONFIRMATION

No.：MHT202006E01
Date：April 26，2021
Place：Guangzhou

The Seller：GUANGXI WUZHOU SENGONG IMPORT AND EXPORT CO.，LTD.
Add：20，East Xinxing Road，Wuzhou，Guangxi，P.R.C.
Tel：0086-774-38205638 Fax：0086-774-38207891
E-Mail：sengong@163.com Web-site：www.sengong.cn

The Buyer：FIREBIRD TRADING CO.，LTD.（CANADA）
Add：350，Brightway Avenue，British Colombia
Tel：001-503 362 2603 Fax：001-503 362 2605
E-mail：bobt@firebird.bc.ca Web-site：www.firebird.ca

This sales confirmation is made by and between the buyer and the seller，whereby the buyer agrees to buy and the seller agrees to sell the under-mentioned commodity according to the terms and conditions stipulated below.

Name of Commodity	Quantity	Unit Price	Total Amount
Manganese Dioxide Powder	150 M/T（±5% at the seller's option）	USD4 500.00/MT CIF Montreal,Canada	USD675 000.00

1.Way of packing：In plastic woven bags of about 50 kgs net each，40 bags to a wooden pallet.

2.Time of shipment：In June and July 2021.

3.Insurance：To be covered by the seller for 110% of invoice value against W.P.A. as per C.I.C. clause.

4.Payment Terms：100% by irrevocable Letter of Credit at sight. The relevant L/C shall be opened 15 days after signing the sales confirmation and shall reach the seller by the end of May，2021.

5.Specification：MnO_2：85% min.

Fe：5% max.

Al_2O_3：4% max.

S_iO_2：10% max.

H_2O：4% max.

Fineness：400 mesh 90% min.passing through.

6.Loading Port：Guangzhou/Wuzhou

7.Destination：Montreal

8.Remarks：Please countersign and return one copy of this confirmation for our file.

Buyer's Signature：	Seller's Signature：
ROB SMITH	LI BIAOBIAO
（deputy manager）	（managing director）

信用证如下：

27：SEQUENCE OF TOTAL
1/1

40A：FORM OF DOCUMENTARY CREDIT
IRREVOCABLE

20：DOCUMENTARY CREDIT NUMBER
2021FTCL06-1401

31C：DATE OF ISSUE
21-06-14

40E：APPLICABLE RULES
UCP LATEST VERSION

31D：DATE AND PLACE OF EXPIRY
21-07-30 IN BENEFICIARY'S COUNTRY

50：APPLICANT：
FIREBIRD TRADING CO.，LTD.（CANADA）
350，BRIGHTWAY AVENUE，BRITISH COLOMBIA

59：BENEFICIARY：
GUANGXI WUZHOU SENGONG I/E CO.，LTD.
20，EAST XINXING ROAD，WUZHOU，GUANGXI，P.R.C.

32B：CURRENCY CODE，AMOUNT
CURRENCY：USD（US DOLLAR）
AMOUNT：USD657 000.00

41D：AVAILABLE WITH...BY...
ANY BANK IN BENEFICIARY'S COUNTRY
BY NEGOTIATION

42C：DRAFTS AT...

SIGHT

FOR 100% OF INVOICE VALUE

42A：DRAWEE：

NORTHEAST AMERICA BANK OF CANADA

43P：PARTIAL SHIPMENTS

ALLOWED

43T：TRANSSHIPMENT

ALLOWED

44E：PORT OF LOADING

GUANGZHOU CHINA

44F：PORT OF DISCHARGE

MONTREAL，CANADA

44C：LATEST DATE OF SHIPMENT

21-07-15

45A：DESCRIPTION OF GOODS &/OR SERVICES

150M/T OF MANGANESE DIOXIDE POWDER

MnO_2：86% MIN. Fe：5% MAX. Al_2O_3：4% MAX. SiO_2：10% MAX.

H_2O：4% MAX. FINENESS：400 MESH 90% MIN.

UNIT PRICE：USD4 500/MT CIFC3% MONTREAL，CANADA

PACKED IN TWO-PLY PLASTIC WOVEN BAGS OF 50 KGS NET EACH，40 BAGS TO A WOODEN PALLET.

AS PER SALES CONFIRMATION NO.MHT202006E01

46A：DOCUMENTS REQUIRED

+ SIGNED COMMERCIAL INVOICE IN THREE COPIES.

+ FULL SET OF CLEAN ON BOARD MARINE BILLS OF LADING IN TWO ORIGINALS AND 3 COPIES，MADE OUT TO ORDER，ENDORSED IN BLANK，MARKED FREIGHT PREPAID AND NOTIFY APPLICANT EVIDENCING SHIPMENT FROM GUANGZHOU TO MONTREAL.

+ INSPECTION CERTIFICATE OF QUALITY AND WEIGHT IN DUPLICATE.

+ PACKING LIST IN THREE COPIES.

+ CERTIFICATE OF ORIGIN G.S.P. FORM A ISSUED BY CORRESPONDING AUTHORITY IN DUPLICATE.

+ INSURANCE POLICY OR CERTIFICATE ENDORSED IN BLANK WITH CLAIMS PAYABLE AT THE DESTINATION WITH THE SAME CURRENCY OF DRAFT AGAINST ALL RISKS AND WAR RISK OF C.I.C. FOR 110% OF INVOICE VALUE.

+ BENEFICIARY'S CERTIFICATE CERTIFYING THAT ONE SET OF NON-NEGOTIABLE SHIPPING DOCUMENTS HAS BEEN SENT TO APPLICANT BY EMS WITHIN 7 DAYS AFTER SHIPMENT HAS BEEN EFFECTED.

47A：ADDITIONAL CONDITIONS

+ ALL DOCUMENTS AND DRAFT（S）MUST BEAR THIS CREDIT NUMBER.

+ SHIPMENT DATE PRIOR TO L/C'S ISSUING DATE IS PROHIBITED.

+ 5 PCT MORE OR LESS IN QUANTITY AND AMOUNT ARE ACCEPTABLE.

+ IF DOCUMENTS PRESENTED UNDER THIS L/C ARE FOUND TO BE DISCREPANT, WE SHALL GIVE ITS NOTICE OF REFUSAL AND SHALL HOLD DOCUMENTS AT YOUR DISPOSAL SUBJECT TO THE FOLLOWING CONDITION:"IF WE HAVE NOT RECEIVED YOUR DISPOSAL INSTRUCTIONS FOR THE DISCREPANT DOCUMENTS PRIOR TO RECEIPT OF THE APPLICANT'S WAIVER OF DISCREPANCIES，WE WILL RELEASE DOCUMENTS TO APPLICANT WITHOUT NOTICE TO YOU."

71B：CHARGES

ALL BANKING CHARGES OUTSIDE CANADA，IF ANY，ARE FOR ACCOUNT OF BENEFICIARY.

48：PERIOD FOR PRESENTATION

DOCUMENTS PRESENTED WITHIN 15 DAYS AFTER SHIPMENT BUT WITHIN THE VALIDITY OF THE CREDIT.

49：CONFIRMATION INSTRUCTIONS

WITHOUT

78：INSTR TO PAYG/ACCPTG/NEGOTG BANK：

+ ALL DOCUMENTS MUST BE SENT TO US IN ONE LOT，OUR ADDRESS：NORTHEAST AMERICA BANK OF CANADA，238 #，BEIXALU，GM，MONTREAL，CANADA.

+ A DISCREPANCY FEE OF USD60.00 SHOULD BE DEDUCTED FROM NEGOTIATION AMOUNT FOR EACH PRESENTATION IF DOCUMENTS DO NOT COMPLY WITH L/C TERMS AND CONDITIONS.

+ ONE COPY OF BILL OF LADING AND COMMERCIAL INVOICE IS REQUIRED FOR ISSUING BANK'S FILE. USD10.00 WILL BE CHARGED IF THESE COPIES ARE NOT PRESENTED.

+ UPON RECEIPT OF DOCUMENTS ALONG WITH DRAFT（S）STRICTLY COMPLYING WITH TERMS AND CONDITIONS OF THIS CREDIT，WE WILL REMIT PROCEEDS LESS OUR HANDLING CHARGES TO YOU AS INSTRUCTED.

57D："ADVISE THROUGH" BANK

BANK OF CHINA WUZHOU BRANCH

72：SENDER TO RECEIVER INFORMATION

PLS RELEASE THE L/C UPON RECEIPT OF ADVISING FEES.

END OF MESSAGE

经对照销售确认书审核信用证，发现信用证存在如下错误：

（1）受益人名称有误，应该写成 GUANGXI WUZHOU SENGONG IMPORT AND EXPORT CO.，LTD.而不是 GUANGXI WUZHOU SENGONG I/E CO.，LTD.

（2）单价有误，应该是 USD4 500/MT CIF MONTREAL，CANADA，而不是 USD4 500/

MT CIFC3% MONTREAL，CANADA.

（3）信用证总金额有误，应该是USD675 000.00，而不是USD657 000.00。

（4）货物规格应该是MnO_2：85% MIN.，而不是MnO_2：86% MIN.。

（5）包装应该是In plastic woven bags of about 50 kgs net each，40 bags to a wooden pallet.，而不是In two-ply plastic woven bags of 50kgs net each，40bags to a wooden pallet.

（6）关于保险，合同只要求投保W.P.A.，而信用证要求投保一切险和战争险。

（7）最晚装船期应为2021年7月31日，而不是2021年7月15日。

2.填写审证记录表

根据前面的审查结果，填写审证记录表（见表1-1）。

表1-1 信用证审查记录表

合同号：______ 信用证号：______

开证银行	名称	信誉（良/中/差）
信用证内容	错误内容	正确表达
	1.	
	2.	
	3.	
	4.	
关于软条款	软条款内容抄录	更改建议
审查结论	执行（打√或×）	修改后执行（打√或×）

审查人：

时间： 年 月 日

第三步 学生做 审证训练

1. 2021年4月20日，广西梧州春江五金矿产进出口有限公司总经理李彪彪参加了春交会，与澳大利亚国际采购公司签订了一份100公吨金属硅的出口合同，回到梧州后交给出口部门执行。5月8日，出口部收到了买方开来的信用证。请根据下面的合同，分小组审查信用证。

SALES CONTRACT

No.：CJ2021E88

Date：April 20，2021

Place：Guangzhou

The Seller：Guangxi Wuzhou Chunjiang Metals and Minerals Import and Export Co.，Ltd.

Address：21，Sijiangwu Road，Wuzhou，Guangxi，P.R.C.

Fax：0086-774-8421 8687

Tel：0086-774-8421 8689

E-Mail：chunjiang@chemicals.com

The Buyer: International Sourcing Company

Address: 358, 29#, New Street, Northbridge, Sydney, Australia

Fax: 0061-2-5653-1170

Tel: 0061-2-5657-1171

E-mail: int' lsource@northbridge.com

The Seller has agreed to sell and the Buyer has agreed to buy the following goods as per the terms and conditions listed below:

Name of Commodity	Specification & Quantity	Unit Price	Total Amount
Silicon Metal	100 M/T(±5% at the seller's option) Si:99.9% min; Fe:0.4% max. Al:0.4% max. Ca:0.1% max. Size:10-100mm 90% min.	USD9 655.00 per M/T CFR Sydney	USD965 500.00

1.Way of Packing: In plastic woven bags of about 1 000kgs net each.

2.Time of Shipment: Shipment from Wuzhou to Sydney via Hong Kong in May and June of 2021. Partial shipment and transshipment are allowed.

3.Insurance: To be covered by the buyer.

4.Payment Terms: By irrevocable Letter of Credit at sight. The said Letter of Credit should be issued by a bank recognized by the Seller and shall reach the Seller not later than May 10, 2021.

5.Inspection

Both the sellers and the buyers mutually agreed that the Certificate of Quality and Weight and/or Quantity issued by related organizations at the port of shipment shall be part of the documents to be presented for negotiation under the relevant L/C. The buyers shall have the right to re-inspect the quality and weight and/or quantity of the cargo at the port of destination. However, the re-inspection fee shall be borne by the buyers.

6.Discrepancy and Claim

Should the quality and/or weight be found not in conformity with that of the contract, the buyers shall be entitled to lodge a claim with the sellers. Such claim should be supported by survey reports issued by a recognized surveyor approved by the sellers. The claim, if any, shall be filed within 30 days after arrival of the cargo at the port of destination specified in the relative Bill of Lading. If the goods have been processed, the buyers shall thereupon lose the right to claim. Claims in respect of matters within responsibility of insurance company and/or shipping company shall not be considered or entertained by the sellers.

7.Arbitration

All disputes arising out of the performance of, or relating to this contract, shall be settled friendly through negotiation. In case no settlement can be reached through negotiation, the case shall then be submitted to the China International Economic and Trade Arbitration Commission, Beijing, China, for arbitration in accordance with its provisional rules for arbitration. The arbitral award is final and binding upon both parties.

8.Force Majeure

In case the contracted goods are prevented or delayed in whole or in part by reason of war、earthquake、flood、fire、storm、heavy snow、tsunami or other causes of Force Majeure, the seller shall not be held responsible for non-shipment or late shipment of the goods under this contract. In that case, the seller shall notify the buyer by cable、fax or telephone and furnish the buyer within 20 days by registered airmail with a certificate issued by the China Council for the Promotion of International Trade attesting such event or events.

9.Remarks

This confirmation is written in English. Both the Seller and the Buyer shall hold one copy of the original. The Seller shall mail this confirmation to the Buyer as soon as possible for signature. The Buyer shall countersign them and return one copy of this confirmation to the Seller for his file.

Buyer's Signature :	Seller's Signature:
Bob Covery	Li biaobiao
(Managing Director)	(Managing Director)

SEQUENCE OF TOTAL: 27 1/1

FORM OF DOC. CREDIT: 40A: IRREVOCABLE

DOC.CREDIT NUMBER: 20: M2021-050012

DATE OF ISSUE 31C: 21-05-07

EXPIRY DATE AND PLACE 31D: 21-07-15 PLACE IN CHINA

APPLICANT 50: INTERNATIONAL SOURCING COMPANY, 358, 29#,
NEW STREET, NORTHBRIDGE, SYDNEY, AUSTRALIA

BENEFICIARY 59: GUANGXI WUZHOU CHUNJIANG METALS AND MINERALS IMPORT AND EXPORT CO., LTD.21, SIJIANGWU ROAD, WUZHOU, GUANGXI, P.R.C.

AMOUNT 32B: CURRENCY USD AMOUNT 956 000.

POS./NEG. TOL. (%) 39A: 5/5

AVAILABLE WITH/BY: 41D: ANY BANK IN CHINA BY NEGOTIATION

DRAFTS AT 42C: 30 DAY'S SIGHT

DRAWEE 42A: COMMONWEALTH BANK OF AUSTRALIA

PARTIAL SHIPMENT 43P: NOT ALLOWED

TRANSSHIPMENT 43T: ALLOWED

LOADING IN CHARGES 44E: GUANGZHOU, CHINA

FOR TRANSPORT TO 44F: NEW YORK, U.S.A.

LATEST DATE OF SHIPMENT 44C：21-06-30

DESCRIPT. OF GOODS 45A：100 M/T OF SILICON METAL

Si：99.99% MIN. Fe：0.4% MAX.

Al：0.4% MAX. Ca：0.1% MAX.

SIZE：10-100MM 95% MIN. PASSING THROUGH

PACKING：IN PLASTIC WOVEN BAGS OF ABOUT 1 000 KGS NET EACH.，40 BAGS TO A WOODEN PALLET.

UNIT PRICE AT USD 9 655.00

PRICE TERM：PER M/T CFR SYDNEY

AS PER SALES CONTRACT NO.GE008

DOCUMENTS REQUIRED：46A：

+SIGNED COMMERCIAL INVOICE IN SEXTUPLICATE.

+ FULL SET OF CLEAN ON BOARD OCEAN BILL OF LADING，IN DUPLICATE, PLUS 5 NON-NEGOTIABLE，MADE OUT TO ORDER OF COMMONWEALTH BANK OF AUSTRALIA，EVIDENCING SHIPMENT FROM WUZHOU TO SYDNEY.MARKED FREIGHT PREPAID AND NOTIFY APPLICANT.

+ SIGNED PACKING LIST IN 1 SET.

+ CERTIFICATE OF ORIGIN IN 1 SET.

+ INSURANCE POLICY OR CERTIFICATE ENDORSED IN BLANK FOR 120 PCT OF INVOICE VALUE WITH CLAIMS PAYABLE AT DESTINATION IN CURRENCY OF DRAFT COVERING C.I.C. ALL RISKS AND WAR RISK

+INSPECTION CERTIFICATE OF QUALITY AND WEIGHT ISSUED BY CORRESPONDING AUTHORITY.

+ SHIPPING ADVICE IN DUPLICATE WITHIN 1 DAY OF SHIPMENT DATE SHOWING TO APPLICANT THE NAME OF CARRYING VESSEL，NAME OF GOODS，DATE OF SHIPMENT，QUANTITY，NET WEIGHT，GROSS WEIGHT，MAKRS，ETD，ETA.

+BENEFICIARY'S CERTIFICATE CERTIFYING THAT ONE SET OF NON-NEGOTIABLE SHIPPING DOCUMENTS HAS BEEN SENT VIA COURIER AND VIA FAX NO：0061-2-5653-1170 DIRECTLY TO APPLICANT WITHIN 7 DAYS AFTER SHIPMENT.

ADDITIONAL CONDITIONS 47A：

+ ALL DOCUMENTS PRESENTED FOR NEGOTIATION SHALL BEAR NO. OF THIS CREDIT.

+ 5 PCT MORE OR LESS IN QUANTITY AND AMOUNT ARE ACCEPTABLE.

DETAILS OF CHARGES 71B：ALL BANK CHARGES OUTSIDE AUSTRALIA ARE FOR THE BENEFICIARY'S ACCOUNT.

CONFIRMATION 49：WITHOUT

INSTRUCTIONS 78：

+ THE NEGOTIATING BANK MUST FORWARD BY EMS THE DRAFTS AND ALL DOCUMENTS IN 1 LOT TO COMMONWEALTH BANK OF AUSTRALIA，599#，NEW

STREET, NORTHBRIDGE, SYDNEY, AUSTRALIA FAX: 0061-2-5253-1780 TEL: 0061-2-5253-1181.

+ UPON RECEIPT OF CREDIT COMMERCIAL DOCUMENTS, WE SHALL REMIT THE PROCEEDS AS PER THE NEGOTIATING BANK'S INSTRUCTIONS.

+ A DISCREPANCY FEE OF USD50.00 WILL BE DEDUCTED FROM PROCEEDS IF DISCREPANT DOCUMENTS ARE PRESENTTED.

+ THE AMOUNT OF ANY DRAFT DRAWN UNDER THIS CREDIT MUST BE ENDORSED ON THE REVERSE OF THE ORIGINAL CREDIT. ALL DRAFTS MUST MARK DRAWN UNDER THIS DOCUMENTARY CREDIT AND BEARING ITS NUMBER AND DATE.

SEND. TO REG.IMFO.72:

+ PLS ACKNOWLEDGE RECEIPT AND ADVISE BENEFICIARY UNGENTLY.

2.请根据合同内容审核下面的信用证，将信用证的不符点全部列出并填写审证记录表(见表1-2)，提出修改意见。

贸易合同条款如下：

SELLER: GUANGXI IMPORT & EXPORT TRADING CORPORATION P.O.BOX, 038, 121, 6TH ZHONGSHAN ROAD, NANNING, GUANGXI, CHINA

BUYER: MAY FLOWER TRADING CO., LTD. P.O. BOX, 18, 18 - 310 KAJI OSAKA JAPAN

COMMODITY: PLUSH TOY BEAR

QUANTITY: 2 500 PCS

UNIT PRICE: USD 18.00 PER PC CIF OSAKA

TOTAL AMOUNT: USD45 000.00

PACKING: POLYTHENE BAGS OF EACH, WITH INNER PAPER BOX, 20 PCS TO A CARTON.

PORT OF SHIPMENT: GUANGZHOU

PORT OF DESTINATION: OSAKA

LATEST TIME OF SHIPMENT: MAY 31, 2021

PARTIAL OF SHIPMENT: ALLOWED

TRANSSHIPMENT: ALLOWED

INSURANCE: COVERING ALL RISKS AND WAR RISKS FOR 120% INVOICE VALUE

PAYMENT: BY IRREVOCABLE DOCUMENTARY LETTER OF CREDIT PAYABLE AT SIGHT, VALID FOR NEGOTIATION IN CHINA UNTIL THE 15TH DAY AFTER THE DAY OF SHIPMENT.

信用证主要条款如下：

FORM OF DOC.CREDIT 40A: IRREVOCABLE

DOC.CREDIT NUMBER 20: WEL18-202008

DATA OF ISSUE 31C: 21-04-01

EXPIRY 31D: DATE 21-06-15 PLACE IN THE COUNTRY OF BENEFICIARY

APPLICANT 50: MAY FLOWER TRADING CO., LTD.

P.O.BOX，18，18-310 KAJI OSAKA JAPAN

BENEFICIARY 59：SHANXI IMPORT & EXPORT TRADE CORPORATION

21，6TH ZHONGSHAN ROAD，NANNING，GUANGXI，CHINA

AMOUNT 32B：USD AMOUNT 44 500.00

AVAILABLE WITH/BY 41D：ANY BANK BY NEGOTIATION

DRAFTS AT 42C：DRAFTS AT 15 DAYS AFTER SIGHT

FOR FULL INVOICE COST

DRAWEE： 42A：FUJI BANK LTD.，TOKYO JAPAN

PARTIAL SHIPMENTS 43P：PROHIBITED

TRANSSHIPMENT 43T：PROHIBITED

LOADING ON BOARD 44E：SHANGHAI

FOR TRANSPORT TO 44F：OSAKA

LATEST DATE OF SHIP 44C：21-05-31

DESCRIPTION OF GOODS 45A：PLUSH TOY BEAR

PTY（PCS）U/PRICE/PC

25 000 USD17.8

TRADE TERM：CIF OSAKA

PACKING：POLYTHENE BAGS OF EACH，WITH INNER PAPER BOX，10 PCS TO A CARTON.

DETAILS OF CHARGES 71B：ALL BANKING CHARGES OUTSIDE JAPAN ARE FOR ACCOUNT OF BENEFICIARY.

PRESENTATION PERIOD 48：DOCUMENTS MUST BE PRESENTED WITHIN 15 DAYS AFTER THE DATE OF SHIPMENT BUT WITHIN THE VALIDITY OF THE CREDIT.

DOCUMENTS REQUIRED 46A：

+ SIGNED COMMERCIAL INVOICE IN TRIPLICATE.

+ FULL SET OF CLEAN ON BOARD OCEAN BILLS OF LADING MADE OUT TO ORDER，BLANK ENDORSED，MARKED FREIGHT PREPAID AND NOTIFY APPLICANT.

+ PACKING LIST IN TRIPLICATE.

+ MARINE INSURANCE POLICY OR CERTIFICATE IN DUPLICATE ENDORSED IN BLANK FOR 120 PCT OF INVOICE VALUE WITH CLAIMS TO BE PAYABLE IN JAPAN IN THE CURRENCY OF THE DRAFT COVERING OCEAN MARINE CARGO CLAUSES ALL RISKS，OCEAN MARINE CARGO CLAUSES OF THE PEOPLE'S INSURANCE COMPANY OF CHINA.

+ PHOTOCOPY OF G.S.P. CERTIFICATE OF ORIGIN FORM A IN DUPLICATE.

+ BENEFICIARY'S CERTIFICATE CERTIFYING THAT ONE SET OF ORIGINAL SHIPPING DOCUMENTS INCLUDING ONE ORIGINAL G. S. P. CERTIFICATE OF ORIGIN FORM A HAVE BEEN SENT DIRECTLY TO APPLICANT BY SPECIAL COURIER SERVICE.

47A：SPECIAL CONDITIONS：

+ ALL SHIPPING DOCUMENTS MUST SHOW THE NUMBER OF THIS CREDIT.

+ B/L SHOULD BEAR VESSEL AGENT'S NAME AND TELEPHONE NUMBER IN JAPAN.

表1-2 信用证审查记录表

合同号：__________ 信用证号：__________

开证银行	名称	信誉（良/中/差）
信用证内容	错误内容	正确表达
	1.	
	2.	
	3.	
	4.	
关于软条款	软条款内容抄录	更改建议
审查结论	执行（打√或×）	修改后执行（打√或×）

审查人：

时间： 年 月 日

任务四 改证

情境导入

2021年4月26日，广西梧州春江五金矿产进出口有限公司总经理李彪彪参加了春交会，与澳大利亚国际采购公司签订了一份100公吨金属硅的出口合同。5月8日，出口部门收到了买方开来的信用证。当天，公司实习单证员谭雅梅仔细审核了信用证，发现客户开来的信用证存在多处与合同不相符的地方。她向出口部经理请示如何应对。出口部经理王瑞荣经过认真核对和思考，回答："给客户发函电要求改证。"

第一步 学生学

一、改证的含义

改证，即信用证的受益人就信用证与合同内容不符的条款要求开证申请人通过开证行对不符内容进行修改。

二、改证的必要性

如果信用证的条款与合同规定不符，卖方不要求修改就直接发货，势必会影响安全收汇和利润实现。

三、改证路径

（1）受益人向开证申请人去函列举不符点，提出改证要求，取得支持。

（2）开证申请人向开证行递交修改申请书，申请改证。

（3）开证行修改信用证，将修改内容用修改书形式通知通知行。

（4）通知行将修改书通知受益人。

出口商必须等信用证修改书到达后，经检查确认修改书的内容合格，才能装运货物出口；不能轻信客户以电话或传真形式做出的承诺而将货物报关出口。如果修改书迟迟不来，而货物又装运出口了，出口商会很被动。出口商必须坚持前面阐述过的原则：信用证不来不备货，修改书不到不装船，单据不合格不交单。

第二步 教师教

一、改证原则

信用证的修改总体上应遵循“利己不损人”的原则，具体包括以下几点：

（1）合同没有规定，但我方可以接受的条款，不改。

（2）对我方有利，不影响对方利益的条款，不改。

（3）对对方有利，不影响我方利益的条款，不改。

（4）对对方有利，影响到货款安全回笼的条款，要改。

（5）虽不符合合同规定，但对双方都没坏处的条款，不改。

（6）本应由对方支出的费用却归由我方支出的条款，要改。

（7）一次性修改，以节省时间和费用。

（8）信用证中的软条款，要改。

二、改证结果

（1）信用证中经过修改的条款，按照修改后的内容执行。

（2）信用证中没有修改的条款，按照原条款执行。

（3）原信用证依然有效，不用开来全新信用证。

（4）办理结汇手续时，信用证原件、修改书原件要一起送交议付银行。

三、改证函电示范（根据项目一任务二审证结果）

To：FIREBIRD TRADING CO.，LTD.（CANADA）

Fm：GUANGXI WUZHOU SENGONG IMPORT AND EXPORT CO.，LTD.

Date：June 16，2021

Attn：Bob Smith

Dear Sir，

Re：Amendment of L/C

We are very glad to have received your L/C No. 2021FTCL06-1401. After checking the clauses carefully according to sales confirmation No.MHT202006E01，we find the following errors and mistakes in your L/C：

1. The name of beneficiary should be GUANGXI WUZHOU SENGONG IMPORT AND EXPORT CO.，LTD instead of GUANGXI WUZHOU SENGONG I/E CO.，LTD..

2.The unit price reads USD4 500/MT CIF MONTREAL，CANADA instead of USD4 500/MT CIFC3% MONTREAL，CANADA.

3.The total amount of L/C should read USD675 000.00 instead of USD657 000.00.

4.The specification should be MnO_2：85% MIN. instead of MnO_2：86% MIN.

5.The way of packing should be “In plastic woven bags of about 50 kgs net each，40 bags to a wooden pallet”.

6. The insurance clause should be: To be covered by the seller for 110% of invoice value against W.P.A. as per C.I.C. clause.

Please rush to make amendment to your L/C through your issuing bank so that we can effect shipment as soon as possible, which is to the mutual benefit of our two companies.

Best regards.

Yours faithfully,

Tan Yamei

（客户回复）

To: GUANGXI WUZHOU SENGONG IMPORT AND EXPORT CO., LTD.

From: FIREBIRD TRADING CO., LTD. (CANADA)

Date: June 17, 2021

Attn: Tan Yamei

Dear Sir,

Thank you for your fax dated June 16, 2021 asking us to amend our L/C No.M2021FTCL06-1401. Much to our surprise and regret, such errors and mistakes happened in our L/C. I think they were made because of the carelessness of our typist. We shall have it amended tomorrow. Please rest assured of it.

Best regards.

Yours faithfully,

Bob Covery

中国银行 BANK OF CHINA

BANK OF CHINA, ×× BRANCH

修 改 通 知 书

NOTIFICATION OF AMENDMENT

1, XINXING YI ROAD

SWJFI: BKCHCNBJ 49ASS

日期：June.17, 2021

TO 致:GUANGXI WUZHOU SENGONG IMPORT AND EXPORT CO.,LTD.		REF.NO AD20107009	
ISSUING BANK 开证行 NORTHEAST AMERICA BANK OF CANADA		TRANSMITTED/TRANSFER TO US THROUGH 转递行/转让行	
L/C NO. 信用证号 2021FTCL06-1401	L/C DATE 开证日期 2021-06-14	L/C TTL AMT 总金额 USD657 000.00	EXPIRY PLACE 有效地 CHINA
EXPIRY DATE 有效期 2021-07-30	TENOR 期限 SIGHT	CHARGE 未付费用 USD00.00	CHARGE BY 费用承担
RECEIVED VIA 修改方式 TELEX	AVAILABLE 修改是否生效 VALID	TEST/SIGN 修改印压是否相符 相符	CONFIRM 我行是否保兑修改
AMEND NO. 修改次数 1	AMEND DATE 修改日期 2021-06-19	INCREASE AMT. 增额 USD18 000.00	DECREASE AMT. 减额

续表

DEAR SIR，迳启者： WE HAVE PLEASURE IN ADVISING YOU THAT WE HAVE RECEIVED FROM THE NORTHEAST AMERICA BANK OF CANADA AMENDMENT TO THE CAPTIONED L/C,CONTENTS OF WHICH ARE AS PER ATTACHED SHEET（S）. 兹通知贵公司，我行自上述银行收到修改书一份，内容见附件。 THIS AMENDMENT SHOULD BE ATTACHED TO THE CAPTIONED L/C ADVISED BY US,OTHERWISE, THE BENEFICIARY WILL BE RESPONSIBLE FOR ANY CONSEQUENCES ARISING THEREFROM. 本修改需附于有关信用证，否则，贵公司需对因此而产生的后果承担责任。 REMARKS 备注： （　）此修改印鉴/密押未核付，我行已对外查询，待复。 （　）此证已由我行加具保兑，但保兑责任不扩展至本次修改。 （　）此证项下银行费用已改为由贵公司承担。 （　）此修改未生效。 （ × ）此证增加金额 USD18 000.00，现信用证总额为 USD675 000.00。

THIS AMENDMENT CONSISTS OF 2 SHEET（S），INCLUDING THE COVERING LETTER AND ATTACHMENTS.

本修改连同面函及附件共2张。

KINDLY TAKE NOTE THAT THE PARTIAL ACCPTANCE OF THE AMENDMENT IS NOT ALLOWED.

本修改不能部分接受。

THIS AMENDMENT IS ADVISED SUBJECT TO ICC UCP PUBLICATION NO. 600.

本修改之通知系遵循国际商会《跟单信用证统一惯例》第600号出版物办理。

YOURS FAITHFULLY,

FOR BANK OF CHINA

第三步　学生做

请根据下面的销售确认书，审查随后的信用证，并写出改证函电。

SALES CONFIRMATION

NO.AN107

DATE：MAR.5TH，2021

THIS SALES CONFIRMATION IS MADE AND ENTERED INTO BY AND BETWEEN SHANGHAI DAXIN TEXTILES IMP.AND EXP. CORPORATION（207 ZHONGSHAN ROAD, 100，SHANGHAI，CHINA，HEREINAFTER REFERRED TO AS THE SELLERS AND ITOCHULU CORPORATION（103，OSAKA，JAPAN，OSAHI，SECTION.E-MAILADDRESS: ITOCHULU@SIFT. SIFT. EDU）HEREINAFTER REFERRED TO AS THE BUYERS. WHEREBY THE SELLERS AGREE TO SELL AND THE BUYERS TO BUY THE COMMODITY MENTIONED IN THIS CONTRACT SUBJECT TO THE TERMS AND CONDITIONS STIPULATED AS FOLLOWS:

NAME OF COMMODITY & SPECIFICATION, PACKING AND SHIPPING MARK	QUANTITY (PCS.)	UNIT PRICE (CIF OSAKA)	AMOUNT
100% PURE COTTON APRON			
ART.NO.29396	4 000	US $ 1.5	US $ 6 000.00
ART.NO.29395	3 600	US $ 1.4	US $ 5 040.00
ART.NO.25306	1 680	US $ 1.25	US $ 2 100.00
PACKING: IN PLASTIC BAGS OF ONE PIECE EACH, 40 BAGS TO A CARTON.		TOTAL:	US $ 13 140.00
TOTAL VALUE:SAY US DOLLARS THIRTEEN THOUSAND ONE HUNDRED AND FORTY ONLY.			

1.TIME OF SHIPMENT：Within 15 days of receipt of letter of credit and not later than the month of MAY，2021 with partial shipments and transshipment allowed.

2.PORT OF LOADING：SHANGHAI CHINA

Port of Destination：OSAKA JAPAN

3.TERMS OF PAYMENT：By 100% Confirmed Irrevocable Sight Letter of Credit opened by the Buyer to reach the Seller not later than April 25TH，2021 and to be available for negotiation in China until the 15th day after the date of shipment.In case of late arrival of the L/C，the Seller shall not be liable for any delay in shipment and shall have the right to rescind the contract and/or claim for damages.

4.INSURANCE：To be effected by the Seller for 110% of the CIF invoice value covering ALL RISKS AND WAR RISK only as per China Insurance Clauses.

5.SHIPPING MARK： ITOCHULU
AN107
OSAKA
C/NO.1-232

The Buyer
ITOCHULU CORPORATION
JMOSU LI

The Seller
SHANGHAI DAXIN TEXTILES IMP.AND EXP.CORP.
刘大贵

与上面的合同对应的信用证如下：

SEQUENCE OF TOTAL 27：1/1
FORM OF DOC.CREDIT 40：IRREVOCABLE
DOC.CREDIT NUMBER 20：ABL-AN107
DATE OF ISSUE 31C：21-04-20
EXIPRY DATE AND PLACE 31D：21-06-15 AT NEGOTIATING BANK'S COUNTER
APPLICANT 50：ITOCHULU CORPORATION，103，OSAKA，JAPAN
OSAHI SECTION
BENEFICIARY 59：SHANGHAI DAXIN TEXTILES IMP.AND EXP.CORP.
207 ZHONGSHAN ROAD，2100，SHANGHAI，CHINA

AMOUNT 32B：CURRENCY USD AMOUNT 13 015.00

MAX.CREDIT AMOUNT 39B：NOT EXCEEDING

AVAILABLE WITH/BY 41D：ANY BANK IN CHINA
BY NEGOTIATION

DRAFTS AT 42C：DRAFTS AT 20 DAYS' SIGHT FOR FULL INVOICE VALUE

DRAWEE 41A：SAIBJPJT ASAHI BANK LTD，TOKYO

PARTIAL SHIPMENTS 43P：ALLOWED

TRANSSHIPMENT 43T：PROHIBITED

LOADING PORT 44E：SHIPMENT FROM CHINESE PORT（S）

FOR TRANSPORT TO 44F：TO OSAKA，JAPAN

LATEST DATE OF SHIPMENT 44C：20-05-31

DESCRIPTION OF GOODS 45A：100% COTTON APRON AS PER S/C NO.AH107

ART NO.	QUANTITY	UNIT PRICE
29396	4 000 PIECES	USD1.5
29395	3 600 PIECES	USD1.4
25306	1 560 PIECES	USD1.25

PRICE TERM：PER PIECE CIF OSAKA

PACKED IN PLASTIC BAGS OF ONE PIECE EACH，40 BAGS TO A CARTON.

AS PER SALES CONFIRMATION NO.AN107

DOCUMENTS REQUIRED 46A：

+ SIGNED COMMERCIAL INVOICE IN TRIPLICATE.

+ FULL SET OF ORIGINAL CLEAN ON BOARD OCEAN BILLS OF LADING MADE OUT TO ORDER OF SHIPPER AND BLANK ENDORSED AND MARKED "FREIGHT PREPAID" NOTIFY APPLICANT（WITH FULL NAME AND ADDRESS）.

+ PACKING LIST IN DUPLICATE.

+ INSURANCE POLICY OR CERTIFICATE IN TWO ORIGINAL ENDORSED IN BLANK，FOR 120 PCT OF THE INVOICE VALUE INCLUDING：THE INSTITUTE CARGO CLAUSES（A），THE INSTITUTE WAR CLAUSES，INSURANCE CLAIMS TO BE PAYABLE IN JAPAN IN THE CURRENCY OF THE DRAFTS.

+ CERTIFICATE OF ORIGIN IN 1 ORIGINAL AND 1 COPY.

+ BENEFICIARY'S CERTIFICATE STATING THAT ONE SET OF NON-NEGOTIABLE SHIPPING DOCUMENTS HAS BEEN SENT DIRECTLY TO THE APPLICANT（ATT.OSAHI SECTION）

ADDITIONAL CONDITION 47：

+ T.T.REIMBURSEMENT IS PROHIBITED.

+ THE GOODS TO BE PACKED IN EXPORT STRONG COLORED CARTONS.

+ INSPECTION IS TO BE EFFECTED BEFORE SHIPMENT AND RELEVANT CERTIFICATES/REPORTS ARE REQUIRED FROM THE INSPECTING AGENCY.

DETAILS OF CHARGES 71B：

SHIPPING MARKS: ITOCHULU
AN107
OSAKA
C/NO.1-232

ALL BANKING CHARGES OUTSIDE JAPAN INCLUDING REIMBURSEMENT / COMMISSIONS, ARE FOR ACCOUNT OF BENEFICIARY.

PRESENTATION PERIOD 48:

DOCUMENTS TO BE PRESENTED WITHIN 15 DAYS AFTER THE DATE OF SHIPMENT BUT WITHIN THE VALIDITY OF THE CREDIT.

CONFIRMATION 49: WITHOUT

INSTRUCTIONS 78:

THE NEGOTIATION BANK MUST FORWARD THE DRAFTS AND ALL DOCUMENTS BY REGISTERED AIRMAIL DIRECT TO US (INT'L OPERATIONS CENTER MAIL ADDRESS: P.O.BOX NO.800 TOKYO 100-91 JAPAN) IN TWO CONSECUTIVE LOTS, UPON RECEIPT OF THE DRAFTS AND DOCUMENTS IN ORDER, WE WILL REMIT THE PROCEEDS AS INSTRUCTED BY THE NEGOTIATING BANK.

任务五 展 证

情境导入

2021年4月28日，广西梧州五金矿产进出口有限公司唐红总经理参加了今年春季中国进出口商品交易会，与英国一家金属进口公司签订了一份250公吨硅锰合金的出口合同。2021年5月27日，公司出口部门收到了买方开来的信用证。可是，信用证规定的装运期很快就要到期了。当天，公司实习单证员谭雅梅仔细审查了信用证，觉得装运期太短了，对卖方不利。她向出口部经理请示如何应对。出口部经理王瑞荣经过认真核对和思考，回答："先赶货，实在不行再要求客户展证。"

第一步 学生学

一、展证的含义

由于信用证的有效期或装运期已经临近，卖方没有足够的时间履行备货或装运等工作，要求买方（开证人）通过其开证银行将信用证的有效期和装运期相应延长。

二、展证的原因

要求展证时，卖方要在函件里充分说明理由以取得买方的理解和支持。一般展证的理由不外乎几种情况：买方没有按时开证；货源紧俏，缺少原材料，备货时间延长；生产力不足；卖方缺乏资金；船源不足；不可抗力等。

第二步 教师教

展证函写作

To: SMITH BROTHERS LTD.（CANADA）

Fm：GUANGXI WUZHOU XINDASUN TRADING CORP.

Date：Sept.20，2021

Attn：Bob Grant

Dear Sir,

Re：Extension of L/C No. ALLC200569-3421

As your L/C No. ALLC200569-3421 did not reach us by the end of August as stipulated in the contract and some errors were found in your L/C，it was impossible for us to execute the contract in such a short period of time. Please kindly extend the time of shipment to Oct. 15，2021 and the expiry date to Oct. 30，2021.

Best regards.

Yours faithfully,

Mo Xiaofu

第三步 学生做

展证函写作

广西梧州虹光化工厂是一家日生产能力只有5公吨钛白粉的小型私企。2021年6月15日该厂与美国星辰化工有限公司签订了一份250公吨钛白粉（TITANIUM DIOXIDE POWDER）出口合同。合同号为HE100988。合同规定2021年7月15日前交货。想不到在合同签订后梧州突发洪水。为保护堤坝安全，梧州港监部门不得不实施封航，洪水期间禁止200公吨以上的船只航行。两周后，洪水退去。这次洪水严重影响了虹光化工厂的生产进度和交货时间。眼看交货时间快到了，全厂上下都很着急。为了不轻易放弃已经签订的出口合同，总经理陈明明决定请求客户展证。请你代虹光化工厂写一份英文展证函电。

综合训练

一、填空题

随堂测1

1. 外贸单证是指对外贸易所涉及的（ ）和文件。
2. 制作外贸单证时，第一个制作的单据一般是（ ）。
3. 就发票的制作时间而言，它是（ ）开出的单据。
4. 就发票的地位而言，它是（ ）单据，起统帅作用。
5. COMMERCIAL INVOICE IN TRIPLICATE的中文含义是（ ）。
6. 唛头上显示的件数号C/NO. 1-UP。这里UP的含义是（ ）。
7. 从形式上看，发票和包装单都是（ ）单据。
8. 收货人栏目显示 TO ORDER，则此提单种类是（ ）提单。
9. 普惠制产地证书上第十一栏目和第十二栏目的内容分别是出口商声明和（ ）。
10. 你学过产地证的种类有（ ）、普惠制产地证、东盟产地证。
11. 出口信用证项下商业发票的抬头应该是（ ）。
12. 收货人栏目显示 TO ORDER，则提单的背书应该是（ ）背书。

二、翻译题

1. DATE OF ISSUE.

2. 普惠制产地证表格A。
3. DOCUMENTS REQUIRED.
4. 商品品质检验证书。
5. 手签商业发票一式三份。
6. 通知开证申请人。
7. 空白抬头，空白背书。
8. 你做好全部单证了么？
9. FULL SET OF CLEAN ON BOARD MARINE BILLS OF LADING IN TWO ORIGINALS AND 3 COPIES.
10. SHIPMENT DATE PRIOR TO L/C'S ISSUING DATE IS PROHIBITED.
11. 我们需要商业发票一式三份。
12. 所有单据必须在月底前做好。
13. 下周一要提交单据给议付行。
14. 没问题的。除了普惠制产地证外，所有单据都做好了。
15. 一个不符点会被扣50美元。
16. 我不太擅长制作商业发票，特别是特约事项不会处理。
17. Bill of Lading.
18. Letter of Credit.
19. Packing List.
20. Discrepancy Fee.
21. LATEST DATE OF SHIPMENT.
22. BILL OF LADING MADE OUT TO ORDER，ENDORSED IN BLANK.
23. PACKING LIST IN DUPLICATE.
24. PRESENTATION PERIOD：WITHIN 15 DAYS AFTER SHIPMENT.
25. ALL DOCUMENTS MUST INDICATE THE NUMBER OF L/C.
26. 开证申请人。
27. 原产地证。
28. USD54 800.00
29. 受益人证明。
30. 卖方应在2021年7月30日前装运。

三、案例分析

某对外贸易进出口公司于5月23日接到一张法国开来的信用证，信用证规定受益人为该对外贸易进出口公司，申请人为法国E贸易有限公司。信用证对装运期和议付有效期条款规定：“Shipment must be effected not prior to 31st May，2021.The Draft must be negotiated not later than 30th June，2021”。

该对外贸易进出口公司发现信用证装运期太紧，23日收到信用证，31日装运就到期。所以有关人员于5月26日（24日和25日系双休日）按装运期5月31日通知储运部安排装运。储运部根据信用证分析单上规定的5月31日装运期向货运代理公司配船。因装运期太紧，经多方努力才设法商洽将其他公司已配上的货退载，换上该对外贸易进出口公司的货，勉强挤上有效的船期。

该对外贸易进出口公司经多方努力，终于在5月30日装运完毕，并取得5月30日签发的提单。6月2日备齐所有单据通过议付行向开证行交单。6月16日开证行来电提出："提单记载5月30日装运货物，不符合信用证规定的装运期限。不同意接受单据。"你怎么看？

四、手工操作题

根据贸易合同审查信用证，并写出改证函电。

1.贸易合同

SALES　CONTRACT

No.: QP11M086

Date: March 28, 2021

Place: Guangzhou

The Seller: GUANGXI WUZHOU SENGONG IMPORT AND EXPORT CO., LTD.

20, EAST QIXING ROAD, WUZHOU, GUANGXI, P.R.C.

Address: 20, EAST QIXING ROAD, WUZHOU, GUANGXI, P.R.C.

Fax: 0086-774-84208688

Tel: 0086-774-84208838

E-mail: sengong@chemicals.com

****

The Buyer: FIREBIRD TRADING CO., LTD.

Address: W. box 3578, 23#, New Street, Northbridge, New York, the United States

Fax: 001-2-5663-1879

Tel: 001-2-5667-1122

E-mail: firebird@northbridge.com

****

The Seller has agreed to sell while the Buyer has agreed to buy the following goods as per the terms and conditions listed below:

Name of Commodity	Quantity	Specifications	Unit Price	Total Amount
Manganese Dioxide Powder	300 M/T(±5% at the seller's option)	MnO_2: 88% MIN. Fe: 5% MAX. Al_2O_3: 4% MAX. SiO_2: 10% MAX. H_2O: 4% MAX. FINENESS: 400 MESHES 90% MIN. PASSING THROUGH	USD1 830.00 per M/T CIF New York	USD549 000.00

1.Packing: In plastic bags of 25 kgs net each, 40 bags to a wooden pallet.

2.Shipment: Shipment from Wuzhou to New York via Hong Kong in June and July 2021. Partial shipment not allowed and transshipment are allowed.

3.Insurance: To be covered by seller against W.P.A.for the full invoice value.

4.Payment Terms: L/C at sight to be opened within one month after signing the sales contract.

5.Inspection

Both the sellers and the buyers mutually agreed that the Certificate of Quality and Weight and/or Quantity issued by related organazations at the port of shipment shall be part of the documents to be presented for negotiation under the relevant S/C. The buyers shall have the right to inspect the quality and weight and/or quantity of the cargo at the port of destination. However, the reinspection fee shall be borne by the buyers.

6.Discrepancy and Claim

Should the quality and/or weight be found not in conformity with that of the contract, the buyers shall be entitled to lodge a claim with the sellers. Such claim should be supported by survey reports issued by a recognized surveyor approved by the sellers. The claim, if any, shall be filed within 30 days after arrival of the cargo at the port of destination specified in the relative Bill of Lading. If the goods have been processed, the buyers shall thereupon lose the right to claim. Claims in respect of matters within responsibility of insurance company and/or shipping company shall not be considered or entertained by the sellers.

7.Arbitration

All disputes arising out of the performance of, or relating to this contract, shall be settled friendly through negotiation. In case no settlement can be reached through negotiation, the case shall then be submitted to the China International Economic and Trade Arbitration Commission, Beijing, China, for arbitration in accordance with its provisional rules for arbitration. The arbitral award is final and binding upon both parties.

8.Force Majeure

In case the contracted goods are prevented or delayed in whole or in part by reason of war, earthquake, flood, fire, storm, heavy snow, tsunami or other causes of Force Majeure, the seller shall not be held responsible for non-shipment or late shipment of the goods under this contract. In that case, the seller shall notify the buyer by cable, fax or telephone and furnish the buyer within 20 days by registered airmail with a certificate issued by the China Council for the Promotion of International Trade attesting such event or events.

9.Remarks

This confirmation is written in English. Both the Seller and the Buyer shall hold one copy of the original. The Seller shall mail this confirmation to the Buyer as soon as possible for signature. The Buyer shall countersign them and return one copy of this confirmation to the Seller for his file.

Buyer's Signature :	Seller's Signature:
Bob Percy	Li Faxiao
(Managing Director)	(Managing Director)

2. 信用证

27: SEQUENCE OF TOTAL: 1/1

40A: FORM OF DOCUMENTARY CREDIT: IRREVOCABLE

20: DOCUMENTARY CREDIT NUMBER: 2021FTCL06-1403

31C: DATE OF ISSUE: 21-05-10

40E: APPLICABLE RULES: UCP LATEST VERSION

31D: DATE AND PLACE OF EXPIRY: 21-08-30 IN BENEFICIARY'S COUNTRY

50：APPLICANT：FIREBIRD TRADING CO. LTD.，W. BOX 3578 ，23# ，NEW STREET ，NORTHBRIDGE，NEW YORK，THE UNITED STATES

59：BENEFICIARY：GUANGXI WUZHOU SENGONG IMPORT AND EXPORT CO. LTD.200，EAST QIXING ROAD，WUZHOU ，GUANGXI，P.R.C.

32B：CURRENCY CODE，AMOUNT

CURRENCY：USD（US DOLLAR）

AMOUNT：#USD549 000.00 #（SAY US FIVE HUNDRED FORTY NINE THOUSAND ONLY）

41D：AVAILABLE WITH...BY...

ANY BANK IN BENEFICIARY'S COUNTRY BY NEGOTIATION

42C：DRAFTS AT...：SIGHT FOR 100% INVOICE VALUE

42A：DRAWEE：NORTHEAST AMERICA BANK OF U.S.

43P：PARTIAL SHIPMENTS：ALLOWED

43T：TRANSHIPMENT：ALLOWED

44E：PORT OF LOADING：GUANGZHOU，CHINA

44F：PORT OF DISCHARGE：MONTREAL，CANADA

44C：LATEST DATE OF SHIPMENT：21-07-25

45A：DESCRIPTION OF GOODS &/OR SERVICES

300 M/T OF MANGANESE DIOXIDE POWDER

MnO_2：88% MIN. Fe：5% MAX. Al_2O_3：4% MAX. SiO_2：10% MAX .

H_2O：4% MAX. FINENESS：400 MESHES 90% MIN.PASSING THROUGH

UNIT PRICE ：USD1380/MT CIF NEW YORK

PACKED IN PLASTIC BAGS OF 25KGS NET EACH，40 BAGS TO A WOODEN PALLET.

AS PER SALES CONTRACT NO. QP11M0806

46A：DOCUMENTS REQUIRED

+ SIGNED COMMERCIAL INVOICE IN THREE COPIES.

+ FULL SET OF CLEAN ON BOARD MARINE BILLS OF LADING IN TWO ORIGINALS AND THREE COPIES，MADE OUT TO ORDER，ENDORSED IN BLANK，MARKED FREIGHT PREPAID AND NOTIFY APPLICANT EVIDENCING SHIPMENT FROM GUANGZHOU TO NEW YORK.

+ INSPECTION CERTIFICATE OF QUALITY AND WEIGHT IN DUPLICATE.

+ PACKING LIST IN THREE COPIES.

+ CERTIFICATE OF ORIGIN ISSUED BY CORRESPONDING AUTHORITY IN DUPLICATE.

+ INSURANCE POLICY IN DUPLICATE ENDORSED IN BLANK COVERING W.P.A.

+ BENEFICIARY'S CERTIFICATE CERTIFYING THAT ONE SET OF NON-NEGOTIABLE SHIPPING DOCUMENTS HAS BEEN SENT TO APPLICANT BY EMS WITHIN 7 DAYS AFTER SHIPMENT HAS BEEN EFFECTED.

47A：ADDITIONAL CONDITIONS

+ ALL DOCUMENTS AND DRAFT（S）MUST BEAR THIS CREDIT NUMBER.

+ SHIPMENT DATE PRIOR TO L/C'S ISSUING DATE IS PROHIBITED.

+ 5 PCT MORE OR LESS IN QUANTITY AND AMOUNT ARE ACCEPTABLE.

+ IF DOCUMENTS PRESENTED UNDER THIS L/C ARE FOUND TO BE DISCREPANT, WE SHALL GIVE ITS NOTICE OF REFUSAL AND SHALL HOLD DOCUMENTS AT YOUR DISPOSAL SUBJECT TO THE FOLLOWING CONDITION: "IF WE HAVE NOT RECEIVED YOUR DISPOSAL INSTRUCTIONS FOR THE DISCREPANT DOCUMENTS PRIOR TO RECEIPT OF THE APPLICANT'S WAIVER OF DISCREPANCIES, WE WILL RELEASE DOCUMENTS TO APPLICANT WITHOUT NOTICE TO YOU."

71B: CHARGES

ALL BANKING CHARGES OUTSIDE THE U.S., IF ANY, ARE FOR ACCOUNT OF BENEFICIARY.

48: PERIOD FOR PRESENTATION: DOCUMENTS PRESENTED WITHIN 15 DAYS AFTER SHIPMENT BUT WITHIN THE VALIDITY OF THE CREDIT.

49: CONFIRMATION INSTRUCTIONS: WITHOUT

78: INSTR TO PAYG/ACCPTG/NEGOTG BANK

(1) ALL DOCUMENTS MUST BE SENT TO US IN ONE LOT, OUR ADDRESS: NORTHEAST AMERICA BANK OF U.S., 238 #, BEIXALU, GM, NEW YORK, THE UNITED STATES OF AMERICA.

(2) A DISCREPANCY FEE OF USD60.00 SHOULD BE DEDUCTED FROM NEGOTIATION AMOUNT FOR EACH PRESENTATION IF DOCUMENTS DO NOT COMPLY WITH L/C TERMS AND CONDITIONS.

(3) ONE COPY OF BILL OF LADING AND COMMERCIAL INVOICE IS REQUIRED FOR ISSUING BANK'S FILE. USD10.00 WILL BE CHARGED IF THESE COPIES ARE NOT PRESENTED.

(4) UPON RECEIPT OF DOCUMENTS ALONG WITH DRAFT (S) STRICTLY COMPLYING WITH TERMS AND CONDITIONS OF THIS CREDIT, WE WILL REMIT PROCEEDS LESS OUR HANDLING CHARGES TO YOU AS INSTRUCTED.

57D: ADVISE THROUGH BANK: BANK OF CHINA WUZHOU BRANCH

项目二

分项制单

能力目标

1. 能制作或办理信用证付款方式下的发票、包装单、商检证、订舱单、提单、保险单、原产地证书、普惠制原产地证、装船通知、受益人证明、船东证明、汇票等各种单据或证单；

2. 能制作或办理汇付和托收付款方式下的发票、包装单、商检证、订舱单、提单、保险单、原产地证书、普惠制原产地证、装船通知、受益人证明、船东证明、汇票等各种单据或证单。

知识目标

1. 熟悉发票、包装单、商检证、订舱单、提单、保险单、原产地证书、普惠制原产地证、装船通知、受益人证明、船东证明、汇票等各种单据或证单的格式；

2. 掌握发票、包装单、商检证、订舱单、提单、保险单、原产地证书、普惠制原产地证、装船通知、受益人证明、船东证明、汇票等各种单据或证单的主要内容及填写方法。

思政目标

通过整个外贸流程分析和外贸单据的分项制作，教导学生在单证实务工作中，必须要按照填制规范进行书写，做到专业、谨慎、认真、规范，不能急躁、大意，更不能弄虚作假，自觉维护企业的利益，树立中国企业的优良形象。

项目引例

制作保险单出错导致无法收款

2021年3月，广州A进出口公司向加拿大B贸易公司出口一批纺织品，合同采用贸易术语CIF Vancouver。信用证上规定：Insurance Policy/Certificate in 2 copies for 110% of the invoice value covering ICC（AN）additional War Risks. 但是A公司的外贸单证员在制作保险单时粗心大意，将战争险漏保，造成单证不符，从而导致银行拒付。

引例评析：本案例告诉我们，单据必须严格按照信用证的要求来缮制，在工作中要有事业心和责任感，不要因为个人的疏忽而给企业带来损失。

任务一　商业发票

情境导入

2021年1月下旬，广西梧州春江五金矿产进出口有限公司拟向加拿大装船出口100公吨特级金属硅。1月18日，出口部经理王瑞荣将一份信用证交给实习单证员谭雅梅，要求她制作议付单据——商业发票。

第一步　学生学

一、商业发票的含义

商业发票（Commercial Invoice），简称发票，是卖方向买方开立的载有货物名称、规格、数量、单价、总金额等内容的正式的购物凭证，是货物买卖的证明，是买方凭以收货、付款、记账和报关完税的依据，是所交货物的总说明。

二、商业发票的地位

无论是在信用证付款方式还是汇付和托收项下，商业发票都是全套议付单据的核心，是基本单证，处于核心和统帅地位。这有以下三点理由：

首先，商业发票排位第一。商业发票是“46A单据要求”中第一个要求的单据。它是受益人第一时间制作的单据，也是议付银行第一个审查的单据。

其次，商业发票内容最为重要。它涉及货物名称、品质、数量、单价、总值等交易最为重要的内容。

最后，商业发票内容影响力很大。制单人首先要确保商业发票的内容正确。如果商业发票的内容有误，其他单据相关栏目的内容也会出现错误。商业发票的内容一旦确定下来，随后制作的其他单据的很多栏目可以直接复制商业发票的内容。例如，货名、品质、数量、包装、唛头、特约事项、运输路线、发票号码、发票日期等。

三、商业发票的作用

（1）可供进口商了解和掌握装运货物的全面情况。发票是一笔交易的全面叙述，它详细列明了该批装运货物的名称、规格、数量、包装、单价、总值等情况，为进口商提供识别该批货物属于哪一批订单项下的依据。进口商可以根据出口商提供的商业发票，核对所签订合同中的项目，了解和掌握合同的履约情况，进行验收。

（2）作为进口商记账，进口报关，海关统计和报关纳税的依据。商业发票是销售货物的凭证。对进口商来说，需要根据发票逐笔登记记账，按时结算货款。进口商在清关时需要向当地海关递交出口商商业发票，海关凭此核算税金，验关放行和海关统计。

（3）在不使用汇票的情况下，商业发票可以代替汇票作为付款依据。

在D/P和T/T即期付款不出具汇票的情况下，商业发票可作为买方支付货款的依据，替代汇票进行核算。在光票付款的方式下，因为没有货运单据跟随，商业发票起着证实装运货物和交易情况的作用。

（4）一旦发生保险索赔时，商业发票还可以作为货物价值的证明。

四、商业发票的格式

商业发票没有统一的格式，是非要式单据。出口商可以自行设计、填写、签字、盖章。不同的进（出）口商往往都有各自不同格式的商业发票，有的格式美丽花哨些，有的格式朴素简单些。虽然格式各有不同，但商业发票填制的项目内容和方法却大同小异。一般的商业发票可以有文档格式、表格格式、文档和表格混合格式。对于商业发票的制作，内容正确是第一位的，格式是第二位的。

第二步　教师教

一、商业发票的内容

1.首文

首文部分应列明发票名称、发票号码、合同号码、出票日期和地点、船名、装运港、卸货港、发货人、收货人等。这部分一般都是印刷好了的项目，留有的空格须填写。

很多教材上都声明商业发票应署有出口单位的全称、详细地址、网址、电话、传真等。我们认为这个做法只是一般习惯做法，找不到任何有说服力的依据，因为各国和联合国法律、法规或国际惯例都没有就发票的详细内容作出规定。

由于商业发票属于非要式单据，本书建议在商业发票的顶头部分不要显示发货人名称、地址、电话、传真、邮箱等信息。因为在发票末尾的落款名称其实就是发货人及其相关信息，上下都填写就显得重复了。

2.文本

商业发票的文本主要包括唛头、商品名称、数量、规格、单价、总价、包装方法、毛重或净重等内容。

3.结文

商业发票的结文部分一般包括信用证中加注的特别条款或文句，出票人的落款和签字。落款和签字一般在发票的右下角。落款就是盖上受益人的单证专用章，以示受益人单位对该发票负责；签字是受益人中经授权人手签，有时也用图章代替手签。

《UCP600》第十八条a款规定：发票无须签字；商业发票中货物、服务或行为的描述必须与信用证中显示的内容相符。

如果来证规定商业发票需要手签的，则不能盖章，必须手签。

二、商业发票的制作要点

1.发票编号（Invoice No.）

由出口商按照自己的习惯和爱好统一编号。发票作为中心单据，其他票据的号码均可与此号码一致，如汇票号码、包装单及附属单据号码等。

2.地址及日期（Place & Date）

出票地址和日期通常在发票右上角。出票地址应为信用证规定的受益人所在地，通常是议付所在地。在全套议付单据中，发票是签发日期最早的单据。它不得早于合同的签订日期，也不得迟于提单的签发日期。

3.合同号（S/C No.）

发票中显示的合同号码应与信用证上列明的合同号码一致，一笔交易牵涉多个合同的，应在发票上表示出来。

4.信用证号（L/C No.）

当采用信用证支付货款时，填写信用证号码。若信用证没有要求在发票上标明信用证号码，此项可以不填。当采用其他支付方式时，此项不填。

5.收货人/抬头人（Consignee）

在此栏目前通常印有“To”“Sold to Messrs”“For Account and Risk of Messrs”等。

抬头人即买方名称，应与信用证中的开证申请人一致。如果信用证中没有特别的规定，即将信用证的开证申请人的名称、地址等信息填入此栏即可。

6.装运港及目的地（From...to...）

起讫地要填上货物自装运港至目的港的地名，有转运情况应予以表示。这些内容应与提单上的相关部分一致。如果货物需要转运则注明转运地。

例如，From Qingdao To New York. U.S.A. W/T Hong Kong.

7.唛头及件数（Marks and Numbers）

唛头一般是由卖方提出，经买方同意后使用。国际标准化组织推荐使用的唛头一般由四部分组成：

（1）买方或收货人名称的简称或缩写。

（2）相关号码。如信用证号、合同号、订单号、发票号等。

（3）目的港。

（4）件数、批号。

注意事项：

（1）如果合同或信用证没有规定唛头，卖方可以自己制作唛头，也可以打上N/M（No mark）。

（2）发票中的唛头应与其他单据上的唛头一致。

（3）如果来证规定了唛头内容，要按照来证规定缮制。

货物件数指按照一定的包装方法，对货物经过大包装后所得的包装件数而不是指货物自然包装件数。

例如，一批出口到欧盟的女式夹克，共12 000件，一个塑料袋装一件夹克，50件夹克装一个纸箱。这里的12 000件就是货物自然包装件数，240箱则是货物包装件数。

唛头中1-UP：合同有溢短装条款，签订合同时，还不知道卖方最终装运数量。“待定”的意思。待卖方最终确定了装多少数量，再根据实际装船数量填写UP的位置。

8.货物描述及数量（Description and Quantity）

根据《UCP600》第十八条规定，商业发票中货物、服务或行为的描述必须与信用证中显示的内容相符。在汇付或托收付款方式下，发票对货物的描述内容可参照合同的规定结合实际情况进行填制。

发票上的货物数量既可以填写货物的自然包装数量，也可以填写货物的大包装数量，或者两者结合起来填写，如“12 000 PIECES/240 CARTONS OF WOMEN’S JACKET.”。

填写货物描述及数量时应注意：

（1）缮制发票时，数量必须反映货物的实际装运数量，做到单证一致。尤其当信用证只给定界限时，例如，“Not Exceed 20 000M/T，Minus 5% Quantity Allowance.”在这样的条件下需要注明实际装运数量。

(2) 如果信用证规定或者实际业务需要，一批货物要分制几套单据，则每套单据应缮制一份发票，各发票的货物数量之和应等于该批货物的总数量。

(3)《UCP600》第三十条规定：a.用“约”或“大约”等用语来表示信用证金额或信用证规定的数量或单价时，应解释为允许有关金额或数量或单价有不超过10%的增减幅度。b.在信用证未以包装单位件数或货物自身件数的方式规定货物数量时，货物数量允许有5%的增减幅度，只要总支取金额不超过信用证金额即可。

9.单价 (Unit price)

单价包括计价货币、计价单位、单位价格金额和贸易术语四部分。如信用证有具体规定，则应与信用证一致。发票金额应与汇票金额相同，且不能超过信用证总金额。

在商业发票正中下方结尾位置，通常印有“有错当查”(E. & O.E.)，即“Errors and Omissions Excepted”，表示在发票一旦出现差错时，发票的制作者可以纠正的意思。

如果成交商品规格较多的，信用证常规定：“AS PER S/C NO. …”，制单时需分别列明各种规格和单价。

10.总值 (Amount)

总值等于单价乘以数量。除非信用证另有规定，否则货物总值不能超过信用证金额。

实际制单时，如果来证要求在发票中扣除佣金，则必须扣除。折扣与佣金的处理方法相同。

例如，来证要求 “From Each Invoice 8 Percent Commission Must Be Deducted 且总额为“USD20 000.00 FOBC8% OSLO”，则填在价格栏中的金额的计算如下：

FOBC8% OSLO USD20 000.00－C8% USD1 600.00

FOB OSLO USD18 400.00

在CFR和CIF价格条件下，佣金一般应按扣除运费和保险费之后的FOB价格计算。

如果来证要求在成交价格为CIF时，分别列出运费、保险费，并显示FOB的价格，制单时可按照如下格式填写：

SIGNED COMMERCIAL INVOICE MANUALLY IN TRIPLICATE AND MUST SHOW BREAKDOWN OF THE AMOUNT AS FOLLOWS: FOB VALUE, FREIGHT CHARGES, PREMIUM AND TOTAL AMOUNT CIF.

FOB VALUE：$20 000.00

FREIGHT：$1 200.00

PREMIUM：$900.00

TOTAL AMOUNT CIF：$22 100.00

11.证明文句

信用证要求在发票内特别注明船名、原产地、进口许可证号码等声明文句，制单时必须一一详列。常用的证明文句有：

(1) 证明所交货物与合同或订单所列货物相符。

We certify that the goods named have been supplied in conformity with Order No.123.

兹证明本发票所列货物与第123号合同相符。

(2) 证明原产地。

We hereby certify that the above mentioned goods are of Korean Origin.

This is to certify that the goods named herein are of Korean Origin.

兹证明所列货物系韩国产。

(3) 证明货物不装载于某国船只，载货船只不停靠某国港口。

We certify that the goods mentioned in this invoice have not been shipped on board of any vessel flying Japanese flag or due to call at any Japanese port.

兹证明本发票所列货物不装载悬挂日本国旗或停靠任何日本港口的船只。

12.特约事项

特约事项就是信用证要求受益人在制作议付单据时特别要注意做到的条款。特约事项的目的是方便进口人办理进口手续。这些信息在进口人办理进口手续时，经常要用到，随便翻看某一个单据就可以找到。有两种情况：

一种情况是要求在所有单据上显示重要号码和内容，如要求显示信用证号码、开证日期、开证银行名称等。

另一种情况是仅仅要求在某一种单据上显示某些重要内容或号码。如要求在发票上显示价格构成部分及货物产地；要求在提单上显示运输路线，显示船公司在目的地的船务代理公司或船公司的分支机构的名称和地址。

如 THE NUMBER AND THE DATE OF THIS CREDIT AND THE NAME OF ISSUING BANK MUST BE QUOTED ON ALL DOCUMENTS.

信用证号码、日期和开证行名称必须在所有单据上显示。

13.出单人签名或盖章

按照《UCP600》的规定，发票无须签字。实际工作中，几乎所有信用证都要求手签发票，不接受盖章式签字。

商业发票只能由信用证中规定的受益人出具。除非信用证另有规定，否则用影印、电脑处理或者复写方法制作出来的发票，应该在作为正本的发票上注明“正”(ORIGINAL)的字样，并且由出单人落款与签字。

三、商业发票的制作原则

根据国际商会《跟单信用证统一惯例》第十八条的规定，出口商制作商业发票要符合以下原则：

(1) 必须在表面上看来系由受益人出具(另有规定者除外)；

(2) 必须做成以申请人的名称为抬头(另有规定者除外)；

(3) 必须将发票币别作成与信用证相同的币种；

(4) 无须签字(另有规定者除外，工作中，信用证一般都要求签名)；

(5) 按照指定行事的被指定银行、保兑行(如有)或开证行可以接受金额超过信用证所允许金额的商业发票，倘若有关银行已兑付或已议付的金额没有超过信用证所允许的金额，则该银行的决定对各有关方均具有约束力；

(6) 商业发票中货物、服务或行为的描述必须与信用证中显示的内容相符。

四、商业发票的制作示范

根据下面的信用证及附后补充信息，制作商业发票。

微课 2-1

商业发票的制作

27：SEQUENCE OF TOTAL：1/1

40A：FORM OF DOCUMENTARY CREDIT：IRREVOCABLE

20：DOCUMENTARY CREDIT NUMBER：EXP2020-1207

31C：DATE OF ISSUE：2021-12-07

40E：APPLICABLE RULES：UCP LATEST VERSION

31D：DATE AND PLACE OF EXPIRY：22-02-15 IN BENEFICIARY'S COUNTRY

50：APPLICANT：GOOD BROTHER RESOURCES CO.，LTD. 2950 HIGHWAY
DRIVE TRAIL BRITISH COLOMBIA，CANADA

59：BENEFICIARY：GUANGXI WUZHOU XINDASHUN TRADING CORP.
555，WEST XINXING ROAD，WUZHOU，GUANGXI，P.R.C.

32B：CURRENCY CODE，AMOUNT

CURRENCY：USD（US DOLLAR）AMOUNT：# 165 000.00 #

41D：AVAILABLE WITH... BY...

ANY BANK IN BENEFICIARY'S COUNTRY BY NEGOTIATION

42C：DRAFTS AT：

SIGHT FOR 100% OF INVOICE VALUE

42A：DRAWEE：NORTHEAST AMERICA BANK OF CANADA

43P：PARTIAL SHIPMENTS：ALLOWED

43T：TRANSSHIPMENT：ALLOWED

44E：PORT OF LOADING：GUANGZHOU，CHINA

44F：PORT OF DISCHARGE：MONTREAL，CANADA

44C：LATEST DATE OF SHIPMENT：22-01-31

45A：DESCRIPTION OF GOODS &/OR SERVICES

100 M/T/100 BAGS OF SILICON METAL

Si：99%　MIN.　Fe：0.4% MAX.　Al：0.4%　MAX.　Ca：0.1% MAX.

SIZE：10-100 MM 90% MIN.

UNIT PRICE：USD1 650/MT CIF MONTREAL，CANADA

AS PER SALES CONTRACT NO.GBR10086

PACKED IN PLASTIC WOVEN BAGS OF ABOUT 1 000 KGS NET EACH

46A：DOCUMENTS REQUIRED

（1）SIGNED COMMERCIAL INVOICE IN DUPLICATE.

（2）FULL SET OF CLEAN ON BOARD MARINE BILLS OF LADING IN TWO ORIGINALS AND 3 COPIES，MADE OUT TO ORDER，ENDORSED IN BLANK，MARKED FREIGHT PREPAID，NOTIFYING APPLICANT EVIDENCING SHIPMENT FROM GUANGZHOU TO MONTREAL.

（3）INSPECTION CERTIFICATE OF QUALITY AND WEIGHT IN DUPLICATE.

（4）PACKING LIST IN TRIPLICATE.

（5） CERTIFICATE OF ORIGIN G. S. P. FORM A ISSUED BY CORRESPONDING AUTHORITY IN DUPLICATE.

（6） INSURANCE POLICY OR CERTIFICATE ENDORSED IN BLANK WITH CLAIMS PAYABLE AT THE DESTINATION WITH THE SAME CURRENCY OF DRAFT AGAINST ALL RISKS AND WAR RISK OF C.I.C. FOR 110 PCT OF INVOICE VALUE.

（7） BENEFICIARY'S CERTIFICATE CERTIFYING THAT ONE SET OF NON-NEGOTIABLE SHIPPING DOCUMENTS HAS BEEN SENT TO APPLICANT BY EMS WITHIN 7 DAYS AFTER SHIPMENT HAS BEEN AFFECTED.

47A： ADDITIONAL CONDITIONS

（1） ALL DOCUMENTS MUST BEAR THIS CREDIT NUMBER.

（2） SHIPMENT DATE PRIOR TO L/C'S ISSUING DATE IS PROHIBITED.

（3） 5 PCT MORE OR LESS IN QUANTITY AND AMOUNT ARE ACCEPTABLE.

（4） GOODS COVERING FREE OF CHARGE ARE ACCEPTABLE.

（5） IF DOCUMENTS PRESENTED UNDER THIS L/C ARE FOUND TO BE DISCREPANT, WE SHALL GIVE ITS NOTICE OF REFUSAL AND SHALL HOLD DOCUMENTS AT YOUR DISPOSAL SUBJECT TO THE FOLLOWING CONDITION： "IF WE HAVE NOT RECEIVED YOUR DISPOSAL INSTRUCTIONS FOR THE DISCREPANT DOCUMENTS PRIOR TO RECEIPT OF THE APPLICANT'S WAIVER OF DISCREPANCIES， WE WILL RELEASE DOCUMENTS TO APPLICANT WITHOUT NOTICE TO YOU."

71B： CHARGES

ALL BANKING CHARGES OUTSIDE CANADA， IF ANY， ARE FOR ACCOUNT OF BENEFICIARY.

48： PERIOD FOR PRESENTATION

DOCUMENTS PRESENTED WITHIN 15 DAYS AFTER SHIPMENT BUT WITHIN THE VALIDITY OF THE CREDIT.

49： CONFIRMATION INSTRUCTIONS

WITHOUT

78： INSTRUCTION TO PAYG/ACCPTG/NEGOTG BANK

（1） ALL DOCUMENTS MUST BE SENT TO US IN ONE LOT， OUR ADDRESS：

NORTHEAST AMERICA BANK OF CANADA， 238#， BEIXALU， GM， MONTREAL， CANADA.

（2） A DISCREPANCY FEE OF USD60.00 SHOULD BE DEDUCTED FROM NEGOTIATION AMOUNT FOR EACH PRESENTATION IF DOCUMENTS DO NOT COMPLY WITH L/C TERMS AND CONDITIONS.

（3） UPON RECEIPT OF DOCUMENTS ALONG WITH DRAFT （S） STRICTLY COMPLYING WITH TERMS AND CONDITIONS OF THIS CREDIT， WE WILL REMIT PROCEEDS LESS OUR HANDLING CHARGES TO YOU AS INSTRUCTED.

（4） ONE COPY OF BILL OF LADING AND COMMERCIAL INVOICE IS REQUIRED FOR ISSUING BANK'S FILE. USD10.00 WILL BE CHARGED IF THESE COPIES ARE NOT PRESENTED.

57D：ADVISE THROUGH BANK

BANK OF CHINA WUZHOU BRANCH

72：SENDER TO RECEIVER INFORMATION

PLS RELEASE THE L/C UPON RECEIPT OF ADVISING FEES.

END OF MESSAGE

补充信息：船名：KUIBEIQUE 12WV；船期：2022-01-28；实装货物数量：金属硅100包；净重100M/T；毛重：100.8 M/T；体积：40M³；货物存放地点：广州黄埔码头2号仓库。要求卖方设计唛头。

COMMERCIAL INVOICE

DATE：JAN.18，2022

NO. CF006

TO：GOOD BROTHER RESOURCES CO.，LTD. 2950 HIGHWAY
DRIVE TRAIL BRITISH COLOMBIA，CANADA
SHIPMENT FROM GUANGZHOU TO MONTREAL BY VESSEL

NAME OF GOODS	SPECIFICATION	QUANTITY	MARKS & NOS.	N.W./G.W.	UNIT PRICE
SILICON METAL	Si:99% MIN. Fe:0.4% MAX. Al:0.4% MAX. Ca:0.1% MAX. SIZE:10-100 MM 90% MIN.	100 BAGS	XINDASHUN GBR10086 MONTREAL C/NO.1-100	100M/T/ 100.8 M/T	USD1 650/MT CIF MONTREAL TOTAL: USD165 000.00

SAY：US DOLLARS ONE HUNDRED AND SIXTY FIVE THOUSAND ONLY.

NO. OF L/C：EXP2020-1207

GUANGXI WUZHOU XINDASHUN TRADING CORP.

莫运金

第三步　学生做　商业发票制作

根据下面的信用证及附加信息，制作商业发票。要求自行设计唛头。

Sequence of Total	*27 ：1/1
Form of Doc. Credit	*40A：IRREVOCABLE
Doc. Credit Number	*20：DICCPM845034
Date of Issue	31C：21-07-20
Applicable Rules	*40E：UCP LATEST VERSION
Expiry	*31D：DATE 21-10-15 PLACE CHINA
Applicant	*50 ：GULF FURNISHING CO.，LTD.， P. O. BOX 61086，RIYADH 11565 SAUDI ARABIA

Beneficiary *59：FOSHAN NANHAI JUNMA IMPORT
AND EXPORT CO.，LTD.

Amount *32B：CURRENCY USD AMOUNT 50 000.00

Pos./Neg.Tol.（%） *39A：10/10

Available with/by *41D：SWIFT：BKCHCNBJ44A
A/C NO.883258643308093014
BY NEGOTIATION

Drafts at ... 42C：SIGHT

Drawee 42A：SAUDI BRITISH BANK，AREA MANAGEMENT OFFICE

Partial Shipment 43P：ALLOWED

Transshipment 43T：ALLOWED

Port of Loading/Airport of Departure 44E：ANY CHINESE PORT，CHINA

Port of Discharge/Airport of Destination 44F：DAMMAM PORT，SAUDI ARABIA

Latest Date of Shipment 44C：21-08-31

Descript. of Goods 45A：

100 CARTONS OF TAISHI CHAIRS
MODEL：L4×3
AS PER ORDER NO. ISL097
BENEFICIARY MUST CERTIFY SO ON THE INVOICES.
PRICE TERM：USD500.00/CARTONS CFR DAMMAM
PACKED IN 120CM×120CM×60CM CARTONS OF 1 CHAIR EACH

Documents Required 46A：

+ MANUALLY SIGNED INVOICES IN TRIPLICATE，ONE OF WHICH SHALL BE CERTIFIED BY CHAMBER OF COMMERCE ABOUT THE ORIGIN OF PRODUCTS EXPORTED.

+ FULL SET OF THREE ORIGINAL CLEAN ON BOARD OCEAN BILLS OF LADING MADE OUT TO ORDER，ENDORSED IN BLANK，MARKED FREIGHT PREPAID AND NOTIFY APPLICANT STATING THE SHIPPING MARK GIVEN BELOW.

SHIPPING MARKS：
GULF FURNISHING
DAMMAM
DICCPM845034
C/NO.1-UP

+ PACKING LIST IN DUPLICATE.

+ SHIPPING ADVICE SHOWING TO THE APPLICANT THE NAME OF CARRYING VESSEL，SHIPMENT DATE，QUANTITY，MARKS，INVOICE VALUE AND DATE，NET WEIGHT AND GROSS WEIGHT WITHIN 1 DAY AFTER SHIPMENT HAS BEEN EFFECTED.

Additional Condition 47A：

+ ALL SHIPPING DOCUMENTS MUST SHOW THIS CREDIT NUMBER.

+ SHIPMENT PRIOR TO DC OPENING DATE NOT ACCEPTABLE.

Details of Charges 71B：ALL CHARGES OUTSIDE COUNTRY OF ISSUER ARE FOR ACCOUNT OF BENEFICIARY/EXPORTER.

Presentation Period 48：WITHIN 21 DAYS AFTER THE DATE OF SHIPMENT BUT WITHIN THE VALIDITY OF THE CREDIT .

Confirmation *49：WITHOUT

Instructions 78：

WE HEREBY ENGAGE WITH THE DRAWERS AND/OR BONA FIDE HOLDERS THAT DRAFTS DRAWN AND NEGOTIATED IN COMFORMITY WITH THE TERMS OF THIS CREDIT WILL BE DULY HONOURED ON PRESENTATION. DOCUMENTS MUST BE DESPATCHED BY DHL COURIER SERVICE IN ONE COVER TO SAUDI BRITISH BANK, AREA MANAGEMENT OFFICE，P.O. BOX 9084，RIYADH 11413，SAUDI ARABIA TEL. 4050677，FAX. 4068715，CHARGES ARE FOR ACCOUNT OF BENEFICIARY.

"Advise through" 57 D：SWIFT：BKCHCNBJ44A
A/C NO. 883258643308093014

Send. to Rec. Info. 72：EXCEPT SO FAR AS OTHERWISE EXPRESSLY STATED，THIS DOCUMENTARY CREDIT IS SUBJECT TO UCP FOR DOCUMENTARY CREDITS（2007 REVISION).

INTERNATIONAL CHAMBER OF COMMERCE PUBLICATION NO.600

附加信息：船名：SWRF DEMARKER 02F；船期：2021-08-19；装运港：佛山南海三山港；目的港：DAMMAM；实际装船数量：100 CARTONS；发票号码：LM1100811；净重：9 000 KGS；毛重：10 000 KGS。

COMMERCIAL INVOICE

DATE：

NO.：

TO：

SHIPMENT FROM　　　　TO　　　　BY VESSEL

NAME OF GOODS	SPECIFICATION	QUANTITY	MARKS & NOS.	N.W./G.W.	UNIT PRICE
					TOTAL：

SAY：US DOLLARS

NO. OF L/C：

×××

任务二 包装单

情境导入

2021年1月下旬，广西梧州春江五金矿产进出口有限公司向加拿大装船出口了100公吨特级金属硅。1月18日，出口部经理王瑞荣要求实习单证员谭雅梅在制作商业发票之后，继续制作另外一种议付单据——包装单。

第一步 学生学

一、包装单的含义

包装单指记载或描述商品包装状况的单据，是商业发票的附属单据，是一种重要的议付单据。

国际贸易是跨国贸易，买卖双方分别在不同国家或地区，距离遥远。国际贸易中的货物只有极小一部分是散装货物或裸装货物，绝大多数货物都需要经过适当包装才能进出口，因为恰当的包装不仅可以保护商品，还可以美化商品，提高售价，促进销售。

在通常情况下，包装单据是必不可少的议付单据。进口地海关验货、公证行检验、进口商清点核对货物都以包装单据为依据，从而了解包装内的具体内容，以便查验、运输和销售。

二、包装单的种类

根据客户的要求，卖方可以使用不同形式、种类的包装单据，如装箱单、包装说明、包装提要、重量单、重量证书、磅码单、尺码单、花色搭配单等。经常使用的包装单据主要有装箱单、重量单和尺码单。

1.装箱单

装箱单（Packing List）又称包装单，是表明出口货物的包装形式、内容、数量、体积或件数的一种单据。

装箱单是海关、进出口商等验货的凭据以及商业发票的补充。装箱单除了需要按装箱情况详细列明商品包装的具体情况，如货号、色号、尺寸搭配、毛净重以及包装的尺码以外，其他项目内容的填写与商业发票的项目填写方法相同。

2.重量单

重量单是按照装货重量（Shipping Weight）成交的货物，在装运时出口商向进口商提供的一种重量证明文件。它证明所装货物的重量与合同规定相符，货到目的港有短重时出口商不负责任。

若按照卸货重量（Delivered Weight）成交的货物，如果货物短重时，进口商必须提供重量证明书，才可以向出口商、轮船公司或保险公司索赔。

重量单上除了记载装箱单的内容外，还需要尽量清楚地表明商品每箱毛、净重以及总重量的情况，供买方安排运输、存仓时参考。

3.尺码单

尺码单（Measurement List）是一种偏重于说明货物每件的尺码和总尺码的包装单据，侧重于在装箱单的基础上再重点说明每件商品、每种商品的尺码和总尺码。

第二步　教师教

一、包装单的内容

包装单是非要式单据，本无固定的格式和内容，一般是由出口商根据货物的种类和进口商的要求仿照商业发票的格式来制作。不同出口商制作的包装单格式可以不尽相同，但基本内容却是大同小异，主要包括单据的名称、编号、出单日期、货物名称、唛头、规格、件数、毛重、净重、签章等，有时还涉及包装材料、包装方式、包装规格等。

1.单据名称（Name of Document）

包装单上应标明“Packing List”字样。在信用证中，经常使用的包装单据名称主要有Packing Summary，Packing Note，Packing Specification，Specification List，Packing Slip，Detail Packing List，Weight List，Weight Note，Weight Certificate，Measurement List，Assortment List等。

2.编号或商业发票编号（No./Invoice No.）

包装单可以有自己的编号，但是因为商业发票是核心单据，因此通常用商业发票的编号作为包装单的编号。

3.出单日期（Date）

出单日期可以按发票日期填写。包装单的制作一般在发票之后，所以也可以晚于发票日期，但是不能晚于提单日期。

4.出口商名称和地址（Exporter's Name and Address）

出口商，即出票人，要求与信用证受益人或合同卖方一致。

5.买方名称和地址（Buyer's Name and Address）

买方，即抬头人，要求与开证申请人或合同买方一致。

6.运输工具和航线（Means of Transport and Route）

包装单上亦可表示运输工具和方式及运输路线，写法可与发票相同。

7.唛头及编号（Marks & Nos.）

唛头应与发票、提单等单据的唛头一致。在单位包装货量或品种不固定的情况下，需注明每个包装件内的包装情况，因此包装件应进行编号。在每个包装件内，一般应尽可能详细列出有关的包装细节，如规格、型号、色泽、内装量等。

8.品名和规格（Name of Commodity & Specification）

根据《UCP600》第十四条审核单据的标准，除商业发票外，其他单据中的货物、服务或行为描述若须规定，可使用统称，但不得与信用证规定的描述相矛盾。

实际工作中，包装单的品名一般都与发票和信用证一致。规格包括商品规格和包装规格。商品规格和包装规格按货物情况和信用证要求详细填列。

9.数量（Quantity）

如果每种规格的包装单位的重量不同，应将不同规格的数量分别表示出来，最后累计出合计数。

10.毛重（Gross Weight）

如果出口一批货物含有多种规格，每种规格的毛重又不同，则应分别列出毛重。如果货物的单件不是定量包装，如粮谷类麻袋包装的商品，一般只能是计算每袋大约的重量。

对于贵重商品，一般要精确包装数据。例如，锡锭的出口，其每捆约为1 000千克。第一捆是999.5千克，第二捆是999.3千克……如果出口100捆，则要将货物一捆捆具体过磅、编码、记录，然后在包装单上列出100个数。这种包装单又称为“磅码单”。

11.净重（Net Weight）

净重指货物自身重量及总净重。

12.尺码（Measurement）

尺码指每件货物的体积及合计体积。

13.签章（Signature）

按照《UCP600》的规定，包装单无须签字，但要落款。实际工作中，一般都要签字以视负责。通常，由出具包装单据的单位和负责人落款和签字，且应与发票的落款和签字一致。如果信用证要求中性包装（Neutral Packing）或规定中性包装单（in white paper or in plain），本栏应空白不落款和签字。

二、制作包装单的注意事项

1.单据名

在包装单据上注明相应的单据名称，如“Packing List”“Weight List”“Measurement List”等。

2.签署

装箱单上一般不用签署，除非信用证条款中有特别规定。

3.出单日

装箱单无须注明出单日，除非信用证上另有规定。

4.抬头人

除非信用证有特别要求，否则银行可以接受无抬头人的装箱单。

5.商品的品名

根据《UCP600》第十四条审核单据的标准，除商业发票外，其他单据中的货物、服务或行为描述若需规定，可使用统称，但不得与信用证规定的描述相矛盾。

现实工作中，装箱单中描述的货物一般都与发票中描述的货物相一致。除非信用证明确规定装箱单必须标明货物描述，否则银行可以接受没有货物描述的装箱单，但是要求装箱单内容与发票有充分的联系。

6.单价及金额

装箱单一般不应显示货物的单价及金额，因为进口商把商品转售给第三方时只交付装箱单和货物，往往不愿泄露其购买成本。

7.唛头

装箱单上必须刷制与发票、信用证及实物完全一致的唛头标识。

8.包装号码

装箱单上的包装号码必须是连号，不可断开或跳号。

9.包装情况

信用证中有关货物的包装描述必须在装箱单上得到完整的反映，如果信用证要求提供详细装箱单，则装箱单的内容应反映每一件商品包装的目录及其他相关信息。

10.特约事项

如果信用证或装船指令规定有特约事项，则包装单也是一个重要的议付单据，也要显示特约事项的内容，才能做到单单一致。

三、包装单制作示范

微课2-2

包装单的制作

根据下面的信用证及补充信息，制作包装单。

27：　SEQUENCE OF TOTAL：1/1

40A：FORM OF DOCUMENTARY CREDIT：IRREVOCABLE

20：　DOCUMENTARY CREDIT NUMBER：EXP2020-1207

31C：DATE OF ISSUE：21-12-07

40E：APPLICABLE RULES：UCP LATEST VERSION

31D：DATE AND PLACE OF EXPIRY：22-02-15 IN BENEFICIARY'S COUNTRY

50：　APPLICANT：GOOD BROTHER RESOURCES CO.，LTD. 2950 HIGHWAY DRIVE TRAIL BRITISH COLOMBIA，CANADA

59：　BENEFICIARY：GUANGXI WUZHOU XINDASHUN TRADING CORP.555，WEST XINXING ROAD，WUZHOU，GUANGXI，P.R.C.

32B：CURRENCY CODE，AMOUNT

CURRENCY：USD（US DOLLAR）

AMOUNT：# 165 000.00 #

41D：AVAILABLE WITH... BY...

ANY BANK IN BENEFICIARY'S COUNTRY BY NEGOTIATION

42C：DRAFTS AT：SIGHT FOR 100% OF INVOICE VALUE

42A：DRAWEE：NORTHEAST AMERICA BANK OF CANADA

43P：PARTIAL SHIPMENTS：ALLOWED

43T：TRANSSHIPMENT：ALLOWED

44A：PORT OF LOADING：GUANGZHOU，CHINA

44E：PORT OF DISCHARGE：MONTREAL，CANADA

44F：LATEST DATE OF SHIPMENT：22-01-31

45A：DESCRIPTION OF GOODS &/OR SERVICES

100 M/T/100 BAGS OF SILICON METAL

Si：99% MIN.　Fe：0.4% MAX.　Al：0.4% MAX.　Ca：0.1% MAX.

SIZE：10-100 MM 90% MIN.

UNIT PRICE：USD1 650/MT CIF MONTREAL，CANADA

AS PER SALES CONTRACT NO.GBR10086

PACKED IN PLASTIC WOVEN BAGS OF ABOUT 1 000 KGS NET EACH.

46A：DOCUMENTS REQUIRED

（1）SIGNED COMMERCIAL INVOICE IN DUPLICATE.

（2）FULL SET OF CLEAN ON BOARD MARINE BILLS OF LADING IN TWO ORIGINALS AND 3 COPIES，MADE OUT TO ORDER，ENDORESED IN BLANK，MARKED FREIGHT PREPAID，NOTIFYING APPLICANT EVIDENCING SHIPMENT FROM GUANGZHOU TO MONTREAL.

（3）INSPECTION CERTIFICATE OF QUALITY AND WEIGHT IN DUPLICATE.

（4）PACKING LIST IN TRIPLICATE.

（5）CERTIFICATE OF ORIGIN G. S. P. FORM A ISSUED BY CORRESPONDING AUTHORITY IN DUPLICATE.

（6）INSURANCE POLICY OR CERTIFICATE ENDORSED IN BLANK WITH CLAIMS PAYABLE AT THE DESTINATION WITH THE SAME CURRENCY OF DRAFT AGAINST ALL RISKS AND WAR RISK OF C.I.C. FOR 110% OF INVOICE VALUE.

（7）BENEFICIARY'S CERTIFICATE CERTIFYING THAT ONE SET OF NON-NEGOTIABLE SHIPPING DOCUMENT HAS BEEN SENT TO APPLICANT BY EMS WITHIN 7 DAYS AFTER SHIPMENT HAS BEEN EFFECTED.

47A：ADDITIONAL CONDITIONS

（1）ALL DOCUMENTS MUST BEAR THIS CREDIT NUMBER.

（2）SHIPMENT DATE PRIOR TO L/C'S ISSUING DATE IS PROHIBITED.

（3）5% MORE OR LESS IN QUANTITY AND AMOUNT ARE ACCEPTABLE.

（4）GOODS COVERING FREE OF CHARGE ARE ACCEPTABLE.

（5）IF DOCUMENTS PRESENTED UNDER THIS L/C ARE FOUND TO BE DISCREPANT，WE SHALL GIVE ITS NOTICE OF REFUSAL AND SHALL HOLD DOCUMENTS AT YOUR DISPOSAL SUBJECT TO THE FOLLOWING CONDITION："IF WE HAVE NOT RECEIVED YOUR DISPOSAL INSTRUCTIONS FOR THE DISCREPANT DOCUMENTS PRIOR TO RECEIPT OF THE APPLICANT'S WAIVER OF DISCREPANCIES，WE WILL RELEASE DOCUMENTS TO APPLICANT WITHOUT NOTICE TO YOU."

71B：CHARGES

ALL BANKING CHARGES OUTSIDE CANADA，IF ANY，ARE FOR ACCOUNT OF BENEFICIARY.

48：PERIOD FOR PRESENTATION

DOCUMENTS PRESENTED WITHIN 15 DAYS AFTER SHIPMENT BUT WITHIN THE VALIDITY OF THE CREDIT.

49：CONFIRMATION INSTRUCTIONS：WITHOUT

78：INSTR TO PAYG/ACCPTG/NEGOTG BANK

（1）ALL DOCUMENTS MUST BE SENT TO US IN ONE LOT，OUR ADDRESS：

NORTHEAST AMERICA BANK OF CANADA，238 #，BEIXALU，GM，MONTREAL，CANADA

（2）UPON RECEIPT OF DOCUMENTS ALONG WITH DRAFT（S）STRICTLY COMPLYING

WITH TERMS AND CONDITIONS OF THIS CREDIT, WE WILL REMIT PROCEEDS LESS OUR HANDLING CHARGES TO YOU AS INSTRUCTED.

(3) ONE COPY OF BILL OF LADING AND COMMERCIAL INVOICE IS REQUIRED FOR ISSUING BANK'S FILE. USD10.00 WILL BE CHARGED IF THESE COPIES ARE NOT PRESENTED.

补充信息：船名：KUIBEIQUE 12WV；船期：2022-01-28；实装货物数量：100包；净重100M/T；毛重：100.8M/T；体积：40M³；货物存放地点：广州黄埔码头2号仓库；要求自行设计唛头。

PACKING LIST

DATE：JAN.18，2022

NO. CF006

TO：GOOD BROTHER RESOURCES CO.，LTD. 2950 HIGHWAY DRIVE TRAIL

BRITISH COLOMBIA，CANADA

SHIPMENT FROM GUANGZHOU TO MONTREAL BY VESSEL

NAME OF GOODS	WAYS OF PACKING	QUANTITY/ MEASUREMENT	MARKS & NOS.	N.W./G.W.
SILICON METAL	PACKED IN PLASTIC WOVEN BAGS OF ABOUT 1 000 KGS NET EACH.	100 BAGS / 40M³	XINDASHUN GBR10086 MONTREAL C/NO.1-100	100M/T 100.8M/T

SAY：ONE HUNDRED BAGS ONLY

NO. OF L/C：EXP2020-1207

GUANGXI WUZHOU XINDASHUN TRADING CORP.

莫运金

第三步　学生做　制作包装单

根据下面的信用证及附加信息，制作包装单。

Sequence of Total	*27：1/1
Form of Doc. Credit	*40A：IRREVOCABLE
Doc. Credit Number	*20：DICCPM845034
Date of Issue	31C：21-07-20
Applicable Rules	*40E：UCP LATEST VERSION
Expiry	*31D：DATE 21-09-30 PLACE CHINA
Applicant	*50：GULF FURNISHING CO.，LTD. P. O. BOX 61086，RIYADH 11565 SAUDI ARABIA
Beneficiary	*59：FOSHAN NANHAI JUNMA IMPORT AND EXPORT CO.，LTD.

Amount *32B：CURRENCY USD AMOUNT 50 000.00

Pos./Neg.Tol.（%） *39A：10/10

Available with/by *41D：SWIFT：BKCHCNBJ44A
A/C NO.883258643308093014
BY NEGOTIATION

Drafts at... 42C：SIGHT

Drawee 42A：SAUDI BRITISH BANK，AREA
MANAGEMENT OFFICE

Partial Shipment 43P：ALLOWED

Transshipment 43T：ALLOWED

Port of Loading/Ariport of Departure 44A：ANY CHINESE PORT，CHINA

Port of Discharge/Airport of Destination 44E：DAMMAM PORT，SAUDI ARABIA

Latest Date of Shipment 44C：21-08-31

Descript. of Goods 45A：

100 CARTONS OF TAISHI CHAIRS MODEL：L4×3
AS PER ORDER NO. ISL097
BENEFICIARY MUST CERTIFY SO ON THE INVOICES.
PRICE TERM：USD500.00/CARTONS CFR DAMMAM
PACKED IN 120CM×120CM×60CM CARTONS OF 1 CHAIR EACH

Documents Required 46A：

+ MANUALLY SIGNED INVOICES IN TRIPLICATE，ONE OF WHICH IS CERTIFIED BY CHAMBER OF COMMERCE ABOUT THE ORIGIN OF PRODUCTS EXPORTED.

+ PACKING LIST IN DUPLICATE.

+ FULL SET OF THREE ORIGINAL CLEAN ON BOARD OCEAN BILLS OF LADING MADE OUT TO ORDER，ENDORSED IN BLANK，MARKED FREIGHT PREPAID AND NOTIFY APPLICANT STATING THE SHIPPING MARKS GIVEN BELOW.

SHIPPING MARKS：
GULF FURNISHING
DAMMAM
DICCPM845034
C/NO.1-UP

+ SHIPPING ADVICE SHOWING TO THE APPLICANT THE NAME OF CARRYING VESSEL，SHIPMENT DATE，QUANTITY，MARKS，INVOICE VALUE AND DATE，NET WEIGHT AND GROSS WEIGHT WITHIN 1 DAY AFTER SHIPMENT HAS BEEN EFFECTED.

Additional Condition 47A：

+ ALL SHIPPING DOCUMENTS MUST SHOW THIS CREDIT NUMBER.

+ SHIPMENT DATE PRIOR TO DC OPENING DATE IS NOT ACCEPTABLE.

Details of Charges 71B：ALL CHARGES OUTSIDE COUNTRY OF ISSUER ARE FOR ACCOUNT OF BENEFICIARY/EXPORTER.

Presentation Period 48：WITHIN 21 DAYS AFTER THE DATE OF SHIPMENT BUT WITHIN THE VALIDITY OF THE CREDIT.

Confirmation *49：WITHOUT

Instructions 78：

WE HEREBY ENGAGE WITH THE DRAWERS AND/OR BONA FIDE HOLDERS THAT DRAFTS DRAWN AND NEGOTIATED IN COMFORMITY WITH THE TERMS OF THIS CREDIT WILL BE DULY HONOURED ON PRESENTATION. DOCUMENTS MUST BE DESPATCHED BY DHL COURIER SERVICE IN ONE COVER TO SAUDI BRITISH BANK, AREA MANAGEMENT OFFICE，P. O. BOX 9084，RIYADH 11413，SAUDI ARABIA，TEL. 4050677 FAX. 4068715. CHARGES ARE FOR ACCOUNT OF BENEFICIARY.

"Advise through"　57D：SWIFT：BKCHCNBJ44A A/C NO. 883258643308093014

附加信息：船名：SWRF DEMARKER 02F；船期：2021-08-19；装运港：佛山南海三山港；目的港：DAMMAM；实际装船数量：100 CARTONS；发票号码：LM1100811；净重：9 000 KGS；毛重：10 000 KGS。

PACKING LIST

DATE：

NO.：

TO：

SHIPMENT FROM__________ TO__________ BY VESSEL

MARK & NOS.	NAME OF COODS	WAY OF PACKING	QUANTITY	N.W./G.W.	MEASUREMENT
					TOTAL：

SAY：

NO. OF L/C：

×××

任务三　订舱单与提单

情境导入

2021年1月下旬，广西梧州春江五金矿产进出口有限公司向加拿大装船出口了100公吨特级金属硅。1月24日上午，实习单证员谭雅梅所在的出口部经理王瑞荣要求她在制作商业发票、包装单并取得商检证书之后，抓紧时间办理租船订舱手续。

第一步　教师教

一、订舱单的含义

订舱单（Shipping Order）俗称下货纸，有的地方还叫托运单（Booking Note），是承运人或其代理人在接受发货人或托运人订舱时，根据发货人或托运人口头或书面申请货物托运的情况安排货物运输而制作的单证。该单证一经承运人确认，便作为承运人、托运人双方订舱的凭证，相当于订舱合同。

二、订舱单的内容

不管是订舱单还是托运单，其格式可能因为不同的船公司而有所不同。其作用是向船东或船代订舱，主要内容大同小异。订舱单的主要内容有：

1.Shipping Order No.（订舱号）

订舱号按照托运人自己的方式和习惯编写。

2.托运日期

托运日期指托运人托运时的实际日期。

3.提单编号

提单编号由船公司出具提单时进行编写。

4.船期

托运时，由于船公司还未安排好船只，故不用填写，由船公司安排。

5.船名

船名由船公司安排后进行填写。

6.Export License No.（出口企业营业登记号）

出品企业营业登记号，即营业执照注册号，此栏是让船公司了解托运人的名称和地址。

7.Shipper（发货人）

发货人一栏填写托运人名称和地址。

8.Consignee（收货人）

提单收货人即提单抬头，有记名抬头、不记名抬头和指示抬头三种。

（1）记名抬头

在收货人栏填写特定的收货人名称，如GREAT NORTHEAST INTERNATIONAL RESOURCES COMPANY。在目的地，只能由记名的人办理提货手续，其他人就算拥有提单也不能提货。其安全性很高，但灵活性不够。此类提单由于不能流通转让，现实中很少使用。记名提单收货人栏不能出现“ORDER”字样。

（2）指示抬头

在提单收货人一栏内载明“凭指示”（to order）或“凭某人指示”（to the order of...）字样。此类提单在目的地只能通过背书才能转让，既有流通性又有安全性，是实务中使用最多的提单。如To Order，to order of shipper，to order of issuing bank。

注意：这里的order是指示提单的标志，不能缺少。在收货人栏只显示to order叫空白抬头。空白抬头提单只能空白背书。

（3）不记名提单

不记名提单又称为来人提单，在提单收货人栏不填任何内容或只填To order。此类提单流通性太强，不用背书就可以转让，任何人拥有提单，不管是何种途径得来的，都可以办理提货手续，实务中很少使用。

9.Notify Party（通知人）

在货物到达目的地时，船公司会发送到货通知给通知人。通知人接到船公司的到货通知后，通知收货人前去办理提货手续。此栏如何填写，信用证或装船指令中的装运条款会给出要求。

10.Pre-carriage by（首程运输）

若要转船，填写第一程船名和航次编号。在转船的情形下，该程填写第一程船东名字。如从广西梧州到香港，然后转大船开往欧洲，第一程运输就是梧州到香港。

11. 装运期限

该栏填写信用证或合同规定的装运货物的时间范围。

12.Place of Receipt（收货地点）

该栏填写船方接收货物的地点。

13.Vessel/ Voy. No.（船名/航次）

装载货物的船名和航次编号。船名/航次由船公司提供，托运人填写订舱单时不用填。

14.Port of LDading（装货港）

该栏填写装货港名称。

15.Port of Discharge（卸货港）

该栏填写卸货港名称。

16.Place of Delivery（交货地点）

该栏填写最后交货地点。

17.Marks & Numbers（标记及号码）

该栏应与发票上的唛头保持一致。

18.No. of Packages（货物件数）

件数指货物外包装数量。该栏填写货物大包装件数。

19.Description of Goods（货物描述）

该栏填写商品名称。

20.Gross Weight（Kgs）（毛重（千克））

该栏填写总毛重。

21.Measurement（CBM）（尺码（立方米））

该栏填写总体积。

22.Number of Original Bill of Ladings（正本提单的份数）

该栏一般填写信用证或合同规定的份数。如果信用证或装船指令没有规定，一般要求船公司出具2份正本、3份副本。

23.Services Required（装柜方式）

（1）整箱（Full Container Load，FCL），是指货主自行将货物装满整箱以后，以箱为单位托运的集装箱。除有些大的货主自己置备有集装箱外，一般都是向承运人或集装箱租赁公司租用集装箱。空箱运到工厂或仓库后，在海关人员的监管下，货主把货物装入箱内，加锁、铝封后交给承运人并取得场站收据，最后凭收据换取提单或运单。

（2）拼箱（Less than Container Load，LCL），是指承运人（或代理人）接受货主托运

的数量不足整箱的小票货运后，根据货物性质和目的地进行分类整理，把去往同一目的地的货物集中到一定数量后拼装入箱。由于一个箱内有不同货主的货拼装在一起，所以叫拼箱。拼箱货的分类、整理、集中、装箱（拆箱）、交货等工作均在承运人码头集装箱货运站或内陆集装箱转运站进行。

24.Freight（运费）

运费支付方式有两种：Prepaid（预付）和Collect（到付）。

25.特别约定事项

特别约定事项是指信用证或合同对卖方提出的特别要求事项。一般是要求在单据上显示号码或其他重要内容，以方便办理进口手续。如要求所有议付单据显示信用证号码、开证日期和开证行名称等。

26.Shipper's Authorized Signature（发货人签名/盖单）

该栏填写发货人所在公司授权人的名字、联系人的联系方式、联系人的名字、电话和传真号码等。

第二步　学生学

一、集装箱货物交接方式

如上所述，集装箱货运分为整箱和拼箱两种，因此在交接方式上也有所不同。纵观当前国际上的做法，集装箱货物交接方式大致有以下四类：

1.整箱交，整箱接（FCL/FCL）

货主在工厂或仓库把装满货后的整箱交给承运人，收货人在目的地以同样整箱接货。换言之，承运人以整箱为单位负责交接。货物的装箱和拆箱均由货主负责。

2.拼箱交，拆箱接（LCL/LCL）

货主将不足整箱的小票托运货物在集装箱货运站或内陆转运站交给承运人，由承运人负责拼箱和装箱（Stuffing，Vanning），然后运到目的地货站或内陆转运站，由承运人负责拆箱（Unstuffing，Devanning）。拆箱后，收货人凭单接货。货物的装箱和拆箱均由承运人负责。

3.整箱交，拆箱接（FCL/LCL）

货主在工厂或仓库把装满货后的整箱交给承运人，在目的地的集装箱货运站或内陆转运站由承运人负责拆箱后，各收货人凭单接货。

4.拼箱交，整箱接（LCL / FCL）

货主将不足整箱的小票托运货物在集装箱货运站或内陆转运站交给承运人，由承运人分类调整，把同一收货人的货集中拼装成整箱，运到目的地后，承运人以整箱交，收货人以整箱接。

二、集装箱货物交接地点

集装箱货物的交接，根据贸易条件所规定的交接地点不同，主要分为如下四种方式：

1.门到门

这种运输方式的特征是：在整个运输过程中完全是集装箱运输，并无翻装接运，故最适宜于整箱交，整箱接。

2.门到场站

这种运输方式的特征是：由门到场站为集装箱运输，由场站到门是货物运输，故适宜于整箱交、拆箱接。

3.场站到门

这种运输方式的特征是：由门至场站是货物运输，由场站至门是集装箱运输，故适宜于拼箱交、整箱接。

4.场站到场站

这种运输方式的特征是：除中间一段为集装箱运输外，两端的内陆运输均为货物运输，故适宜于拼箱交、拆箱接。

三、海运订舱流程

出口方填写由轮船公司或轮船代理公司打印好的托运单，盖上出口方单位公章后送给轮船公司或轮船代理公司。

托运单上的托运人名称和地址、收货人名称和地址、通知人名称和地址、货物名称、重量、容积、数量、目的地、转运、分批、船期、付款方式、结汇期限等详细内容，出口人要一一填好。

轮船公司收到出口方直接递交的托运单/轮船代理公司转交的托运单后，根据船只、航线、航期、货物等情况，配置船只和船期，向出口方签发装货单（Shipping Order，S/O），要求出口方将货物存放在指定的码头仓库。

如果出口方自己将货物送到指定仓库不方便的，可以要求轮船公司安排拖柜公司把货物拖到码头进仓。当然，这要支付一定的拖柜费用。

出口方在托运前，要认真研读信用证中的提单条款，特别是要弄懂托运单上的收货人和通知人栏目的填写方法，还要看信用证是否有特约条款，以及这些特约条款与船公司有无关系。如果有关的话，要在托运单中向货运代理或轮船公司声明，要求其在签发提单等单据的时候予以配合。

（一）委托货运代理订舱

1.在货、证备好后，查询运费，对比船公司，选一家运费合理、服务好的船公司，与其货代公司联系，取得该船公司的订舱委托书。

2.托运人填写订舱委托书，发给货代公司。

3.货代公司接到订舱委托书后，反馈信息给船公司。

4.船公司根据船源、航线等配置船只和船期，发送订舱单回执给代理公司。

5.货代公司反馈订舱回执给托运人，要求其将货物进仓，需要拖柜的，安排拖柜。

6.托运人用订舱回执办理代理报关或自理报关手续。

7.报关后，海关在S/O和报关单上盖章，放行货物。

8.海关放行后，货物装船。

9.装完货物，由货运代理公司领取提单后，转交托运人。

（二）出口方自理订舱

货、证备好后，如果货物数量比较大，或者出口方自身与船公司比较熟悉，出口方也可以自理租船订舱。

1.出口方填写托运单一式五份，交给货运公司，将货物的详细情况告诉货运公司。

2.货运公司根据自身的船源、航线等情况，配置船只，在托运单上写上船名、船期等信息，盖章后退回部分托运单给出口方。

3.出口方将货物按照船公司的要求放进船公司指定的仓库，或由拖柜公司到托运人公司/仓库/工厂接货；向托运人反馈订舱单回执。

4.托运人凭S/O办理自理报关或代理报关手续。

5.报关后，海关在S/O和报关单上盖章放行。

6.海关放行后，船公司按照S/O所列内容将货物装上船。

7.托运人凭M/R到船公司领取提单。

（三）注意事项

1.船货衔接

出口租船订舱时，要注意与备货、备证环节协调好，不要在没有备好货物的情况下就租船，让船等货；也不要在货物备好后一直配不上船，让货等船。这两种情况会产生仓租、利息、空仓费等费用，对迅速出口、回笼资金不利。

2.特约事项

出口方托运时，要注意信用证或装船指令中的特约事项。许多新近从事外贸的人弄不懂什么是特约事项，不知道信用证条款或客户的装船指令中哪些条款是特约事项内容。

所谓特约事项（Special Instructions），就是信用证或装船指令中要求出口方特别注意要做到的事项。有的信用证只有一点或两点特约事项，有的信用证有数项特约事项，有的信用证一个特约事项都没有。

如信用证要求出口方在发票或提单上显示某某号码、日期、某某句子。又如，有的信用证要求所有的单据都要显示开证行的名称和信用证号码。

例如：

（1）ALL DOCUMENTS PRESENTED FOR NEGOTIATION SHALL BEAR NO.OF THIS CREDIT AND THE NAME OF ISSUING BANK.

（2）ALL DOCUMENTS AND DRAFT（S）MUST BEAR THIS CREDIT NUMBER.

3.特约条款的重要性

订舱单或托运单是根据信用证的内容和要求填写的。船公司签发的提单又是以出口方的订舱单/托运单为基础的。如果托运单的内容不符合信用证的要求，将来船公司签发的提单也一定不符合信用证的要求，势必影响单据质量，进而影响收汇安全。

为了避免日后修改提单，出口方在租船订舱前，一定要仔细弄清楚信用证或客户的装船指令有何特殊要求，特别是在信用证付款方式下，出口方要格外留意该信用证中的提单条款和特约事项是如何规定的，然后在托运单的特约事项中详细清楚地将特约条款内容转述给船公司，要求其在出具提单的时候照办。信用证与船公司不相关，船公司通常不知道信用证的要求。

很多议付单据都是出口方自己制作的，要显示什么内容很容易做到，而有的单据如提单、保险单等是外单位出具的，如果不告之特约事项，对方就不会按照要求做，就不能做到单单相符，势必要改单，既耗时又耗钱，影响交单速度。

例如，针对前面的两个特约事项中的第一个要求，托运人可在托运单的特殊事项栏目中显示“请在提单上显示以下内容：NO.OF LETTER OF CREDIT：EXIM06-0070/2004”。

四、订舱单与提单的关系

1.不同船公司，其订舱单形式各有不同，内容大同小异。

2.订舱单是由托运人根据信用证等资料填写；填写后交给船代或船公司。

3.提单是由船公司根据订舱单内容开具，订舱单的内容必须完全正确。

4.托运人凭大副收据领取提单。

第三步　教师示范填写订舱单

根据下面的信用证及附后补充信息，填制订舱单，然后根据订舱单模拟出具提单。

微课 2-3

订舱单的制作

27:　SEQUENCE OF TOTAL: 1/1

40A:　FORM OF DOCUMENTARY CREDIT: IRREVOCABLE

20:　DOCUMENTARY CREDIT NUMBER: EXP2021-1207

31C:　DATE OF ISSUE : 21-12-07

40E:　APPLICABLE RULES : UCP LATEST VERSION

31D:　DATE AND PLACE OF EXPIRY: 22-02-15 IN BENEFICIARY'S COUNTRY

50:　APPLICANT: GOOD BROTHER RESOURCES CO., LTD., 2950 HIGHWAY DRIVE TRAIL BRITISH COLOMBIA, CANADA

59:　BENEFICIARY: GUANGXI WUZHOU XINDASHUN TRADING CORP. 555, WEST XINXING ROAD, WUZHOU, GUANGXI, P.R.C.

32B:　CURRENCY CODE, AMOUNT

CURRENCY: USD (US DOLLAR)

AMOUNT: # 165 000.00 #

41D:　AVAILABLE WITH/BY

ANY BANK IN BENEFICIARY'S COUNTRY

BY NEGOTIATION

42C:　DRAFTS AT: SIGHT FOR 100% OF INVOICE VALUE

42A:　DRAWEE: NORTHEAST AMERICA BANK OF CANADA

43P:　PARTIAL SHIPMENTS: ALLOWED

43T:　TRANSSHIPMENT: ALLOWED

44E:　PORT OF LOADING: GUANGZHOU, CHINA

44F:　PORT OF DISCHARGE: MONTREAL, CANADA

44C:　LATEST DATE OF SHIPMENT: 22-01-31

45A:　DESCRIPTION OF GOODS &/OR SERVICES

100M/T/100 BAGS OF SILICON METAL

Si: 99%MIN.　　Fe: 0.4% MAX.

Al: 0.4%MAX.　　Ca: 0.1% MAX.

SIZE: 10-100MM 90% MIN.

UNIT PRICE: USD1 650/MT CIF MONTREAL, CANADA

AS PER SALES CONTRACT NO.GBR10086

PACKED: IN PLASTIC WOVEN BAGS OF ABOUT 1 000 KGS NET EACH

46A：DOCUMENTS REQUIRED

（1）SIGNED COMMERCIAL INVOICE IN DUPLICATE.

（2）FULL SET OF CLEAN ON BOARD MARINE BILLS OF LADING IN TWO ORIGINALS AND 3 COPIES，MADE OUT TO ORDER，ENDORSED IN BLANK，MARKED FREIGHT PREPAID，NOTIFYING APPLICANT EVIDENCING SHIPMENT FROM GUANGZHOU TO MONTREAL.

（3）INSPECTION CERTIFICATE OF QUALITY AND WEIGHT IN DUPLICATE.

（4）PACKING LIST IN TRIPLICATE.

（5）CERTIFICATE OF ORIGIN G. S. P. FORM A ISSUED BY CORRESPONDING AUTHORITY IN DUPLICATE.

（6）INSURANCE POLICY OR CERTIFICATE ENDORSED IN BLANK WITH CLAIMS PAYABLE AT THE DESTINATION WITH THE SAME CURRENCY OF DRAFT AGAINST ALL RISKS AND WAR RISK OF C.I.C. FOR 110 PCT OF INVOICE VALUE.

（7）BENEFICARY'S CERTIFICATE CERTIFYING THAT ONE SET OF NON-NEGOTIABLE SHIPPING DOCUMENTS HAVE BEEN SENT TO APPLICANT BY EMS WITHIN 7 DAYS AFTER SHIPMENT HAS BEEN EFFECTED.

47A：ADDITIONAL CONDITIONS

（1）ALL DOCUMENTS MUST BEAR THIS CREDIT NUMBER.

（2）SHIPMENT DATE PRIOR TO L/C'S ISSUING DATE IS PROHIBITED.

（3）5% MORE OR LESS IN QUANTITY AND AMOUNT ARE ACCEPTABLE.

（4）GOODS COVERING FREE OF CHARGE ARE ACCEPTABLE.

（5）IF DOCUMENTS PRESENTED UNDER THIS L/C ARE FOUND TO BE DISCREPANT，WE SHALL GIVE ITS NOTICE OF REFUSAL AND SHALL HOLD DOCUMENTS AT YOUR DISPOSAL SUBJECT TO THE FOLLOWING CONDITION：“IF WE HAVE NOT RECEIVED YOUR DISPOSAL INSTRUCTIONS FOR THE DISCREPANT DOCUMENTS PRIOR TO RECEIPT OF THE APPLICANT'S WAIVER OF DISCREPANCIES，WE WILL RELEASE DOCUMENTS TO APPLICANT WITHOUT NOTICE TO YOU.”

71B：DETAILS OF CHARGES

ALL BANKING CHARGES OUTSIDE CANADA，IF ANY，ARE FOR ACCOUNT OF BENEFICIARY

48：PERIOD FOR PRESENTATION

DOCUMENTS PRESENTED WITHIN 15 DAYS AFTER SHIPMENT BUT WITHIN THE VALIDITY OF THE CREDIT

49：CONFIRMATION：WITHOUT

78：INSTR TO PAYG/ACCPTG/NEGOTG BANK

（1）ALL DOCUMENTS MUST BE SENT TO US IN ONE LOT，OUR ADDRESS：NORTHEAST AMERICA BANK OF CANADA，238 #，BEIXALU，GM，MONTREAL，CANADA.

（2）A DISCREPANCY FEE OF USD 60.00 SHOULD BE DEDUCTED FROM NEGOTIATION AMOUNT FOR EACH PRESENTATION IF DOCUMENTS DO NOT COMPLY WITH L/C TERMS AND CONDITIONS.

（3）UPON RECEIPT OF DOCUMENTS ALONG WITH DRAFT(S) STRICTLY COMPLYING WITH TERMS AND CONDITIONS OF THIS CREDIT，WE WILL REMIT PROCEEDS LESS OUR HANDLING CHARGES TO YOU AS INSTRUCTED.

（4）ONE COPY OF BILL OF LADING AND COMMERCIAL INVOICE IS REQUIRED FOR ISSUING BANK'S FILE. USD 10.00 WILL BE CHARGED IF THESE COPIES ARE NOT PRESENTED.

57D：ADVISE THROUGH BANK
BANK OF CHINA WUZHOU BRANCH

72：SEND TO RECEIVER INFORMATION
PLS RELEASE THE L/C UPON RECEIPT OF ADVISING FEES
END OF MESSAGE

补充信息：船名：KUIBEIQUE 12WV；船期：2022-01-28；实装货物：数量100包、净重100M/T、毛重100.8M/T、体积40M³；货物存放地点：广州黄埔码头2号仓库；要求自行设计唛头。

出口货物订舱单

提单编号 ZWB11018　托运日期 2022.01.14　托运单编号 HKL201101006

船　　名 KUIBEIQUE 12W　船　　期 2022.01.28　运 往 地 点 蒙特利尔

托运人：GUANGXI WUZHOU XINDASHUN TRADING CORP. 555，WEST XINXING ROAD，WUZHOU，GUANGXI，P.R.C.

受货人：TO ORDER

通知人：GOOD BROTHER RESOURCES CO.，LTD.，2950 HIGHWAY DRIVE TRAIL BRITISH COLOMBIA，CANADA

<table>
<tr><td rowspan="2">标记及号码</td><td rowspan="2">件数</td><td rowspan="2" colspan="2">货　　名</td><td colspan="2">重量</td><td rowspan="2" colspan="2">体/容积吨</td></tr>
<tr><td>净重</td><td>毛重</td></tr>
<tr><td>XINDASHUN
GBR10086
MONTREAL
C/NO.1-100</td><td>100 BAGS</td><td colspan="2">SILICON METAL</td><td>100M/T</td><td>100.8M/T</td><td colspan="2">40M³</td></tr>
<tr><td colspan="4">合计:SAY ONE HUNDRED BAGS ONLY</td><td colspan="4">共重:100M/T</td></tr>
<tr><td>特约事项</td><td colspan="7">请在提单上显示:
L/C NO.EXP2021-1207</td></tr>
<tr><td>可否转船</td><td colspan="7">可以　　　　（托运人盖章）</td></tr>
<tr><td>可否分批</td><td colspan="2">可以</td><td colspan="5">需要提单正本2份,副本5份</td></tr>
<tr><td>货物堆存地点</td><td>广州/黄埔/梧州</td><td>装船期限</td><td>2022.01.31</td><td colspan="2">结汇期限</td><td colspan="2">2022.02.15</td></tr>
<tr><td>运费缴付方式</td><td colspan="3">AT DESTINATION/PAID/PREPAID√</td><td colspan="2">运费账单开送</td><td colspan="2">梧工艺</td></tr>
<tr><td>信用证号码</td><td colspan="2">L/C NO.:EXP2021-1207</td><td colspan="5">货价:FOB　　CIF</td></tr>
<tr><td>运往香港船名</td><td colspan="3"></td><td colspan="2">实际装船日期</td><td colspan="2"></td></tr>
<tr><td colspan="8">运费吨:　　　　运费率:　　　　运费金额:</td></tr>
</table>

BILL OF LADING

Shipper GUANGXI WUZHOU XINDASHUN TRADING CORP. 555,WEST XINXING ROAD,WUZHOU,GUANGXI,P.R.C.		B/L NO. ZWB11018	
Consignee TO ORDER		Combined transport BILL OF LADING	
Notify Address GOOD BROTHER RESOURCES CO.,LTD.,2950 HIGHWAY DRIVE TRAIL BRITISH COLOMBIA , CANADA		For delivery of goods please apply to:	
Pre-carriage by	Place of Receipt GUANGZHOU		
Ocean Vessel Voy.No. KUIBEIQUE 12W	Port of Loading GUANGZHOU		
Port of Discharge MONTREAL	Place of Delivery MONTREAL	Final Destination for the Merchant's Reference only	
Container,Seal No.& Marks & Nos. XINDASHUN GBR10086 MONTREAL C/NO.1-100	No.of Package & Description of Goods SILICON METAL L/C NO. EXP2021-1207 SAY:ONE HUNDRED BAGS ONLY	Gross Weight (KGS) 100 000	Measurement (M^3) 40
FREIGHT & CHARGES	Revenue Tons / Rate Per	Prepaid √	Collect
Ex. Rate: / Prepaid at GUAGNZHOU	Payable at GUANGZHOU	Place and Date of Issue GUANGZHOU:JAN 28，2022	
Total Prepaid	No. of Original B(s)/L:TWO	Stamp & Signature ×××	
LADEN ON BOARD THE VESSEL			
Date JAN 28，2022		By	

第四步　学生做

一、根据下面的信用证及附加信息，制作订舱单，然后根据订舱单模拟填写提单。

Sequence of Total	*27：1/1
Form of Doc. Credit	*40A：IRREVOCABLE
Doc. Credit Number	*20：DICCPM845034
Date of Issue	31C：21-07-20
Applicable Rules	*40E：UCP LATEST VERSION

Expiry *31D：DATE 21-09-30 PLACE CHINA

Applicant *50：GULF FURNISHING CO.，LTD.
PO. BOX 61086，RIYADH 11565
SAUDI ARABIA
TEL：2782590 FAX：2782926

Beneficiary *59：FOSHAN NANHAI JUNMA IMPORT AND EXPORT CO.，LTD.

Amount *32B：CURRENCY USD AMOUNT 50 000.00

Pos./Neg. Tol.(%) *39A：10/10

Available with/by *41D：SWIFT：BKCHCNBJ44A
A/C NO.883258643308093014
BY NEGOTIATION

Drafts at… 42C：SIGHT

Drawee 42A：SAUDI BRITISH BANK，AREA MANAGEMENT OFFICE

Partial Shipments 43P：ALLOWED

Transshipment 43T：ALLOWED

Port of Loading/Ariport of departure 44E：ANY CHINESE PORT，CHINA

Port of Discharge/Ariport of destination 44F：DAMMAM PORT，SAUDI ARABIA

Latest Date of Shipment 44C：21-08-31

Description of Goods 45A：100 CARTONS OF TAISHI CHAIRS MODEL：L4×3
AS PER ORDER NO.ISL097
BENEFICIARY MUST CERTIFY SO ON THE INVOICES
PRICE TERM：USD 500.00/CARTONS CFR DAMMAM
PACKED IN 120CM×120CM×60CM CARTONS OF 1 CHAIR EACH

Documents required 46A：

+ MANUALLY SIGNED INVOICES IN TRIPLICATE，ONE OF WHICH SHALL BE CERTIFIED BY CHAMBER OF COMMERCE ABOUT THE ORIGIN OF PRODUCTSEXPORTED.

+ PACKING LIST IN DUPLICATE.

+ FULL SET OF THREE ORIGINAL CLEAN ON BOARD OCEAN BILLS OF LADING MADE OUT TO ORDER，ENDORSED IN BLANK，MARKED FREIGHT PREPAID AND NOTIFY APPLICANT STATING THE SHIPPING MARK GIVEN BELOW.

SHIPPING MARKS：
GULF FURNISHING
DAMMAM
DICCPM845034
C/NO.1-UP

+ SHIPPING ADVICE SHOWING TO THE APPLICANT THE NAME OF CARRYING VESSEL，SHIPMENT DATE，QUANTITY，MARKS，INVOICE VALUE AND DATE，NET WEIGHT AND GROSS WEIGHT WITHIN 1 DAY AFTER SHIPMENT HAS BEEN EFFECTED.

Additional Conditions　　47A:

+ ALL SHIPPING DOCUMENTS MUST SHOW THIS CREDIT NUMBER.

+ SHIPMENT PRIOR TO DC OPENING DATE NOT ACCEPTABLE.

Details of Charges　　71B: ALL CHARGES OUTSIDE COUNTRY OF ISSUER ARE FOR ACCOUNT OF BENEFICIARY/EXPORTER

Presentation Period　　48: WITHIN 21 DAYS AFTER THE DATE OF SHIPMENT BUT WITHIN THE VALIDITY OF THE CREDIT

Confirmation　　49: WITHOUT

补充信息：船名：SWRF DEMARKER 02F；船期：2021-08-19；装运港：佛山南海三山港；目的港：DAMMAM；实际装船：数量100 CARTONS、净重9 000 KGS、毛重10 000 KGS；发票号码：LM1100811。

出口货物订舱单

提单编号＿＿＿＿＿　托运日期＿＿＿＿＿　托运单位编号＿＿＿＿＿

船　　名＿＿＿＿＿　船　　期＿＿＿＿＿　运 往 地 点＿＿＿＿＿

托运人：

受货人：

通知人：

标记及号码	件数	货　　名	重量		体/容积吨
			净重	毛重	
合计：			共重：		
特约事项					

可否转船			（托运人盖章）		
可否分批			需要提单正本　　份，副本　　份		
货物堆存地点	广州/黄埔/梧州	装船期限		结汇期限	
运费缴付方式	AT DESTINATION/PAID/PREPAID		运费账单开送		梧工艺
信用证号码		货价：FOB		CIF	
运往目的港船名			实际装船日期		
运费吨：		运费率：		运费金额：	

二、根据下面给出的信用证及相关补充资料，填写出口订舱单，然后根据出口订舱单模拟填写提单。

SEQUENCE OF TOTAL	27：	1/1
FORM OF DOC. CREDIT	40A：	IRREVOCABLE
DOC. CREDIT NUMBER	20：	EX1070/2021
DATE OF ISSUE	31C：	21-07-30
EXPIRY DATE AND PLACE	31D：	21-09-15 PLACE IN CHINA
APPLICANT	50：	NORTHEAST INTERNATIONAL RESOURCES COMPANY, BG STREET，W.BOX 3578，NEW YORK，U.S.A.
BENEFICIARY	59：	GUANGXI WUZHOU GUANGDA METALS EXPORT GROUP COMPANY, 235 WEST XINXING ROAD, WUZHOU, CHINA
AMOUNT	32B：	CURRENCY USD AMOUNT 800 000. 00
POS./NEG. TOL.（%）	39A：	5/5
AVAILABLE WITH/BY	41D：	ANY BANK IN CHINA BY NEGOTIATION
DRAFTS AT	42C：	SIGHT
DRAWEE	42A：	EXPORT-IMPORT BANK OF NEW YORK
PARTIAL SHIPMENTS	43P：	NOT ALLOWED
TRANSSHIPMENT	43T：	NOT ALLOWED
LOADING IN CHARGES	44E：	GUANGZHOU，CHINA
FOR TRANSPORT TO	44F：	NEW YORK，U.S.A.
LATEST DATE OF SHIPMENT	44C：	21-08-30
DESCRIPTION OF GOODS	45A：	50M/T TIN INGOT SPECIFICATION Sn：99.90% MIN. PACKING：IN BUNDLES OF ABOUT 1 000 KGS NET EACH UNIT PRICE AT USD 16 000.00 PRICE TERM：PER M/T CIF NEW YORK AS PER SALES CONTRACT NO.WLE1008
DOCUMENTS REQUIRED	46A：	

+ SIGNED COMMERCIAL INVOICE IN SEXTUPLICATE，SHOWING PRICE CIF NEW YORK.

+ FULL SET OF CLEAN ON BOARD OCEAN BILL OF LADING，IN DUPLICATE，PLUS 5 NON-NEGOTIABLE，MADE OUT TO ORDER OF EXPORT-IMPORT BANK OF NEW YORK，EVIDENCING SHIPMENT FROM GUANGZHOU TO NEW YORK，MARKED FREIGHT PREPAID AND NOTIFY APPLICANT.

+ SIGNED PACKING LIST IN TRIPLICATE.

+ CERTIFICATE OF ORIGIN IN 1 SET.

+ INSURANCE POLICY OR CERTIFICATE ENDORSED IN BLANK FOR 110 PCT OF INVOICE VALUE WITH CLAIMS PAYABLE AT DESTINATION IN CURRENCY OF DRAFT COVERING C.I.C. ALL RISKS AND WAR RISK.

+ INSPECTION CERTIFICATE OF QUALITY ISSUED BY CORRESPONDING AUTHORITY.

+ BENEFICIARY'S CERTIFICATE CERTIFYING THAT ONE SET OF NON-NEGOTIABLE SHIPPING DOCUMENTS HAS BEEN SENT VIA COURIER AND VIA FAX NO.（001）-203-785-1879 DIRECTLY TO APPLICANT WITHIN 7 DAYS AFTER SHIPMENT.

ADDITIONAL CONDITIONS　47A：

+ALL DOCUMENTS PRESENTED FOR NEGOTIATION SHALL BEAR NO.OF THIS CREDIT.

+ 5 PCT MORE OR LESS IN QUANTITY AND AMOUNT ARE ACCEPTABLE.

DETAILS OF CHARGES　71B：ALL BANK CHARGES OUTSIDE U.S. A. ARE FOR THE BENEFICIARY'S ACCOUNT

CONFIRMATION　49：WITHOUT

INSTRUCTIONS　78：

+ THE NEGOTIATING BANK MUST FORWARD THE DRAFTS AND ALL DOCUMENTS IN 1 LOT TO EXPORT-IMPORT BANK OF NEW YORK，MAMA 2 BRACH，111/917-919 MOO. RAMA 2 RD.SAMAEDUN，NEW YORK，U.S.A..

+ UPON RECEIPT OF CREDIT COMMERCIAL DOCUMENTS，WE SHALL REMIT THE PROCEEDS AS PER THE NEGOTIATING BANK'S INSTRUCTIONS.

+ A DISCREPANCY FEE OF USD 50.00 WILL BE DEDUCTED FROM PROCEEDS IF DISCREPANT DOCUMENTS ARE PRESENTED.

+ THE AMOUNT OF ANY DRAFT DRAWN UNDER THIS CREDIT MUST BE ENDORSED ON THE REVERSE OF THE ORIGINAL CREDIT. ALL DRAFTS MUST MARK DRAWN UNDER THIS DOCUMENTARY CREDIT AND BEARING ITS NUMBER AND DATE.

SEND TO REG. IMFO.　72：

+ PLS ACKNOWLEDGE RECEIPT AND ADVISE BENEFICIARY UNGENTLY.

货物原始资料如下：

唛头：NORTHEAST INTL
L/C NO. EX1070/2021
NEW YORK
C/NO.1-50

货存地点：广州黄埔码头1号仓库；实装货物：净重50M/T、毛重50.1M/T、体积30M³；产地：贺州市钟山县冶炼厂；运输工具：DONGFENG 001；发货日期：2021-08-16；锡锭（如图2-1所示）H.S.编码：80011000.00；订舱联系人：莫小梅；联系电话：0774-20003788。

托运人：GUANGXI WUZHOU GUANGFA METALS EXPORT GROUP COMPANY；地址：广西梧州市西江四路7号。

图2-1　锡锭

出口货物订舱单

提单编号＿＿＿＿＿　托运日期＿＿＿＿＿　托运单位编号＿＿＿＿＿

船　　名＿＿＿＿＿　船　　期＿＿＿＿＿　运 往 地 点＿＿＿＿＿

托运人：

受货人：

通知人：

<table>
<tr><td rowspan="2">标记及号码</td><td rowspan="2">件数</td><td rowspan="2" colspan="3">货　　名</td><td colspan="2">重量</td><td rowspan="2">体/容积吨</td></tr>
<tr><td>净重</td><td>毛重</td></tr>
<tr><td></td><td></td><td colspan="3"></td><td></td><td></td><td></td></tr>
<tr><td colspan="5">合计：</td><td colspan="3">共重：</td></tr>
<tr><td>特约事项</td><td colspan="7"></td></tr>
<tr><td>可否转船</td><td colspan="7">（托运人盖章）</td></tr>
<tr><td>可否分批</td><td colspan="2"></td><td colspan="5">需要提单正本　　份，副本　　份</td></tr>
<tr><td>货物堆存地点</td><td>广州/黄埔/梧州</td><td>装船期限</td><td colspan="2"></td><td>结汇期限</td><td colspan="2"></td></tr>
<tr><td>运费缴付方式</td><td colspan="3">AT DESTINATION/PAID/PREPAID</td><td colspan="3">运费账单开送</td><td>梧工艺</td></tr>
<tr><td>信用证号码</td><td colspan="2"></td><td colspan="2">货价：FOB</td><td colspan="3">CIF</td></tr>
<tr><td>运往目的港船名</td><td colspan="3"></td><td colspan="3">实际装船日期</td><td></td></tr>
<tr><td colspan="3">运费吨：</td><td colspan="3">运费率：</td><td colspan="2">运费金额：</td></tr>
</table>

任务四　装船通知

情境导入

2022年1月下旬，广西梧州春江五金矿产进出口有限公司向加拿大装船出口了100吨一号锡锭。1月28日上午，货物装船后，公司取得了提单。下午，实习单证员谭雅梅所在的出口部副经理刘瑞荣要求她在制作了商业发票、包装单、商检证书后，抓紧时间向客户发出装船通知。

第一步　学生学

一、装船通知的定义

出口人在货物装船、领取提单后，要及时向买方发出有关货物装船情况的通知，将船名、航次编号、船期、货物名称、数量、航线、ETD、ETA等细节告知买方，让买方做好接货付款的准备或办理投保手续。

在CFR或CPT成交方式下，卖方在货物装船后首要任务就是向买方发出装船通知，让买方及时投保；否则，由此带来的一切损失由卖方负责，不能因为货物已经装船而将风险转移给买方。

二、装船通知的格式

装船通知是出口人在货物已经装船的情况下，向买方发出通知即货物装船详细情况的一种单据。它是非要式单据，没有固定的格式，出口人可以凭自己的喜好设计。装船通知也是一种议付单据。

三、出具装船通知的时间

货物装船之后，无论是从礼貌的角度还是从义务和责任的角度来看，卖方都要向买方发出装船通知。在CFR或CPT成交方式下，卖方要在装船后的当天向买方或买方的保险公司发出装船通知。在CIF或CIP成交方式下，卖方一般在装船后3～7天向买方发出装船通知。

四、装船通知的内容

不同信用证对装船通知的内容有不同要求。在CFR和CPT成交方式下，信用证会对装船通知的具体内容作出规定。一般包括以下内容：

1.单据名称：装船通知（Shipping Advice）。

2.出具装船通知时间：按信用证要求。一般与提单日期相同或稍后两三天。

3.相关性：对应的合同号码或信用证号码。

4.发票号码与金额：买方投保时需要。

5.货物：显示提单上的货物名称及数量。

6.船名：与提单上的船名一致。

7.船期：与提单上的日期一致。

8.运输路线：从装运港到目的港，中间是否转船，与提单显示的内容一致。

9.ETD：估计开航时间。

10.ETA：估计到港时间。

11.唛头：与提单上的唛头一致。没有唛头的，则填写N/M。

12.特约事项：若信用证有特约事项，要显示特约事项内容，做到单单一致。

13.落款签名：盖章签名。

微课 2-4

装船通知的制作

第二步　教师示范制作装船通知

请教师根据本任务第二步提供的资料，制作装船通知。

SHIPPING　ADVICE

DATE：JAN 28，2022

TO：GOOD BROTHER RESOURCES CO.，LTD.，2950 HIGHWAY DRIVE TRAIL
BRITISH COLOMBIA，CANADA，FAX：001-5143645605

ATTN：MR. HENRY KAZI

RE：100 BAGS （100M/T） SILICON METAL UNDER L/C NO.EXP2021-1207 AND B/L NO.ZWB11018 AND INVOICE NO. CF006 AND INVOICE VALUE USD165 000.00.

WE HEREBY ADVISE YOU THAT ABOVE GOODS HAVE BEEN SHIPPED ON BOARD KUIBEIQUE 12W WHICH IS DUE TO SAIL FROM GUANGZHOU TO MONTREAL ON JAN 28，2022.

ETD：JAN 28，2022　　　　ETA：FEB 26，2022

NO. OF L/C：EXP2021-1207

MARKS：XINDASHUN
GBR10086
MONTREAL
C/NO.1-100

GUANGXI WUZHOU XINDASHUN TRADING CORP.

莫运金

第三步　学生根据资料发装船通知

请各小组的学生根据下面提供的提单、发票等资料，发装船通知。

1.商业发票

COMMERCIAL INVOICE

NO.CF006

DATE：JAN 18，2022

TO：GOOD BROTHER RESOURCES CO.，LTD.，2950 HIGHWAY
DRIVE TRAIL BRITISH COLOMBIA，CANADA
SHIPMENT FROM GUANGZHOU TO MONTREAL BY VESSEL

NAME OF GOODS	SPECIFICATION	QUANTITY	MARKS & NOS.	N.W./G.W.	UNIT PRICE
SILICON METAL	Si：99%　MIN. Fe：0.4% MAX. Al：0.4% MAX. Ca：0.1%　MAX. SIZE:10-100 MM 90% MIN.	100 BAGS	XINDASHUN GBR10086 MONTREAL C/NO.1-100	100M/T/ 100.8M/T	USD1 650/MT CIF MONTREAL TOTAL: USD165 000

SAY：U.S. DOLLARS ONE HUNDRED AND SIXTY FIVE THOUSAND ONLY.

NO. OF L/C：EXP2021-1207

GUANGXI WUZHOU XINDASHUN TRADING CORP.

莫运金

2.提单

BILL OF LADING

<table>
<tr><td colspan="2">Shipper
GUANGXI WUZHOU XINDASHUN TRADING CORP.
555,WEST XINXING ROAD,WUZHOU,GUANGXI,P.R.C.</td><td colspan="2">B/L NO. ZWB11018</td></tr>
<tr><td colspan="2">Consignee
TO ORDER</td><td colspan="2">Combined transport
BILL OF LADING</td></tr>
<tr><td colspan="2">Notify Address
GOOD BROTHER RESOURCES CO.,LTD.,2950 HIGHWAY
DRIVE TRAIL BRITISH COLOMBIA , CANADA</td><td colspan="2">For delivery of goods please apply to:</td></tr>
<tr><td>Pre-carriage by</td><td>Place of Receipt
GUANGZHOU</td><td colspan="2"></td></tr>
<tr><td>Ocean Vessel Voy.No.
KUIBEIQUE 12W</td><td>Port of Loading
GUANGZHOU</td><td colspan="2"></td></tr>
<tr><td>Port of Discharge
MONTREAL</td><td>Place of Delivery
MONTREAL</td><td colspan="2">Final Destination for the Merchant's Reference only</td></tr>
<tr><td>Container, Seal No. & Marks & Nos.
XINDASHUN
GBR10086
MONTREAL
C/NO.1-100</td><td>No.of Package & Description of Goods
SILICON METAL
L/C NO. EXP2021-1207
SAY: ONE HUNDRED BAGS ONLY</td><td>Gross Weight (KGS)
100 000</td><td>Measurement (M^3)
40</td></tr>
<tr><td>FREIGHT & CHARGES</td><td>Revenue Tons / Rate Per</td><td>Prepaid √</td><td>Collect</td></tr>
<tr><td>Ex. Rate: / Prepaid at
GUAGNZHOU</td><td>Payable at
GUANGZHOU</td><td colspan="2">Place and Date of Issue
GUANGZHOU: JAN 28, 2022</td></tr>
<tr><td>Total Prepaid</td><td>No. of Original B(s)/L: TWO</td><td colspan="2">Stamp & Signature
×××</td></tr>
<tr><td colspan="4">LADEN ON BOARD THE VESSEL</td></tr>
<tr><td colspan="2">Date JAN 28, 2022</td><td colspan="2">By</td></tr>
</table>

任务五　保险单

情境导入

2022年1月下旬，广西梧州春江五金矿产进出口有限公司向加拿大装船出口了100吨一号锡锭。1月28日上午，货物装船后，公司取得了提单。下午，实习单证员谭雅梅所在的出口部副经理刘瑞荣要求她在制作了商业发票、包装单、商检证书、装船通知后，抓紧时间办理货物保险手续。

第一步　学生学

一、保险的意义

国际贸易是跨国交易。货物从出口国运输到进口国，路途遥远，危机四伏，风险重重。保险的真正目的和意义就是为了“保险”。海洋货物运输保险是发展最早的一种保险，它不仅为国际贸易活动提供风险保障，也促进了远洋航运事业及国际贸易的发展。海洋货物运输保险以海洋运输财产为保险标的，补偿被保险人的货物在海洋运输过程中因自然灾害或意外事故等所遭受的经济损失。

二、保险时间

在CIF或CIP成交方式下，出口人取得提单后，要着手办理保险事宜。很多书上都说，保险必须在装船前办理，这与实际工作不相符。一般情况下，保险都是在货物装船完毕、取得提单后办理的。因为在装船前投保时，保险公司并不清楚装船过程的具体情况（如货物是否真的装船了、装多少货物、货物状况是否完好等）。但是，在出口人已经知道了船名、航次、柜号等情况下，且货物尚未装船时，出口人也可以及早办理货物投保事宜，保险公司本着灵活原则也是受理的。

三、保险单据

1.保险单

保险单俗称“大保单”，简称保单，是保险人与被保险人订立保险合同的正式书面证明。保险单必须完整地记载保险合同双方当事人的权利、义务和责任。保险单记载的内容是合同双方履行的依据，保险单是保险合同成立的证明。

2.保险凭证

保险凭证俗称“小保单”，又称保险条，是保险人签发给投保人的，表明其已接受其投保的证明文件，是一种简化的保险单。保险凭证上不载明保单背面的保险条款，其余内容与大保单完全相同。凡保险凭证上没有列明的内容均以同类的大保单为准。虽然保险凭证的法律效力与大保单相同，但是不能作为对保险人提起诉讼的依据，因此在国际上使用不多。在实务中，保险凭证既可由保险人签发，也可由保险经纪人作为预约保险单代为签发。

四、保险随附单据

1.发票副本：查看货物名称、数量、金额、包装和买卖双方公司名称。

2.提单副本：查看提单是否是清洁的，以及船名、船期、航线、货名、数量。

3.保险单据：大保单或小保单（按信用证的要求选择。如果没有要求，则两种单据可任意选用）是投保人与保险人之间的保险合同。

4.保险联系单：在此单上，投保人告诉保险公司要保险的条款、险别或特约条款等内容。

第二步 教师教

一、海运货物保险流程

1.货物装船取得提单后，选择一家有国际货物运输保险业务的保险公司。

2.阅读信用证或合同中的保险条款，根据条款要求填写保险单或保险凭证。

3.填写保险联系单。

4.收集商业发票、提单副本。

5.将商业发票、提单副本、保险单一起送交保险公司。

6.保险公司审查核实，盖章签名，退还被保险人。

7.被保险人缴纳保险费。

二、保险金额

1.投保加成

如果信用证或合同中有投保加成比例规定的，按照规定的比例加成投保；如果信用证或合同中没有投保加成比例规定的，按照国际保险市场惯例，加成10%，即按照发票金额的110%进行投保。

2.保险金额的计算

保险金额=发票金额×投保加成

一般情况下，投保加成率是10%，投保加成是110%。

三、特约事项处理

在信用证支付方式下，开证人经常会对受益人提出某些特别要求，这种条款就是特约事项。在办理投保时，出口人需要仔细阅读特约条款。保险单是保险公司出具的，而不是出口人自己出具的，它是一种重要的议付单据。在办理保险时，若出口人自己制作保险单，则在制单时显示特约事项就可以了；若保险公司出具保险单，出口人则要将信用证中特约事项转告保险公司，要求其在出具保险单时照办，才能保证单单一致。

例如，信用证规定“ALL DOCUMENTS MUST BEAR THIS CREDIT NUMBER.”，出口人办理保险时，可以在保险联系单上这样转告保险公司：请在保险单/凭证上显示以下内容：NO.OF LETTER OF CREDIT：EXP2021-1207。

四、保险金额的表达

1.保险金额不实行四舍五入，发票金额乘以投保加成后，尾数有小数的，应保留小数点后两位数。

2.保险金额有小数点的，小数点不能用“point”表示，应该用货币的分“cent”表示，且句末不能用“only”。

例如，USD 1 388.6

U.S. A. DOLLARS：ONE THOUSAND THREE HUNDRED EIGHTY EIGHT POINT SIX ONLY. ×

U.S. A. DOLLARS：ONE THOUSAND THREE HUNDRED EIGHTY EIGHT AND CENTS SIXTY. √

五、教师填写保险单

微课 2-5

保险单的制作

请教师根据本任务第一步骤提供的资料，填写保险单。要求各小组的学生将自己所做单据中错误的地方改正过来。

PICC

中国人民财产保险股份有限公司

PICC PROPERTY AND CASUALTY COMPANY LIMITED

保险联系单

被保险人：GUANGXI WUZHOU XINDASHUN TRADING CORP.

地　　址：555，WEST XINXING ROAD，WUZHOU，GUANGXI，P.R.C.

联 系 人：莫运金

电　　话：13138623183

信用证或合同中关于保险的条款：

INSURANCE POLICY OR CERTIFICATE ENDORSED IN BLANK WITH PAYABLE AT THE DESTINATION WITH THE SAME CURRENCY OF DRAFT AGAINST ALL RISKS AND WAR RISK OF C.I.C. FOR 110% OF INVOICE VALUE.

中保条款（C.I.C）（请打√）	伦敦协会条款（I.C.C）（请打√）
（1）平安险（F.P.A）	（1）协会货物条款（A）
（2）水渍险（W.P.A 或 W.A）	（2）协会货物条款（B）
（3）一切险（All Risks）√	（3）协会货物条款（C）
	（4）协会战争险条款（货物）（IWCC）
附加险：	（5）协会罢工险条款（货物）（ISCC）
（1）战争险√	附加险：
（2）罢工险	恶意损害险（Malicious Damage Clause）
（3）其他	

被保险人提供单据名称：（请打√）

（1）商业发票副本 1 份√　　（2）提单副本 1 份√

（3）保险单正本 2 份，副本 3 份√　　（4）保险凭证正本　　份，副本　　份

（5）其他

海洋货物运输保险单

MARINE CARGO TRANSPORTATION INSURANCE POLICY

NUMBER OF ORIGINAL I/P：TWO

发票号码 CF006　　　　保险单号次

Invoice No.　　　　Policy No.

中国人民保险公司（以下简称本公司）根据广西梧州新达顺贸易有限公司（以下简称被保险人）的要求，由被保险人向本公司缴付约定的保险费，按照本保险单承担的险别和背后所载条款与下列条款承担下述货物运输保险，特立本保险单。

This Policy of Insurance witnesses that the People’s Insurance Company of China（herein-after called “The Company”），at the request of GUANGXI WUZHOU XINDASHUN TRADING CORP.（herein-after called the “Insured”）and in consideration of the agreed premium being paid to the company by the Insured，undertakes to insure the under-mentioned goods in transportation subject to the conditions of this policy as per the Clauses printed overleaf and other special Clauses attached hereon.

标记 Marks & Nos.	包装及数量 Packing & Quantity	保险货物项目 Description of Goods	保险金额 Amount Insured
XINDASHUN GBR10086 MONTREAL C/NO.1-100	100 BAGS	SILICON METAL NO. OF L/C:EXP2021-1207 DATE OF L/C:DEC 07,2021	USD 181 500.00

总保险金额：

Total Amount Insured：U.S. DOLLARS ONE HUNDRED EIGHTY ONE THOUSAND AND FIVE HUNDRED ONLY.

保费　　　　　　　　费率　　　　　　　　装载工具

Premium as arranged　　Rate as arranged　　per conveyance S.S.KUIBEIQUE 12W

开航日期　　　　　　　自　　　　　　　　至

Slg.on or abt. JAN 28，2022　from GUANGZHOU　to MONTREAL

承保险别：

Conditions：

（注：险别条款由保险公司盖上险别章）

所保货物如遇风险，本公司凭本保险单及其有关证件给付赔款。所保货物如发生保险单项下负责赔偿的损失或事故，应立即通知本公司下述代理人查勘。

Claims，if any，payable in surrender of this Policy together with other relevant documents. In the event of accident whereby loss or damage may result in a claim under this Policy immediate notice applying for survey must be given to Company's Agent as mentioned hereunder.

中国人民保险公司

THE PEOPLE'S INSURANCE COMPANY OF CHINA

赔款偿付地点

Claim payable at MONTREAL

出单公司地址　　　　　　　　　　　　　　日期

Address of Issuing Office　　　　　　　　Date：JAN 28，2022

第三步　学生制作保险单

请根据下面给出的信用证及相关补充资料，制作保险单。

SEQUENCE OF TOTAL　　27：1/1

FORM OF DOC. CREDIT　　40A：IRREVOCABLE

DOC. CREDIT NUMBER　　20：EX1070/2021

DATE OF ISSUE　　31C：21-07-30

EXPIRY DATE AND PLACE　　31D：21-09-15 PLACE IN CHINA

APPLICANT　50：NORTHEAST INTERNATIONAL RESOURCES COMPANY，

BG STREET，W. BOX 3578，NEW YORK，U.S.A.

BENEFICIARY　59：GUANGXI WUZHOU GUANGDA METALS EXPORT GROUP COMPANY，

235 WEST XINXING ROAD，WUZHOU，CHINA

AMOUNT　32B：CURRENCY USD AMOUNT 800 000.00

POS./NEG. TOL.（%）39A：5/5

AVAILABLE WITH/BY 41D: ANY BANK IN CHINA BY NEGOTIATION

DRAFTS AT 42C: SIGHT

DRAWEE 42A: EXPORT-IMPORT BANK OF NEW YORK

PARTIAL SHIPMENT 43P: NOT ALLOWED

TRANSSHIPMENT 43T: NOT ALLOWED

LOADING IN CHARGES 44E: GUANGZHOU, CHINA

FOR TRANSPORT TO 44F: NEW YORK, U.S.A

LATEST DATE OF SHIPMENT 44C: 21-08-30

DESCRIPT OF GOODS 45A: 50M/T TIN INGOT

SPECIFICATION Sn: 99.90% MIN.

PACKING: IN BUNDLES OF ABOUT 1 000 KGS NET EACH

UNIT PRICE AT USD 16 000.00

PRICE TERM: PER M/T CIF NEW YORK

AS PER SALES CONTRACT NO.WLE1008

DOCUMENTS REQUIRED46A:

+ SIGNED COMMERCIAL INVOICE IN SEXTUPLICATE, SHOWING PRICE CIF NEW YORK.

+ FULL SET OF CLEAN ON BOARD OCEAN BILL OF LADING, IN DUPLICATE, PLUS 5 NON-NEGOTIABLE, MADE OUT TO ORDER OF EXPORT-IMPORT BANK OF NEW YORK, EVIDENCING SHIPMENT FROM GUANGZHOU TO NEW YORK, MARKED FREIGHT PREPAID AND NOTIFY APPLICANT.

+ SIGNED PACKING LIST IN TRIPLICATE.

+ CERTIFICATE OF ORIGIN IN 1 SET.

+ INSURANCE POLICY OR CERTIFICATE ENDORSED IN BLANK FOR 110 PCT OF INVOICE VALUE WITH CLAIMS PAYABLE AT DESTINATION IN CURRENCY OF DRAFT COVERING C.I.C. ALL RISKS AND WAR RISK.

+ INSPECTION CERTIFICATE OF QUALITY ISSUED BY CORRESPONDING AUTHORITY.

+ BENEFICIARY'S CERTIFICATE CERTIFYING THAT ONE SET OF NON-NEGOTIABLE SHIPPING DOCUMENTS HAS BEEN SENT VIA COURIER AND VIA FAX NO. (001) -203-785-1879 DIRECTLY TO APPLICANT WITHIN 7 DAYS AFTER SHIPMENT.

ADDITIONAL CONDITIONS 47A:

+ ALL DOCUMENTS PRESENTED FOR NEGOTIATION SHALL BEAR NO.OF THIS CREDIT.

+ 5 PCT MORE OR LESS IN QUANTITY AND AMOUNT ARE ACCEPTABLE.

DETAILS OF CHARGES 71B: ALL BANK CHARGES OUTSIDE U.S. A. ARE FOR THE BENEFICIARY'S ACCOUNT

CONFIRMATION 49: WITHOUT

INSTRUCTIONS 78:

+ THE NEGOTIATING BANK MUST FORWARD THE DRAFTS AND ALL DOCUMENTS IN 1 LOT TO EXPORT-IMPORT BANK OF NEW YORK, MAMA 2 BRACH, 111/917-919 MOO. RAMA 2 RD. SAMAEDUN, NEW YORK, U.S.A..

+ UPON RECEIPT OF COMMERCIAL DOCUMENTS，WE SHALL REMIT THE PROCEEDS AS PER THE NEGOTIATING BANK'S INSTRUCTIONS.

+ A DISCREPANCY FEE OF USD 50.00 WILL BE DEDUCTED FROM PROCEEDS IF DISCREPANT DOCUMENTS ARE PRESENTED.

+ THE AMOUNT OF ANY DRAFT DRAWN UNDER THIS CREDIT MUST BE ENDORSED ON THE REVERSE OF THE ORIGINAL CREDIT. ALL DRAFTS MUST MARK DRAWN UNDER THIS DOCUMENTARY CREDIT AND BEARING ITS NUMBER AND DATE.

SEND TO REG. IMFO. 72：

+ PLS ACKNOWLEDGE RECEIPT AND ADVISE BENEFICIARY UNGENTLY.

货物原始资料如下：

唛头：NORTHEAST INTL
L/C NO. EX1070/2021
NEW YORK
C/NO.1-50

发票号码：M2010087；提单编号：WLY10021；提单日期：2021-08-16；货存地点：广州黄埔码头1号仓库；实装货物：净重50M/T、毛重50.1M/T、体积30M^3；产地：贺州市钟山县冶炼厂；运输工具：DONGFENG 001；发货日期：2021-08-16；锡锭H.S.编码：80011000.00；订舱联系人：莫小梅；联系电话：0774-20003788。

海洋货物运输保险单
MARINE CARGO TRANSPORTATION INSURANCE POLICY

NUMBER OF ORIGINAL I/P：TWO

发票号码 保险单号次
Invoice No. Policy No.

中国人民保险公司（以下简称本公司）根据____________（以下简称被保险人）的要求，由被保险人向本公司缴付约定的保险费，按照本保险单承担的险别和背后所载条款与下列条款承担下述货物运输保险，特立本保险单。

This Policy of Insurance witnesses that the People's Insurance Company of China（herein-after called "The Company"），at the request of...（herein-after called the "Insured"）and in consideration of the agreed premium being paid to the company by the Insured，undertakes to insure the under-mentioned goods in transportation subject to the conditions of this policy as per the Clauses printed overleaf and other special Clauses attached hereon.

标记 Marks & Nos.	包装及数量 Packing & Quantity	保险货物项目 Description of Goods	保险金额 Amount Insured

总保险金额：
Total Amount Insured：

保费	费率	装载工具
Premium as arranged	Rate as arranged	per conveyance S.S.
开航日期	自	至
Slg.on or abt.	from	to

承保险别：

Conditions：

（注：险别条款由保险公司盖上险别章）

所保货物如遇风险，本公司凭本保险单及其有关证件给付赔款。所保货物如发生保险单项下负责赔偿的损失或事故，应立即通知本公司下述代理人查勘。

Claims, if any, payable in surrender of this Policy together with other relevant documents. In the event of accident whereby loss or damage may result in a claim under this Policy immediate notice applying for survey must be given to Company's Agent as mentioned hereunder.

中国人民保险公司

THE PEOPLE'S INSURANCE COMPANY OF CHINA

赔款偿付地点

Claim payable at

出单公司地址　　　　日期

Address of Issuing Office　　　　Date

任务六　一般原产地证

情境导入

2022年1月下旬，广西梧州春江五金矿产进出口有限公司向加拿大装船出口了100公吨一号锡锭。1月28日上午，货物装船后，公司取得了提单。下午，实习单证员谭雅梅所在的出口部副经理王瑞荣要求她在制作商业发票、包装单、装船通知、保险单后，抓紧时间申领原产地证。

第一步　学生学

一、原产地证的含义

原产地证（Certificate of Origin）是用以证明出口货物国籍和制造地的一种证明文件。

在当前新冠肺炎疫情全球蔓延、世界经济复苏乏力、贸易保护主义抬头的情况下，各国根据各自的对外贸易政策，普遍实行进口贸易管制，对进口商品实施差别关税和数量限制，由海关执行统计，进口国要求出口国出具货物的原产地证明已成为国际惯例。

二、原产地证的作用

1.关税征收依据

原产地证俗称“纸黄金”，是各国海关据以征收关税和实施差别关税待遇的有效凭证。原产地证可以确定产品关税待遇，提高商品在进口国市场的竞争力。

2.产地和品质证明

原产地证可以证明商品的产地和品质，提高商品在进口国的竞争力。许多商品的品质和产地是密切相关的，产地往往就是品质的代名词。

例如，在国际市场上，持有中国原产地证的丝绸比持有其他国家产地证的丝绸更能卖出好价钱。

3. 重要的议付单据

原产地证还是贸易双方进行货物交接、结汇的重要单据。买方在申请信用证时，常常要求卖方提供原产地证作为重要的议付单据，以确保其自身利益。

4. 海关统计依据

原产地证是各国海关凭以对进口货物进行统计的重要依据。

5. 贸易管制工具

世界各国根据其贸易政策，出于保护本国工业生产和国际贸易竞争的需要，往往对某些进口货物采取控制措施，如进口配额、许可证、反倾销、反补贴等制度。要实行这些控制措施，需要先确定进口货物的原产地，而原产地证就是实施这些控制措施的重要工具。

三、原产地证的格式

（1）原产地证是一种要式单据，有设计好的格式和规定的内容，有规定的各栏目填写方法，还有专门的签发机构。出口人不能自行设计和变更。

（2）原产地证样本。

ORIGINAL

<table>
<tr><td colspan="2">1.Exporter</td><td colspan="3" rowspan="2">Certificate No.
CERTIFICATE OF ORIGIN
OF
THE PEOPLE'S REPUBLIC OF CHINA</td></tr>
<tr><td colspan="2">2.Consignee</td></tr>
<tr><td colspan="2">3.Means of transport and route</td><td colspan="3" rowspan="2">5.For certifying authority use only</td></tr>
<tr><td colspan="2">4.Country/region of destination</td></tr>
<tr><td>6.Marks and numbers</td><td>7.Number and kind of packages; description of goods</td><td>8.H.S.code</td><td>9.Quantity</td><td>10. Number and date of invoices</td></tr>
<tr><td colspan="2">11.Declaration by the exporter
The undersigned hereby declares that the above details and statements are correct,that all the goods were produced in China and that they comply with the Rules of Origin of the People's Republic of China.</td><td colspan="3">12.Certification
It is hereby certified that the declaration by the exporter is correct.</td></tr>
<tr><td colspan="2">Place and date,signature and stamp of authorized signatory</td><td colspan="3">Place and date,signature and stamp of certifying authority</td></tr>
</table>

第二步　教师教

一、原产地证的内容

1.Exporter （出口商）

此栏填写出口商的名称、地址、国别。出口商的名称必须是在海关登记注册的，且名称、地址必须与注册档案一致。

2.Consignee （收货人）

此栏一般应填写最终收货人的名称，即提单通知人或信用证上特别声明的收货人。当最终收货人不明确或为中间商时，可填写“TO ORDER”字样。

3.Means of transport and route（运输方式和路线）

此栏填写装货港、目的港的名称及运输方式（海运、空运或陆运）。经转运的，应注明转运地，其格式为“FROM...TO...BY...（VIA...）”。多式联运的，要分段说明。

4.Country/region of destination （目的地所在国家/地区）

目的地是指货物最终运抵港或国家/地区，一般应与最终收货人（第2栏）一致。不能填写中间商所在的国家名称。

5.For certifying authority use only（签证机构专用栏）

此栏留空。签证机构在签发证书、补发证书或加注其他声明时使用。

6.Marks and numbers（唛头及包装号）

此栏应照实填写出口发票上所列唛头的完整的图案、文字标记及包装号。如果唛头较多，此栏填写不下，可填写在第7、8、9栏的空白处；如果还不够用，可以附页填写。如果图案文字无法缮制，可附复印件，但须加盖签证机构印章。如果无唛头，则应填写“N/M”字样。此栏不得出现“香港、台湾地区或其他国家和地区制造”等的字样。

7.Number and kind of packages；description of goods（包装数量及种类、商品名称）

此栏应填写商品总称和具体名称。在商品名称后须加上大写的英文数字并用括号加上阿拉伯数字及包装种类或度量单位。如果同批货物有不同品种，则要有总包装数。最后应加上结束符号“***”，以防止他人添加伪造内容。

关于特约事项在原产地证中的填写位置，即国外信用证要求每种单据上都填写信用证号码等内容，按照原产地证填写规范要求，应填写在结束符号之后的空白处。在实务中，特约事项一般应放在结束符号之前的空白处，说明结束符号后面都是空白，没有内容。

8.H.S. code （商品编码）

此栏要求填写6位数的H.S.税目号，若同一证书含有多种商品，应将相应的税目号全部填列上。

9.Quantity（数量和重量）

此栏应填写商品的计量单位。以重量计算的，要填写毛重或净重。若同一证书包含多种商品，则量值的填写必须与第7、8栏中的商品名称、商品编码相对应，有的还必须填写总数。

10.Number and date of invoices（发票号与日期）

此栏不得留空，必须按照所申请出口货物的商业发票填写。此栏中日期的填写应早于或等同于第11、12栏的申报和签发日期，且月份的书写一律用英文缩写形式。

11.Declaration by the exporter （出口商声明）

此栏由申领单位中已在签证机构注册的人员签字并加盖企业中英文印章，且签字与印章不得重合。同时，此栏需要填写申领地点和日期，日期不得早于发票日期（第10栏）。

12.Certification （签证机构证明）

申请单位在此栏填写签证日期和地点，然后由签证机构已授权的签证人签名、盖章。签发日期不得早于发票日期（第10栏）和申请日期（第11栏）。若有信用证要求填写签证机关名称、地址、电话、传真以及签证人员姓名，则需要仔细核对，要求准确无误。

微课 2-6

原产地证的制作

二、原产地证的签发机构

根据《中华人民共和国出口货物原产地规则》《中华人民共和国出口货物原产地规则实施办法》的规定，由各地海关签发原产地证。

第三步 教师示范制作原产地证

ORIGINAL

<table>
<tr><td colspan="2">1.Exporter
GUANGXI WUZHOU GUANGDA METALS EXPORT GROUP COMPANY, 235 WEST XINXING ROAD, WUZHOU, CHINA</td><td colspan="3" rowspan="2">Certificate No.

CERTIFICATE OF ORIGIN
OF
THE PEOPLE'S REPUBLIC OF CHINA</td></tr>
<tr><td colspan="2">2.Consignee
NORTHEAST INTERNATIONAL RESOURCES COMPANY, BG STREET, W.BOX 3578, NEW YORK, U.S.A.</td></tr>
<tr><td colspan="2">3.Means of transport and route
BY VESSEL FROM GUANGZHOU TO NEWYORK</td><td colspan="3" rowspan="2">5.For certifying authority use only</td></tr>
<tr><td colspan="2">4.Country/region of destination
U.S.A.</td></tr>
<tr><td>6.Marks and numbers
GUANGDA
GE008
NEWYORK
C/NO.1-100</td><td>7.Number and kind of packages; description of goods
100(ONE HUNDRED)BUNDLES OF TIN INGOT
NO. OF L/C:EXIM06-0070/2021
************</td><td>8.H.S.code
800110</td><td>9.Quantity
N.W.:100M/T</td><td>10.Number and date of invoices
G080515
JUNE 20, 2021</td></tr>
<tr><td colspan="2">11.Declaration by the exporter
The undersigned hereby declares that the above details and statements are correct, that all the goods were produced in China and that they comply with the Rules of Origin of the People's Republic of China.

Place and date, signature and stamp of authorized signatory
GUANGZHOU:JUNE 20, 2021 刘芳芳</td><td colspan="3">12.Certification
It is hereby certified that the declaration by the exporter is correct.

Place and date, signature and stamp of certifying authority
GUANGZHOU:JUNE 21, 2021 黄雅梅</td></tr>
</table>

第四步 学生制作原产地证

请各小组的学生根据以下信用证及补充材料，填写原产地证申请表及原产地证明书各一份。

SEQUENCE OF TOTAL	27：	1/1
FORM OF DOC. CREDIT	40A：	IRREVOCABLE
DOC. CREDIT NUMBER	20：	EX1070/2021
DATE OF ISSUE	31C：	21-07-30
EXPIRY DATE AND PLACE	31D：	21-09-15 PLACE IN CHINA
APPLICANT	50：	NORTHEAST INTERNATIONAL RESOURCES COMPANY, BG STREET, W. BOX 3578, NEW YORK, U.S.A.
BENEFICIARY	59：	GUANGXI WUZHOU GUANGDA METALS EXPORT GROUP COMPANY, 235 WEST XINXING ROAD, WUZHOU, CHINA
AMOUNT	32B：	CURRENCY USD AMOUNT 800 000. 00
POS./NEG. TOL.（%）	39A：	5/5
AVAILABLE WITH/BY	41D：	ANY BANK IN CHINA BY NEGOTIATION
DRAFTS AT	42C：	SIGHT
DRAWEE	42A：	EXPORT-IMPORT BANK OF NEW YORK
PARTIAL SHIPMENTS	43P：	NOT ALLOWED
TRANSSHIPMENT	43A：	NOT ALLOWED
LOADING IN CHARGES	44E：	GUANGZHOU, CHINA
FOR TRANSPORT TO	44F：	NEW YORK, U.S.A.
LATEST DATE OF SHIPMENT	44C：	21-08-30
DESCRIPTION OF GOODS	45A：	50M/T TIN INGOT SPECIFICATION Sn：99.90% MIN. PACKING：IN BUNDLES OF ABOUT 1 000 KGS NET EACH UNIT PRICE AT USD 16 000.00 PRICE TERM：PER M/T CIF NEW YORK AS PER SALES CONTRACT NO.WLE1008
DOCUMENTS REQUIRED	46A：	

+ SIGNED COMMERCIAL INVOICE IN SEXTUPLICATE, SHOWING PRICE CIF NEW YORK.

+ FULL SET OF CLEAN ON BOARD OCEAN BILL OF LADING, IN DUPLICATE, PLUS 5 NON-NEGOTIABLE, MADE OUT TO ORDER OF EXPORT-IMPORT BANK OF NEW YORK, EVIDENCING SHIPMENT FROM GUANGZHOU TO NEW YORK, MARKED FREIGHT PREPAID AND NOTIFY APPLICANT.

+ SIGNED PACKING LIST IN TRIPLICATE.

+ CERTIFICATE OF ORIGIN IN 1 SET.

+ INSURANCE POLICY OR CERTIFICATE ENDORSED IN BLANK FOR 110 PCT OF

INVOICE VALUE WITH CLAIMS PAYABLE AT DESTINATION IN CURRENCY OF DRAFT COVERING C.I.C. ALL RISKS AND WAR RISK.

+ INSPECTION CERTIFICATE OF QUALITY ISSUED BY CORRESPONDING AUTHORITY.

+ BENEFICIARY'S CERTIFICATE CERTIFYING THAT ONE SET OF NON-NEGOTIABLE SHIPPING DOCUMENTS HAS BEEN SENT VIA COURIER AND VIA FAX NO.（001）-203-785-1879 DIRECTLY TO APPLICANT WITHIN 7 DAYS AFTER SHIPMENT.

ADDITIONAL CONDITION　　47A：

+ ALL DOCUMENTS PRESENTED FOR NEGOTIATION SHALL BEAR NO. OF THIS CREDIT.

+ 5 PCT MORE OR LESS IN QUANTITY AND AMOUNT ARE ACCEPTABLE.

DETAILS OF CHARGES　　71B：ALL BANK CHARGES OUTSIDE U.S.A. ARE FOR THE BENEFICIARY'S ACCOUNT

CONFIRMATION　　49：WITHOUT

INSTRUCTIONS　　78：

+ THE NEGOTIATING BANK MUST FORWARD THE DRAFTS AND ALL DOCUMENTS IN 1 LOT TO EXPORT-IMPORT BANK OF NEW YORK，MAMA 2 BRACH，111/917-919 MOO. RAMA 2 RD. SAMAEDUN，NEW YORK，U.S.A..

+ UPON RECEIPT OF COMMERCIAL DOCUMENTS，WE SHALL REMIT THE PROCEEDS AS PER THE NEGOTIATING BANK'S INSTRUCTIONS.

+ A DISCREPANCY FEE OF USD 50.00 WILL BE DEDUCTED FROM PROCEEDS IF DISCREPANT DOCUMENTS ARE PRESENTED.

+ THE AMOUNT OF ANY DRAFT DRAWN UNDER THIS CREDIT MUST BE ENDORSED ON THE REVERSE OF THE ORIGINAL CREDIT. ALL DRAFTS MUST MARK DRAWN UNDER THIS DOCUMENTARY CREDIT AND BEARING ITS NUMBER AND DATE.

SEND TO REG. IMFO.　　72：

+ PLS ACKNOWLEDGE RECEIPT AND ADVISE BENEFICIARY UNGENTLY.

货物原始资料如下：

唛头：NORTHEAST INTL
L/C NO. EX1070/2021
NEW YORK
C/NO.1-50

发票号码：M2010087；提单编号：WLY10021；提单日期：2021-08-16；货存地点：广州黄埔码头1号仓库；实装货物：净重50M/T、毛重50.1M/T、体积$30M^3$；产地：贺州市钟山县冶炼厂；运输工具：DONGFENG 001；发货日期：2021-08-16；锡锭H.S.编码：80011000.00；订舱联系人：莫小梅；联系电话：0774-20003788。

第五步　课后训练

1.请根据下面的信用证制作原产地证。

船期：2021年5月20日；发票号：L10119；Plush Toy Bear的H.S.编码：9503006000（可

只填写前面6位数字）。

SEQUENCE OF TOTAL　　27：1/1

FORM OF DOC. CREDIT　40A：IRREVOCABLE

DOC. CREDIT NUMBER　20：WEL18-202008

DATA OF ISSUE　31C：21-04-10

DATE AND PLACE OF EXPIRY　31D：21-06-15 IN THE COUNTRY OF BENEFICIARY

APPLICANT　50：JAPAN TAKAMULA TRADE CO.，LTD.，18-310MAJI，OSAKA，JAPAN

BENEFICIARY　59：GUANGXI IMPORT & EXPORT TRADE CORPORATION，21，6TH ZHONGSHANROAD，NANNING，GUANGXI，CHINA

AMOUNT　32B：USD AMOUNT 375 000.00

AVAILABLE WITH/BY　41D：ANY BANK BY NEGOTIATION

DRAFTS AT　42C：DRAFTS AT 15 DAYS AFTER SIGHT FOR FULL INVOICE COST

DRAWEE　42A：FUJI BANK LTD.，TOKYO，JAPAN

PARTIAL SHIPMENTS　43P：PROHIBITED

TRANSSHIPMENT　43T：PROHIBITED

LOADING ON BOARD　44E：SHANGHAI

FOR TRANSPORT TO...　44F：OSAKA

LATEST DATE OF SHIPMENT　44C：21-05-31

DESCRIPTION OF GOODS　45A：

COMMODITY PTY（PCS）U/PRICE/PC

PLUSH TOY BEAR 25 000　　USD 15.00

TRADE TERM：CIF OSAKA

DETAILS OF CHARGES　　71B：ALL BANKING CHARGES OUTSIDE JAPAN，IF ANY，ARE FOR ACCOUNT OF BENEFICIARY

PRESENTATION PERIOD　48：DOCUMENTS MUST BE PRESENTED WITHIN 15 DAYS AFTER THE DATE OF SHIPMENT BUT WITHIN THE VALIDITY OF THE CREDIT

DOCUMENTS REQUIRED　46A：

+ SIGNED COMMERCIAL INVOICE IN TRIPLICATE.

+ FULL SET OF CLEAN ON BOARD OCEAN BILLS OF LADING MADE OUT TO ORDER OF ISSUING BANK AND BLANK ENDORSED AND MARKED FREIGHT PREPAID AND NOTIFY APPLICANT.

+ PACKING LIST IN TRIPLICATE.

+ CERTIFICATE OF ORIGIN IN DUPLICATE.

+ MARINE INSURANCE POLICY OR CERTIFICATE ENDORSED IN BLANK FOR 120 PCT OF INVOICE VALUE WITH CLAIMS TO BE PAYABLE IN JAPAN IN THE CURRENCY OF THE DRAFT COVERING OCEAN MARINE CARGO CLAUSES ALL RISK，OCEAN MARINE CARGO CLAUSES OF THE PEOPLE'S INSURANCE COMPANY OF CHINA.

+ BENEFICIARY'S CERTIFICATE CERTIFYING THAT ONE SET OF NON-NEGOTIABLE SHIPPING DOCUMENTS HAVE BEEN SENT DIRECTLY TO APPLICANT BY SPECIAL COURIER SERVICE WITHIN 7 DAYS AFTER SHIPMENT HAS BEEN EFFECTED.

SPECIAL CONDITIONS 47A :

+ ALL SHIPPING DOCUMENTS MUST SHOW THE NUMBER OF THIS CREDIT.

+ B/L SHOULD BEAR VESSEL AGENT'S NAME AND TELEPHONE NUMBER IN OSAKA JAPAN.

ORIGINAL

<table>
<tr><td colspan="2">1.Exporter</td><td colspan="3">Certificate No. 040921430</td></tr>
<tr><td colspan="2">2.Consignee</td><td colspan="3">CERTIFICATE OF ORIGIN
OF
THE PEOPLE'S REPUBLIC OF CHINA</td></tr>
<tr><td colspan="2">3.Means of transport and route</td><td colspan="3" rowspan="2">5.For certifying authority use only</td></tr>
<tr><td colspan="2">4.Country/region of destination</td></tr>
<tr><td>6.Marks and numbers</td><td>7.Number and kind of packages; description of goods</td><td>8.H.S.code</td><td>9.Quantity</td><td>10.Number and date of invoices</td></tr>
<tr><td colspan="2">11.Declaration by the exporter
The undersigned hereby declares that the above details and statements are correct, that all the goods were produced in China and that they comply with the Rules of Origin of the People's Republic of China.
Place and date,signature and stamp of authorized signatory</td><td colspan="3">12.Certification
It is hereby certified that the declaration by the exporter is correct.
Place and date,signature and stamp of certifying authority</td></tr>
</table>

2.根据合同、装船指令填写原产地证

请根据下面的合同、装船指令及补充资料，先制作商业发票、包装单、订舱单，然后填写原产地证申请表。Manganese Dioxide Powder 的H.S. 编码：8111001000（可只填写前面6位数字）。

1.合同

SALES CONTRACT

No. QP11M086

Date：April 28，2021

Place：Guangzhou

The Seller：Guangxi Wuzhou Chunwang Chemicals Manufacturer

Address：2233，Sijiangsi Road，Wuzhou，Guangxi，P.R.C.

Fax：0086-774-84208688

Tel：0086-774-84208838

E-mail：chunwang@chemicals.com

****

The Buyer：International Sourcing Company

Address：W. box 3578 ，23# ，New Street，Northbridge，Sydney，Australia

Fax：0061-02-5663-1879

Tel：0061-02-5667-1122

E-mail：int' lsource@northbridge.com

****

The Seller has agreed to sell while the Buyer has agreed to buy the following goods as per the terms and conditions listed below：

Name of Commodity	Quantity	Unit Price	Total Amount
Manganese Dioxide Powder	36M/T （±5% at the seller's option）	USD 885.00 per M/T CFR Sydney	USD 31 860.00

1.Packing：In plastic bags of 25 kgs net each，40 bags to a wooden pallet.

2.Shipment：Shipment from Wuzhou to Sydney via Hong Kong in May and June of 2021. Partial shipment and transshipment are not allowed.

3.Insurance：To be covered by the buyer.

4.Payment Terms：D/P at sight.

5.Specification：MnO_2：75% min.

Fe：0.3% max.

P：0.15% max.

S：0.15% max.

Fineness：325 mesh 98% passing through

6.Inspection

Both the seller and the buyer mutually agreed that the Certificate of Quality and Weight and/ or Quantity issued by related organiaztion at the port of shipment shall be part of the documents to be presented for negotiation under the relevant S/C. The buyer shall have the right to re-inspect the quality and weight and/or quantity of the cargo at the port of destination. However，the re-inspection fee shall be borne by the buyer.

7.Discrepancy and Claim

Should the quality and/or weight be found not in conformity with that of the contract，the buyer shall be entitled to lodge a claim with the seller. Such claim should be supported by survey reports issued by a recognized surveyor approved by the seller. The claim，if any，shall be filed within 30 days after arrival of the cargo at the port of destination specified in the relative Bill of Lading. If the goods have been processed，the buyer shall there upon lose the right to claim. Claims in respect of matters within responsibility of insurance company and/or shipping company shall not be considered or entertained by the seller.

8.Arbitration

All disputes arising out of the performance of，or relating to this contract，shall be settled friendly through negotiation. In case no settlement can be reached through negotiation, the case shall then be submitted to the China International Economic and Trade Arbitration Commission, Beijing, China, for arbitration in accordance with its provisional rules for arbitration. The arbitral award is final and binding upon both parties.

9.Force Majeure

In case the contracted goods are prevented or delayed in whole or in partby reason of war, earthquake, flood, fire, storm, heavy snow, tsunami or other causes of Force Majeure, the seller shall not be held responsible for non-shipment or late shipment of the goods under this contract. In that case, the seller shall notify the buyer by cable, fax or telephone and furnish the buyer within 20 days by registered airmail with a certificate issued by the China Council for the Promotion of International Trade attesting such event or events.

10.Remarks

This confirmation is written in English. Both the seller and the buyer shall hold one copy of the original. The seller shall mail this confirmation to the buyer as soon as possible for signature. The buyer shall countersign them and return one copy of this confirmation to the seller for his file.

Buyer's Signature :	Seller's Signature:
Bob Percy	Li Faxiao
(Managing Director)	(Managing Director)

2.装船指令

SHIPPING INSTRUCTION

To: Guangxi Wuzhou Chunwang Chemicals Manufacturer
2233, Sijiangsi Road, Wuzhou, Guangxi, P.R.C.
fax: 0086-774-84208688
E-mail: chunwang@chemicals.com

From: International Sourcing Company
W.box 3578, 23#, New Street, Northbridge, Sydney, Australia
Fax: 0061-02-5663-1879
E-mail: int' lsource@northbridge.com

Date: May 8, 2021

Attn: Li Faxiao

Dear Sirs,

We were very happy to have met you in the Spring Guangzhou Fair last month and signed contract No.QP11M086 with your company for 36M/T of Manganese Dioxide Powder. To tell you the truth, we are in urgent need of this product. In order to help you execute the contract, we fax you the following details of shipping instructions. Please effect shipment as soon as possible.

The followings are the documents we require. You are requested to send us the full set of original shipping documents through your bank. Upon receipt of them, we shall remit the proceeds by telegraphic transfer.

1.Name and Address of our Banker:

International Private Group Banker, W. box 2578, 53#, New Street, Northbridge, Sydney, Australia, fax: 0061-02-7663-3871.

2.Name of commodity:　36M/T Manganese Dioxide Powder

MnO_2: 75% min.

Fe: 0.3% max.

P: 0.15% max.

S: 0.15% max.

Fineness: 325 mesh 98% passing through

3.Time of shipment: in May and June, 2021

4.Documents required:

(1) Commercial invoice in six copies, showing the Nos. of commercial invoice and bill of lading.

(2) Packing list in triplicate.

(3) Full set of ocean bills of lading made out to order, endorsed in blank, marked freight prepaid, notifying the full name and address of the contract buyer.

(4) Certificate of origin issued by corresponding authority in duplicate.

(5) Inspection certificate issued by corresponding authority in duplicate.

(6) Beneficiary's certificate certifying that one set of non-negotiable shipping documents has been sent to us by EMS within 7 days after shipment.

Best regards.

Bob Percy

Managing director

ORIGINAL

<table>
<tr><td colspan="2">1.Exporter</td><td colspan="3" rowspan="2">Certificate No. 040921430
CERTIFICATE OF ORIGIN
OF
THE PEOPLE'S REPUBLIC OF CHINA</td></tr>
<tr><td colspan="2">2.Consignee</td></tr>
<tr><td colspan="2">3.Means of transport and route</td><td colspan="3" rowspan="2">5.For certifying authority use only</td></tr>
<tr><td colspan="2">4.Country/region of destination</td></tr>
<tr><td>6.Marks and numbers</td><td>7.Number and kind of packages; description of goods</td><td>8.H.S.code</td><td>9.Quantity</td><td>10. Number and date of invoices</td></tr>
<tr><td colspan="2">11.Declaration by the exporter
The undersigned hereby declares that the above details and statements are correct, that all the goods were produced in China and that they comply with the Rules of Origin of the People's Republic of China.</td><td colspan="3">12.Certification
It is hereby certified that the declaration by the exporter is correct.</td></tr>
<tr><td colspan="2">Place and date,signature and stamp of authorized signatory</td><td colspan="3">Place and date,signature and stamp of certifying authority</td></tr>
</table>

任务七　普惠制原产地证

情境导入

2022年1月下旬，广西梧州春江五金矿产进出口有限公司向加拿大装船出口了100公吨一号锡锭。1月28日上午，货物将装船。1月25日下午，实习单证员谭雅梅所在的出口部副经理王瑞荣要求她抓紧时间申领普惠制原产地证书。

第一步　教师教

一、普惠制的含义

普惠制全称为普遍优惠制度（Generalized System of Preferences，G.S.P）是发达国家给予发展中国家的出口制成品和半制成品（包括某些初级产品）一种普遍的、非歧视的、非互惠的关税优惠待遇。

世界各国对进口商品都要征收关税。就同一个国家而言，对同样的进口商品，由于其原产地不同，征税的税率并不是完全相同的。

发达国家对进口商品征税有三种税率标准：一般税率、最惠国待遇税率、普惠制税率。一般税率通常是针对没有正常的外交或贸易关系的国家的。最惠国待遇税率通常适用具有正常贸易关系的国家，这是国家之间互相给予对方的正常关税待遇。普惠制税率是比最惠国待遇税率更低的一种税率。

二、普惠制原则

1.普遍的：所有发达国家都给惠。

2.非歧视的：对于原产于所有发展中国家的商品，在最惠国待遇的基础上，对进口关税再进行削减或免除。

3.非互惠的：发达国家单方面对发展中国家做出特别的关税减让，不要求受惠国对给惠国做出任何减免关税的回报。

三、普惠制原产地证的作用

1.降低进口商品税率，进口商品在市场上的竞争力大大增强。

2.降低发展中国家出口商品价格，成本下降，增加发展中国家收益，促进发展中国家出口贸易发展，增加外汇收入，加快工业化进程，加速发展中国家的经济增长。

3.发达国家能以低关税进口发展中国家商品，促进发达国家经济发展和人民生活水平提高。

2021年10月25日，海关总署发布2021年第84号公告称：根据《中华人民共和国普遍优惠制原产地证明书签证管理办法》，海关总署决定，自2021年12月1日起，对输往欧盟成员国、英国、加拿大、土耳其、乌克兰和列支敦士登等已不再给予中国普惠制关税优惠待遇国家的货物，海关不再签发普惠制原产地证书。输往上述国家的货物发货人需要原产地证明文件的，可以申请领取非优惠原产地证书。

四、普惠制毕业制度

普惠制不是永久的。当发展中国家或地区的产品在优惠政策下出口越来越多，经济增长速度相应加快并达到一定程度时，发达国家认为这些国家或地区可以“毕业”，就会取消此种优惠。

五、普惠制目标

1. 增加发展中国家出口收益。

2. 促进发展中国家工业化进程。

3. 提高发展中国家的经济增长率。

六、给惠国与受惠国

1. 给惠国普惠制原产地证在国际贸易中被称为“有价证券”和开启国际市场的“金钥匙”。目前全世界只有少数几个国家是给惠国，它们是：瑞士、新西兰、澳大利亚、俄罗斯、白俄罗斯、哈萨克斯坦。

2. 受惠国。目前世界上共170多个发展中国家和地区受惠。中国是受惠国。

七、普惠制原产地证与一般产地证的区分

1. 一般产地证是享受最惠国待遇的有效证件、证明产地。

2. 普惠制原产地证，则是享受普惠制减、免税待遇的有效证件。

八、享受普惠制待遇条件

1. 原产地标准。一切商品均可分为两类，一类为“完全原产地”商品，即商品完全是受惠国出产或制造，没有使用任何进口原料或零部件；另一类为全部或部分使用了进口原料或零部件（包括来源不明的原料和零部件）生产的产品。从普惠制的角度来说，受惠国出口的商品要获权享受普惠制关税的待遇，该出口商品必须在受惠国进行生产和制造，其中所使用的进口原料或零部件必经过充分的加工，使这些进口原料或零部件有了实质性的改变，或者符合给惠国提出的其他条件。

2. 直接运输原则。出口商品不但要在受惠国生产或制造，而且必须直接从受惠国运往给惠国。通过过境国的，必须在过境国海关监管之下，没有投入当地市场销售或交付当地使用，更不能在那里进行其他再加工。

3. 提供有效的证明文件。这包括普惠制原产地证书（申报和证明联合）格式A（简称G.S.P FORM A）及其他有关的单证。G.S.P FORM A 产地证书是受惠国的原产地产品出口到给惠国时享受减、免关税优惠待遇的法律凭证。

九、申领企业

根据海关总署制定的普惠制签证管理办法及其实施细则的规定，以下机构和企业可以申领普惠制原产地证书：

1. 有进出口经营权的国内企业；

2. 中外合资、中外合作和外商独资企业；

3. 国外企业、商社常驻中国代表机构；

4. 对外承接来料加工、来图来样加工、来件装配和补偿贸易业务的企业；

5. 经营旅游商品的销售部门；

6. 参加国际经济、文化交流及拍卖等活动需出售展品、样品等的有关单位。

十、签发机构

根据大多数给惠国的规定，享受普惠制必须持有受惠国政府指定机构签署的普惠制原产地证书。中国普惠制原产地证书由各地海关签发。

十一、申领时间

一般提前3天办理。先用九城软件或信诚通来做产地证的电子申领，做好后，发到各地海关，等收到正确回执后，才能去海关领取纸质证。

第二步 学生学

一、普惠制原产地证的内容

1.第一栏：注册企业的英文名称、地址、国家（强制性添加，不得以任何理由删改）

中文地名采用汉语拼音。国家名称不可以有“ROC”字样。

2.第二栏：收货人名称、地址、国家

必须填写给惠国最终收货人名称，不可填中间转口商名称。到日本、加拿大的货物必须填写最终收货人名称、地址。除此之外如有特殊要求可填“to order”，不得留空。

3.第三栏：运输方式及路线

填写货物最终离境口岸和到货口岸。如有转运可分段填写。转口国须在申请书信息内显示。

例：From Dalian to Hamberg by sea

From Dalian to Hamberg by sea，final destination is Basel（分段描述）

From Dalian to Basel by sea and land（海空联运或海陆联运）

4.第四栏：后发证书

正常情况下此栏空白。

此栏显示“ISSUED RETROSPECTIVELY”（系统自动生成）。如证书遗失、被盗或损毁，签发“复本”证书时显示“THIS CERTIFICATE IS IN REPLACEMENT OF CERTIFICATE OF ORIGIN NO. ...DATED ...WHICH IS CANCELLED”（系统自动生成）。

5.第五栏：商品顺序号

按照商品品名顺序“1”“2”“3”“4”“5”等，以此类推。单项商品此栏填“1”，也可以留空。

6.第六栏：唛头及包装号

此栏应与货物外包装和发票唛头一致，不得出现他国制造字样，也不得出现中国香港地区、澳门地区、台湾地区原产字样。如无唛头应填“N/M”或“NO MARK”。

7.第七栏：包装数量及种类、商品的名称

包装数量必须用英文和阿拉伯数字同时表示，品名必须具体填明，不能笼统填“machine”“garments”等模糊的名称，应具体到可以判断出其前四位税目号。化工产品等必须填具体品名，不能只填如“B-11”这样的代号。商品名称等列完后，应紧接着加上结束符号，防止加添伪造内容。

如有信用证要求填具合同、信用证号码等特殊条款，可填在结束符号下的空白处，也可以填在结束符号上面空白处。一般填写在结束符号上面空白处。

散装应注明“IN BULK”。裸装“IN NUDE”应在申请书备注栏注明。

8.第八栏：产地标准

（1）完全原产填“P”。

（2）加拿大：在两个或以上受惠国内加工填“G”，利用给惠国成分填“F”。原产地标准：非原产成分的价值未超过产品出厂价的40%。

（3）日本、挪威、瑞士、欧盟、土耳其、波兰：填“W”和产品的四位H.S.品目号。

（4）俄罗斯、白俄罗斯、乌克兰、哈萨克斯坦、捷克、斯洛伐克：填“Y”和非原产成分占产品FOB百分比。原产地标准：非原产成分的价值未超过产品离岸价的50%。

9.第九栏：以商品正常计量单位填，如“只”“件”“打”等。以重量计算的则填毛重，只有净重的，填净重，但要标上“N.W.”或“net weight”字样。

10.第十栏：发票号码及日期

月份用英文显示，此栏的日期必须与商业发票一致，发票日期不得迟于出货日期。发票号码之间不得留空格。

11.第十一栏：签证当局的证明

此栏填写签证当局的签证地点、日期。如有企业异地签证必须填写签证所在地的签证地点。

12.第十二栏：出口商声明

申请单位手签人员在此栏右下角签字，此栏盖单位中英文对照印章，除单位名外不得出现任何其他字样。申请日期必须早于签证日期、晚于发票日期，极特殊情况下这三个日期可以是同一天。要特别注意，此处位置比较小，盖章时印章不能与进口国名、出口国名、签名重叠。

二、普惠制原产地证的申领流程

1.注册登记

由申请签发普惠制原产地证书的企业（公司）事先向当地海关办理注册登记手续。登记时须提交下列证件：

（1）经营出口业务的批准文件；

（2）国家市场监督管理部门核发的营业执照；

（3）由申请签证单位法定代表人签署的、委托该单位人员办理普惠制原产地证书申请及手签事宜的委托书一份，以及被委托之手签人免冠半身一寸近照两张。

上述证件，经海关初步审核后，发给“申请签发普惠制原产地证书注册登记表”和“普惠制FORM A原产地证书申报人注册登记卡”各一式两份，由申请单位如实填写，并在规定的时间内将上述表格递交海关审核。海关确认该单位具有申请签证资格后将准予注册，申请单位应在同时交付规定的注册费。

由海关在指定时间内，对普惠制申请手签人员进行业务培训，考核合格后，签发申报证件。申报人可在当年度内凭证件向各地海关办理普惠制申请签证业务。注册地海关每2年对已注册单位及手签人员进行审核。

2.申请出证

申报手签人在本批货物出运前5日到海关办理申请事宜。申请时一般应提交：

（1）普惠制原产地证书申请书一份；

（2）出口商业发票（副本）一份；

（3）装箱单一份；

（4）普惠制原产地证书一套；

（5）对含有进口成分的出口商品，申请人应填写“含进口成分商品成本明细单”；

（6）海关认为有必要提供的其他有关单证（如信用证、合同、报关单等），并如实解答海关提出的有关问题。

对于首次申请签证的单位，海关将派员到生产现场作例行调查。对于非首次申请签证的单位，海关对申报内容有疑问或认为有必要时，也可派员对产品的生产企业进行抽查。

3.签发证书

海关在调查或抽查的基础上，逐一审核申请单位提交的有关单证，确认无误后签发“普惠制原产地证”，交申请单位。

普惠制原产地证申请书样本

申请单位（签章）： 证书号：

注册号：

申请人郑重声明：

本人是被正式授权代表出口单位办理和签署本申请书的。

本申请书及普惠制原产地证格式A所列内容正确无误，如发现弄虚作假，冒充格式A所列货物，擅改证书，自愿接受签证机关的处罚及负法律责任。现将有关情况申报如下：

生产单位		生产单位及联系人电话		
商品名称 （中英文）		H.S.税目号(以 六位数码计)		
商品(FOB)总值(以美元计)		发票号		
最终销售国		证书种类(打“✓”)	加急证书	普通证书
货物拟出运日期				
贸易方式(请在适用处打“✓”)				
一般贸易 C	灵活贸易 L	零售 Y	展卖 M	
包装数量或毛重或其他数量				
原产地标准： 本项商品系在中国生产，完全符合该给惠国给惠方案的规定，其原产地情况符合以下第(　　)条： (1)“P”(完全国产,未使用任何进口原材料) (2)“W”(其H.S.税目号为________ 含进口成分________) (3)“F”(对加拿大出口产品,其进口成分不超过产品出厂价值的40%) 本批产品系：(1)直接运输从____________到____________ (2)转口运输从________ 中转国(地区)________到________				
申请人说明：			领证人(签名)： 电话： 日期： 年 月 日	

ORIGINAL

<table>
<tr><td colspan="3">1. Goods consigned from (Exporter's business name, address, country)</td><td colspan="3" rowspan="2">Reference No.
GENERALIZED SYSTEM OF PREFERENCES
CERTIFICATE OF ORIGIN
(Combined declaration and certificate)
FORM A
Issued in THE PEOPLE'S REPUBLIC OF CHINA
(country)
See notes overleaf</td></tr>
<tr><td colspan="3">2.Goods consigned to (Consignee's name,address,country)</td></tr>
<tr><td colspan="3">3.Means of transport and route (as for as known)</td><td colspan="3">4.For official use</td></tr>
<tr><td>5. Item number</td><td>6. Marks and numbers of packages</td><td>7. Number and kind of packages; description of goods</td><td>8.Origin criterion (see notes overleaf)</td><td>9.Gross weight or other quantity</td><td>10. Number and date of invoices</td></tr>
<tr><td colspan="3">11.Certification
It is hereby certified,on the basis of control carried out, that the declaration by the exporter is correct.

Place and date,signature and stamp of certifying authority</td><td colspan="3">12.Declaration by the exporter
The undersigned hereby declares that the above details and statements are correct;that all the goods were produced in CHINA
(country)
and that they comply with the origin requirements specified for those goods in the Generalized System of preferences for goods exported to
(importing country)
place and date,signature of authorized signatory</td></tr>
</table>

第三步　教师示范制作普惠制原产地证

根据所给的资料，由教师示范填写普惠制原产地证申领表和普惠制原产地证。

27:　SEQUENCE OF TOTAL: 1/1

40A: FORM OF DOCUMENTARY CREDIT: IRREVOCABLE

20:　DOCUMENTARY CREDIT NUMBER: EXP2021-1207

31C: DATE OF ISSUE : 21-12-07

40E: APPLICABLE RULES : UCP LATEST VERSION

31D: DATE AND PLACE OF EXPIRY :

22-02-15 IN BENEFICIARY'S COUNTRY

50: APPLICANT:

GOOD BROTHER RESOURCES CO., LTD., 2950 HIGHWAY DRIVE TRAIL

BRITISH COLOMBIA, CANADA

微课 2-7

普惠制产地证的制作

59：BENEFICIARY：

GUANGXI WUZHOU XIANDASHUN TRADING CORP.

555，WEST XINXING ROAD，WUZHOU，GUANGXI，P.R.C.

32B：CURRENCY CODE，AMOUNT：

CURRENCY：USD（US DOLLAR）

AMOUNT ：# 165 000.00 #

41D：AVAILABLE WITH/BY：

ANY BANK IN BENEFICIARY'S COUNTRY

BY NEGOTIATION

42C：DRAFTS AT：

SIGHT FOR 100% OF INVOICE VALUE

42A：DRAWEE：NORTHEAST AMERICA BANK OF CANADA

43P：PARTIAL SHIPMENT：

ALLOWED

43T：TRANSSHIPMENT：

ALLOWED

44E：PORT OF LOADING：

GUANGZHOU，CHINA

44F：PORT OF DISCHARGE：

MONTREAL，CANADA

44C：LATEST DATE OF SHIPMENT：

22-01-31

45A：DESCRIPTION OF GOODS AND/OR SERVICES：

100M/T/100 BAGS OF SILICON METAL

Si：99% MIN. Fe：0.4% MAX.

Al：0.4% MAX. Ca：0.1% MAX.

SIZE：10-100 MM 90% MIN.

UNIT PRICE：USD1 650/MT CIF MONTREAL，CANADA

AS PER SALES CONTRACT NO.GRB10086

PACKED IN PLASTIC WOVEN BAGS OF ABOUT 1 000 KGS NET EACH

46A：DOCUMENTS REQUIRED：

（1）SIGNED COMMERCIAL INVOICE IN DUPLICATE.

（2）FULL SET OF CLEAN ON BOARD MARINE BILLS OF LADING IN TWO ORIGINALS AND 3 COPIES，MADE OUT TO ORDER，ENDORSED IN BLANK，MARKED FREIGHT PREPAID，NOTIFYING APPLICANT EVIDENCING SHIPMENT FROM GUANGZHOU TO MONTREAL BY VESSEL.

（3）INSPECTION CERTIFICATE OF QUALITY AND WEIGHT IN DUPLICATE.

（4）PACKING LIST IN TRIPLICATE.

（5）CERTIFICATE OF ORIGIN G.S.P. FORM A ISSUED BY CORRESPONDING AUTHORITY

IN DUPLICATE.

(6) INSURANCE POLICY OR CERTIFICATE ENDORSED IN BLANK WITH PAYABLE AT THE DESTINATION WITH THE SAME CURRENCY OF DRAFT AGAINST ALL RISKS AND WAR RISK OF C.I.C. FOR 110% OF INVOICE VALUE.

(7) BENEFICIARY ' S CERTIFICATE CERTIFYING THAT ONE SET OF NON - NEGOTIABLE SHIPPING DOCUMENTS HAS BEEN SENT TO APPLICANT BY EMS WITHIN 7 DAYS AFTER SHIPMENT HAS BEEN EFFECTED.

47A: ADDITIONAL CONDITIONS:

(1) ALL DOCUMENTS MUST BEAR THIS CREDIT NUMBER.

(2) SHIPMENT DATE PRIOR TO L/C'S ISSUING DATE IS PROHIBITED.

(3) 5% MORE OR LESS IN QUANTITY AND AMOUNT ARE ACCEPTABLE.

(4) GOODS COVERING FREE OF CHARGE ARE ACCEPTABLE.

(5) IF DOCUMENTS PRESENTED UNDER THIS L/C ARE FOUND TO BE DISCREPANT, WE SHALL GIVE ITS NOTICE OF REFUSAL AND SHALL HOLD DOCUMENTS AT YOUR DISPOSAL SUBJECT TO THE FOLLOWING CONDITION: "IF WE HAVE NOT RECEIVED YOUR DISPOSAL INSTRUCTIONS FOR THE DISCREPANT DOCUMENTS PRIOR TO RECEIPT OF THE APPLICANT'S WAIVER OF DISCREPANCIES, WE WILL RELEASE DOCUMENTS TO APPLICANT WITHOUT NOTICE TO YOU."

71B: CHARGES:

ALL BANKING CHARGES OUTSIDE CANADA, IF ANY, ARE FOR ACCOUNT OF BENEFICIARY.

48: PERIOD FOR PRESENTATION:

DOCUMENTS PRESENTED WITHIN 15 DAYS AFTER SHIPMENT BUT WITHIN THE VALIDITY OF THE CREDIT.

49: CONFIRMATION INSTRUCTIONS:

WITHOUT.

78: INSTR. TO PAYG/ACCPTG/NGGOTG BANK:

(1) ALL DOCUMENTS MUST BE SENT TO US IN ONE LOT, OUR ADDRESS:

NORTHEAST AMERICA BANK OF CANADA, 238#, BEIXALU, GM, MONTREAL, CANADA

(2) A DISCREPANCY FEE OF USD60.00 SHOULD BE DEDUCTED FROM NEGOTIATION AMOUNT FOR EACH PRESENTATION IF DOCUMENTS DO NOT COMPLY WITH L/C TERMS AND CONDITIONS.

(3) UPON RECEIPT OF DOCUMENTS ALONG WITH DRAFT (S) STRICTLY COMPLYING WITH TERMS AND CONDITIONS OF THIS CREDIT, WE WILL REMIT PROCEEDS LESS OUR HANDLING CHARGES TO YOU AS INSTRUCTED.

(4) ONE COPY OF BILL OF LADING AND COMMERCIAL INVOICE IS REQUIRED FOR ISSUING BANK'S FILE. USD10.00 WILL BE CHARGED IF THESE COPIES ARE NOT PRESENTED.

57D: "ADVISE THROUGH" BANK:

BANK OF CHINA, WUZHOU BRANCH.

72：SENDER TO RECEIVER INFORMATION：

PLS RELEASE THE L/C UPON RECEIPT OF ADVISING FEES.

END OF MESSAGE.

补充信息：船名：KUIBEIQUE 12WV；船期：2022-01-28；发票号码：M110188；发票日期：2022-01-18；实装货物数量：100包；净重100M/T；毛重：100.8M/T；体积：40M³；货物存放地点：广州黄埔码头2号仓库；申请单位注册号：4504E201101933；金属硅H.S.编码：28046 90000。

普惠制原产地证书申请书样本

申请单位（签章）：广西梧州先达顺贸易有限公司　　　　证书号：

注册号：4504E201101933

申请人郑重声明：

本人是被正式授权代表出口单位办理和签署本申请书的。

本申请书及普惠制原产地证格式A所列内容正确无误，如发现弄虚作假、冒充格式A所列货物、擅改证书，自愿接受签证机关的处罚及负法律责任。现将有关情况申报如下：

生产单位	广西贺州有色金属有限公司	生产单位联系人及电话	莫运隆 2234××××
商品名称（中英文）	金属硅/SILICON METAL	H.S.税目号（以六位数码计）	2804690
商品（FOB）总值（以美元计）	160 000	发票号	M110188

最终销售国	加拿大	证书种类（打"✓"）	加急证书	✓普通证书
货物拟出运日期	2022.01.28			

贸易方式（请在适用处打"✓"）

一般贸易 C	灵活贸易 L	零售 Y	展卖 M
✓			

包装数量或毛重或其他数量	净重100M/T；毛重：100.8M/T

原产地标准：

本项商品系在中国生产，完全符合该给惠国给惠方案的规定，其原产地情况符合以下第（1）条：

（1）"P"（完全国产，未使用任何进口原材料）

（2）"W"（其H.S.税目号为__________ 含进口成分__________）

（3）"F"（对加拿大出口产品，其进口成分不超过产品出厂价值的40%）

本批产品系：（1）直接运输从 广州 到 蒙特利尔

（2）转口运输从________中转国（地区）________到________

申请人说明：

领证人（签名）：莫运金

电话：131××××3183

日期：2022年1月13日

现提交中国出口商业发票副本一份、普惠制原产地证书格式S（FORM A）一正二副，以及其他附件 3 份，请予审核签证。

注：凡含有进口成分的商品，必须按要求提交"含进口成分受惠商品成本明细单"。

灵活贸易包括来料加工、补偿贸易、进料加工贸易。

ORIGINAL

<table>
<tr><td colspan="3">1.Goods consigned from (Exporter's business name,address,country)
GUANGXI WUZHOU XIANDASHUN TRADING CORP.
555 ,WEST XINXING ROAD,WUZHOU,GUANGXI,P.R.C.</td><td colspan="3" rowspan="2">Reference No.
GENERALIZED SYSTEM OF PREFERENCES
CERTIFICATE OF ORIGIN
(Combined declaration and certificate)
FORM A
Issued in THE PEOPLE'S REPUBLIC OF CHINA
(country)
See notes overleaf</td></tr>
<tr><td colspan="3">2.Goods consigned to (Consignee's name,address,country)
GOOD BROTHER RESOURCES CO., LTD., 2950 HIGHWAY DRIVE TRAIL BRITISH COLOMBIA , CANADA</td></tr>
<tr><td colspan="3">3.Means of transport and route (as for as known)
BY VESSEL FROM GUANGZHOU TO MONTREAL</td><td colspan="3">4.For official use</td></tr>
<tr><td>5.Item Number</td><td>6.Marks and numbers of packages</td><td>7.Number and kind of packages; description of goods</td><td>8.Origin criterion (see notes overleaf)</td><td>9.Gross weight or other quantity</td><td>10.Number and date of invoices</td></tr>
<tr><td>1</td><td>GOOD
BROTHER
EXP2022-12-07
MONTREAL
C/NO.1-100</td><td>100 (ONE HUNDRED) BAGS OF SILICON METAL
L/C NO.: EXP2021-12-07
*** *** *** ***</td><td>"P"</td><td>G.W.:
100.8 M/T</td><td>M110188
JAN.18,2022</td></tr>
<tr><td colspan="3">11.Certification
It is hereby certified,on the basis of control carried out, that the declaration by the exporter is correct.

WUZHOU:JAN. 18, 2022　王伟大
Place and date,signature and stamp of certifying authority</td><td colspan="3">12.Declaration by the exporter
The undersigned hereby declares that the above details and statements are correct;that all the goods were produced in CHINA
(country)
and that they comply with the origin requirements specified for those goods in the Generalized System of preferences for goods exported to
CANADA
(importing country)
WUZHOU:JAN.18, 2022　莫运金
place and date,signature of authorized signatory</td></tr>
</table>

第四步　学生填制普惠制原产地证

请各个小组学生根据所给的资料，用纸质版表格或电子版表格，共同填写普惠制原产地证申领表和普惠制原产地证，在网上交给老师（L/C付款方式。货物包装用纸箱，每只重2.5千克。发票号码和日期自编）。

SEQUENCE OF TOTAL 27:　1/1
FORM OF DOC., CREDIT 40A:　IRREVOCABLE
DOC.CREDIT NUMBER　20:　ABL-AN107
DATE OF ISSUE　31C:　21-04-05
EXPIRY　31D:　DATE 21-06-15 AT NEGOTIATING BANK'S COUNTER
APPLICANT　50:　ITOCHULU CORPORATION, 103, OSAKA, JAPAN
OSACY SECTION
BENEFICIARY　59:　SHANGHAI DAXIN TEXTILES IMP. AND EXP. CORP.

		207 ZHONGSHAN ROAD，2100，SHANGHAI，CHINA
AMOUNT	32B：	CURRENCY USD AMOUNT 13 140.00
MAX.CREDIT AMOUNT	39B：	NOT EXCEEDING
AVAILABLE WITH/BY	41D：	ANY BANK IN CHINA BY NEGOTIATION
DRAFTS AT	42C：	DRAFTS AT 30 DAYS SIGHT FOR FULL INVOICE VALUE
DRAWEE	42A：	SAIBJPJT ASAHI BANK LTD.，TOKYO
PARTIAL SHIPMENT	43P：	ALLOWED
TRANSSHIPMENT	43T：	PROHIBITED
LOADING PORT	44E：	SHIPMENT FROM CHINESE PORT(S)
FOR TRANSPORTATION TO...	44F：	OSAKA，JAPAN
LATEST DATE OF SHIPMENT	44C：	21-05-31
DESCRIPT.OF GOODS	45A：	100% COTTON APRON AS PER S/C NO.AH107

ART NO.	QUANTITY	UNIT PRICE
29396	4 000 PIECES	USD1.5
29395	3 600 PIECES	USD1.4
25306	1 680 PIECES	USD1.25

PRICE TERM：CIF OSAKA

PACKED IN CARTONS OF 40 PIECES EACH AS PER SALES CONTRACT NO. NT201090

DOCUMENTS REQUIRED 46A：

+ FULL SET OF ORIGINAL CLEAN ON BOARD OCEAN BILLS OF LADING MADE OUT TO ORDER OF SHIPPER AND BLANK ENDORSED AND MARKED “FREIGHT PREPAID” NOTIFY APPLICANT（WITH FULL NAME AND ADDRESS）.

+ ORIGINAL SIGNED COMMERCIAL INVOICE IN 5 COPIES INDICATING S/C NO.

+ INSURANCE POLICY OR CERTIFICATE IN TWO ORIGINAL ENDORSED IN BLANK, FOR 120 PCT OF INVOICE VALUE INCLUDING：THE INSTITUTE CARGO CLAUSES（A），THE INSTITUTE WAR CLAUSES，INSURANCE CLAIMS TO BE PAYABLE IN JAPAN IN THE CURRENCY OF THE DRAFTS.

+ CERTIFICATE OF ORIGIN G.S.P FORM A IN 1 ORIGINAL AND 1 COPY.

+ PACKING LIST IN 3 COPIES

+ BENEFICIARY'S CERTIFICATE STATING THAT ONE SET OF NON-NEGOTIALLE SHIPPING DOCUMENTS HAS BEEN SENT DIRECT TO THE APPLICANT （ATT.OSACY SECTION）.

ADDITIONAL CONDITIONS 47A：

+ T.T.REIMBURSEMENT IS PROHIBITED.

+ THE GOODS TO BE PACKED IN EXPORT STRONG COLORED CARTONS.

+ INSPECTION IS TO BE EFFECTED BEFORE SHIPMENT AND RELEVANT CERTIFICATES/ REPORTS ARE REQUIRED FROM THE INSPECTING AGENCY.

DETAILS OF CHARGES 71B：

ALL BANKING CHARGES OUTSIDE JAPAN INCLUDING REIMBURSEMENT / COMMISSIONS, ARE FOR ACCOUNT OF BENEFICIARY.

PRESENTATION PERIOD 48:

DOCUMENTS TO BE PRESENTED WITHIN 15 DAYS AFTER THE DATE OF SHIPMENT BUT WITHIN THE VALIDITY OF THE CREDIT.

CONFIRMATION 49: WITHOUT.

INSTRUCTIONS 78:

THE NEGOTIATION BANK MUST FORWARD THE DRAFTS AND ALL DOCUMENTS BY REGISTERED AIRMAIL DIRECT TO US (INT'L OPERATIONS CENTER MAIL ADDRESS: C.P.O.BOX NO.800 TOKYO 100-91 JAPAN) IN TWO CONSECUTIVE LOTS, UPON RECEIPT OF THE DRAFTS AND DOCUMENTS IN ORDER, WE WILL REMIT THE PROCEEDS AS INSTRUCTED BY THE NEGOTIATING BANK.

普惠制原产地证申请书样本

申请单位（签章）：　　　　　　　　　　　　　　证书号：

注册号：

申请人郑重声明：

本人是被正式授权代表出口单位办理和签署本申请书的。

本申请书及普惠制原产地证格式A所列内容正确无误，如发现弄虚作假、冒充格式A所列货物、擅改证书，自愿接受签证机关的处罚及负法律责任。现将有关情况申报如下：

<table>
<tr><td>生产单位</td><td colspan="2"></td><td colspan="2">生产单位联系人及电话</td><td></td></tr>
<tr><td>商品名称
（中英文）</td><td colspan="2"></td><td colspan="2">H.S. 税目号（以
六位数码计）</td><td></td></tr>
<tr><td>商品(FOB)总值(以美元计)</td><td colspan="2"></td><td>发票号</td><td colspan="2"></td></tr>
<tr><td>最终销售国</td><td></td><td colspan="2">证书种类(打"✓")</td><td>加急证书</td><td>普通证书</td></tr>
<tr><td>货物拟出运日期</td><td colspan="5"></td></tr>
<tr><td colspan="6">贸易方式(请在适用处打"✓")</td></tr>
<tr><td>一般贸易
C</td><td colspan="2">灵活贸易
L</td><td colspan="2">零售
Y</td><td>展卖
M</td></tr>
<tr><td></td><td colspan="2"></td><td colspan="2"></td><td></td></tr>
<tr><td>包装数量或毛重或其他数量</td><td colspan="5"></td></tr>
<tr><td colspan="6">原产地标准：
本项商品系在中国生产，完全符合该给惠国给惠方案的规定，其原产地情况符合以下第（　）条：
（1）"P"（完全国产，未使用任何进口原材料）
（2）"W"（其 H.S. 税目号为________ 含进口成分________）
（3）"F"（对加拿大出口产品，其进口成分不超过产品出厂价值的 40%）
本批产品系：（1）直接运输从________到________
（2）转口运输从________中转国（地区）________到________</td></tr>
<tr><td colspan="6">申请人说明：　　　　　　　　　　　　　　　领证人(签名)：
电话：
日期：　　年　　月　　日</td></tr>
</table>

现提交中国出口商业发票副本一份、普惠制原产地证书格式S（FORM A）一正二副，以及其他附件______份，请予审核签证。

注：凡含有进口成分的商品，必须按要求提交"含进口成分受惠商品成本明细单"。

灵活贸易包括来料加工、补偿贸易、进料加工贸易。

ORIGINAL

<table>
<tr><td colspan="3">1.Goods consigned from (Exporter's business name, address,country)</td><td colspan="3" rowspan="2">Reference No.
GENERALIZED SYSTEM OF PREFERENCES
CERTIFICATE OF ORIGIN
(Combined declaration and certificate)
FORM A
Issued in THE PEOPLE'S REPUBLIC OF CHINA
(country)
See notes overleaf</td></tr>
<tr><td colspan="3">2. Goods consigned to (Consignee's name, address, country)</td></tr>
<tr><td colspan="3">3.Means of transport and route (as for as known)</td><td colspan="3">4.For official use</td></tr>
<tr><td>5.Item number</td><td>6.Marks and numbers of packages</td><td>7.Number and kind of packages; description of goods</td><td>8.Origin criterion (see notes overleaf)</td><td>9.Gross weight or other quantity</td><td>10. Number and date of invoices</td></tr>
<tr><td colspan="3">11.Certification
It is hereby certified,on the basis of control carried out, that the declaration by the exporter is correct.

Place and date,signature and stamp of certifying authority</td><td colspan="3">12.Declaration by the exporter
The undersigned hereby declares that the above details and statements are correct; that all the goods were produced in CHINA
(country)
and that they comply with the origin requirements specified for those goods in the Generalized System of preferences for goods exported to
(importing country)
place and date,signature of authorized signatory</td></tr>
</table>

第五步　课后训练

请各位学生课后根据所给的电子版本资料，填写普惠制原产地证书申请表及普惠制原产地证书，在网上交给老师（D/P付款方式）。

1.销售合同

SALES　CONTRACT

No.：EX09M088

Date：April 22，2021

Place：Guangzhou

The Seller：Guangxi Wuzhou Chunwang Chemicals Manufacturer

Address：2233，Sijiangsi Road，Wuzhou，Guangxi，P.R.C.

Fax：0086-774-8420××××

Tel：0086-774-8420××××

E-mail: chunwang@chemicals.com

****

The Buyer: International Sourceing Company

Address: W.box 3578, 23#, New Street, Northbridge, Sydney, Australia

Fax: 0061-2-5663××××

Tel: 0061-2-5667××××

E-mail: int'lsource@northbridge.com

****

The Seller has agreed to sell while the Buyer has agreed to buy the following goods as per the terms and conditions listed below:

Name of Commodity	Quantity	Unit Price	Total Amount
Manganese Dioxide Powder	20M/T (±5% at the seller's option)	USD1 125.00 per M/T CFR Sydney	USD22 500.00

1.Packing: In plastic bags of 25kgs net each, 40 bags to a wooden pallet.

2.Shipment: Shipment from Wuzhou to Sydney via Hong Kong in June and July of 2021.
Partial shipment and transshipment are not allowed.

3.Insurance: To be covered by the buyer.

4.Payment Terms: D/P at sight.

5.Specification: MnO_2: 75% min.
Fe: 0.3% max.
P: 0.15% max.
S: 0.15% max.
Fineness: 325 mesh 98% min.passing through.

6.Inspection

Both the sellers and the buyers mutually agreed that the Certificate of Quality and Weight and/or Quantity issued by related organizations at the port of shipment shall be part of the documents to be presented for negotiation under the relevant S/C. The buyers shall have the right to re-inspect the quality and weight and/or quantity of the cargo at the port of destination. However, the re-inspection fee shall be borne by the buycrs.

7.Discrepancy and Claim

Should the quality and/or weight be found not in conformity with that of the contract, the buyers shall be entitled to lodge a claim with the sellers. Such claim should be supported by survey reports issued by a recognized surveyor approved by the sellers. The claim, if any, shall be filed within 30 days after arrival of the cargo at the port of destination specified in the relative Bill of Lading. If the goods have been processed, the buyers shall thereupon lose the right to claim.

Claims in respect of matters within responsibility of insurance company and/or shipping company shall not be considered or entertained by the sellers.

8.Arbitration

All disputes arising out of the performance of, or relating to this contract, shall be settled friendly through negotiation. In case no settlement can be reached through negotiation, the case shall then be submitted to the China International Economic and Trade Arbitration Commission, Beijing, China, for arbitration in accordance with its provisional rules for arbitration. The arbitral award is final and binding upon both parties.

9.Force Majeure

In case the contracted goods are prevented or delayed in whole or in part by reason of war, earthquake, flood, fire, storm, heavy snow, tsunami or other causes of Force Majeure, the seller shall not be held responsible for non-shipment or late shipment of the goods under this contract. In that case, the seller shall notify the buyer by cable, fax or telephone and furnish the buyer within 20 days by registered airmail with a certificate issued by the China Council for the Promotion of International Trade attesting such event or events.

10.Remarks

This confirmation is written in English. Both the Seller and the Buyer shall hold one copy of the original. The Seller shall mail this confirmation to the Buyer as soon as possible for signature. The Buyer shall countersign them and return one copy of this confirmation to the Seller for his file.

Buyer's Signature :	Seller's Signature:
Bob Percy	Li Faxiao
(Managing Director)	(Managing Director)

2.装船指令

SHIPPING INSTRUCTION

****

To: Guangxi Wuzhou Chunwang Chemicals Manufacturer
2233, Sijiangsi Road, Wuzhou, Guangxi, P.R.C.
E-mail: chunwang@chemicals.com

From: International Sourcing Company
W.box 3578, 23#, New Street, Northbridge, Sydney, Australia
E-mail: int'lsource@northbridge.com

Date: May 15, 2021

Attn: Li Faxiao

Dear Sirs,

We were very happy to have met you in the Spring Guangzhou Fair last month and signed contract No. EX09M088 with your company for 20 M/T of Manganese Dioxide Powder. To tell you the truth, we are in urgent need of this product. In order to help you execute the contract, we fax you the following details of shipping instructions. Please effect shipment as soon as possible.

The followings are the documents we require. You are requested to send us the full set of original shipping documents through your bank. Upon receipt of them, we shall remit the proceeds by telegraphic transfer.

1.Name and address of our bank:

International Private Group Banker, W. box 2578, 53#, New Street, Northbridge, Sydney, Australia, fax: 0061-02-7663-3871.

2.Details of goods: 20 M/T Manganese Dioxide Powder

Packed in plastic bags of 25 kgs net each, 40 bags to a wooden pallet.

3.Loading port and destination: Wuzhou; Sydney

4.Shipment during June and July, 2021

5.Documents required:

(1) Commercial Invoice in six copies.

(2) Packing List in triplicate.

(3) Full set of ocean bills of lading made out to order, endorsed in blank, marked freight prepaid, notifying the full name and address of the contract buyer.

(4) Certificate of Origin G.S.P. FORM A issued by corresponding authority in duplicate.

(5) Inspection Certificate issued by corresponding authority in duplicate.

(6) Beneficiary's Certificate certifying that one set of non-negotiable shipping documents has been sent to us by EMS within 7 days after shipment.

Best regards.

Bob Percy

Managing Director

任务八　东盟产地证

情境导入

位于广西南宁市的Guangxi Daguilin Chemicals Manufacturer今年四月与泰国的一家公司签订了软锰粉的出口合同。泰国是中国-东盟自贸区的成员之一。自2010年1月1日起，原产于中国的产品出口到泰国可以享受到零关税优惠，但是要提供东盟产地证书。这个证书与以往我们学习的一般原产地证书和普惠制原产地证书有什么不同？应该怎么申请和办理呢？

第一步　学生学

一、中国-东盟自贸区简介

中国-东盟自由贸易区（China-ASEAN Free Trade Area，CAFTA，以下简称中国-东盟自贸区），是中国与东盟10国组建的自由贸易区。2010年1月1日自贸区正式全面启动，标志着由中国和东盟10国组成、接近6万亿美元国内生产总值、4.5万亿美元贸易额的区域，进入了零关税时代，达到了完全自由贸易化。中国-东盟自贸区是中国参加的第一个自由贸易区，是目前世界人口最多的自贸区，是发展中国家间最大的自贸区。按照协议，中国与东盟国家实现“零关税”的商品将超过7 000种。

通过实施降税和消除区内贸易壁垒，自贸区实现零关税以及贸易便利化，对企业的产品出口大为有利，使中国和东盟的企业减少关税支出，降低经营成本，减少投资障碍，拓展合作空间，促进自由贸易区内的贸易增长。

2020年11月12日，第23次中国-东盟领导人会议发表《中国-东盟自由贸易区全面建成10周年实施报告》。中国-东盟自贸区成立10多年来，蓬勃发展，双边贸易快步增长，双向投资稳中有升，经济技术合作不断深入。中国-东盟自贸区已经成为全球最具活力、最富成效的自贸区之一，有力促进了世界经济的稳定和繁荣。2020年东盟历史性地成为我国第一大贸易伙伴，进出口总额达4.74万亿元，同比增长7%。其中，我国对东盟出口3 837.2亿美元，自东盟进口3 008.8亿美元。这是东盟继2019年超过美国成为我国第二大贸易伙伴后实现的又一突破。我国已连续12年保持东盟第一大贸易伙伴地位。

二、东盟10国

东盟10国包括文莱、柬埔寨、印度尼西亚、老挝、马来西亚、缅甸、菲律宾、新加坡、泰国、越南10个国家。

三、享受零关税优惠的条件

中国出口到东盟的产品只要具备下列条件之一就可享受零关税待遇：

1.产品完全原产于中国。

2.来自非中国-东盟自贸区成员国的原材料货值不超过出口产品的货值的60%。

3.来自非中国-东盟自贸区成员国的原材料经过充分加工后制得的产品。

4.满足以上条件之一的出口产品，在运输途中未经过任何非中国-东盟自贸区成员国境内。

5.满足以上条件之一的出口产品，在运输途中途经非中国-东盟自贸区成员国境内时，不论是否在这些国家转换运输工具或作临时储存，产品在这些国家未经任何其他操作（装卸或其他为了使产品保持良好状态的处理，不算为加工）。

四、免税手续办理

满足上述条件的货物，须到海关总署设在各地的海关申请签发中国-东盟自贸区优惠关税原产地证书。持有该证书，进口国海关即给予进口关税减免待遇。

东盟产地证书FORM E从内容和格式上看，与G.S.P.普惠制原产地证书格式差不多。

FORM E注册手续办理所需资料：

1.注册登记表，由企业填写。

2.企业营业执照复印件，需由申请人加注“与原件一致”字样。

3.对外贸易经营者备案登记表（或中华人民共和国外商投资企业批准证书）复印件，双面复印。

4.注册公司章程复印件。

5.公司空白出口发票复印件（税务局提供出口专用发票或公司制作出口形式发票）。

6.企业组织机构代码证复印件。

7.产地证书申报员授权书，注明身份证号码，粘贴近期一寸免冠照片，需有申报员手签笔迹。

8.出口货物生产厂家为本地企业的，需提供厂家出具的“产品成本明细单”，以及与厂家签订的购销合同；出口货物生产厂家为异地企业的，提供生产企业当地海关出具的“原产地标准调查结果单”，以及与厂家签订的购销合同。

9.其他资料。根据注册调查需要决定。

注册时间：3～5个工作日。注册费用：500元（银联卡支付）。

五、FORM E证书申领办法

1.从网上向本地的海关发送数据申报。

2.打印纸质交单给海关确认，盖章、领证。当天或第二天得证。费用60元。

第二步　教师教

一、创立中国-东盟自贸区的目标

中国-东盟自贸区的创立目标是用10年的时间完成所有关税和非关税的削减，消除双方之间存在的关税及非关税壁垒；建立一个综合框架，包含市场一体化等一系列措施，如投资促进、贸易便利化以及和谐的贸易及投资规则与标准。

二、中国-东盟自贸区产地证

自从2010年1月1日中国-东盟自贸区正式建立以来，中国与东盟双方有超过90%的贸易产品享受零关税待遇。如果没有中国-东盟自贸区原产地证书（FORM E），进出口的产品都不能享受零关税或关税减免待遇，只能按照正常关税税率交税。

1.中国-东盟自贸区原产地证书使得出口到东盟国家的商品享受到零关税或减免税政策，降低费用，降低成本，增强市场竞争力。

2.中国-东盟自贸区原产地证书使得进口的商品享受到零关税或减免税待遇，价廉物美，满足人民生活需要。

3.通过实施降税和消除区内贸易壁垒，自贸区实现零关税以及贸易便利化，对企业的产品出口大为有利，中国和东盟的企业减少了关税支出，降低了经营成本，减少了投资障碍，拓展了合作空间，促进了自由贸易区内的贸易增长。

三、签发机构

各地海关。

四、签发时间

货物出口前后3天内办理，属于正常出证。货物出口3天后办理则属于后发证书。

五、填制规范

证书的正本和第二副本应由出口人提供给进口人，以供其在进口国通关时使用。第一副本应由出口成员方签证机构留底。第三副本由出口人留存。进口国海关对收到的FORM E证书产生怀疑时，会将FORM E证书第二副本退给签证机构以备核查。FORM E证书所用文字为英语。

新版FORM E产地证填制规范：

1.原产地证书号

标题栏（右上角），填上海关规定的证书号。编号规则如下：E+年份代码（2位）+申请单位备案号（9位）+流水号（4位）。

例如：证书号E203800000050045是备案号为380000005的单位2020年办理的第45票FORM E证书。注意：重发证的号码与新证的编码规则一致，但改变流水号。

2.第一栏：出口商的名称、地址、国家

例如：NINGBO ××× GROUP CO.，LTD. ROOM ×××，××× MANSION，93 ××× ROAD，NINGBO CHINA

（1）填写在中国境内的出口商或生产商名称、地址、国家等。出口商或生产商必须是已办理原产地证备案的企业，且公司英文名称应与备案一致。此栏显示生产商（不是出口商）信息时，应在第十一栏加盖生产商的中英文章，同时需在第一栏加注出口商的名称、地址。

（2）注册在中国台湾、香港、澳门地区的公司不能作为出口商。

3.第二栏：收货人的名称、地址、国家

例如：××× CO.，LTD，
LAN GE ×××，F-2000，
SURABAYA，INDONESIA

注意：此栏是带有强制性的，应填东盟最终收货人名称、地址、国家。

4.第三栏：运输方式及路线（就所知而言）

离港日期（Departure date）：OCT. 26，2021

船舶名称/飞机等（Vessel's name/Aircraft etc）：KMCT ULA V.46S

卸货口岸（Port of discharge）：SURABAYA，INDONESIA

5.第四栏：供官方使用（进口方海关使用）

由进口成员方的海关在该栏简要说明根据协定是否给予优惠待遇。申请单位应将此栏留空。

6.第五栏：商品顺序号

在收货人、运输条件相同的情况下，如同批出口货物有不同品种，则可按不同品种分列“1”“2”“3”……以此类推。

7.第六栏：唛头及包装号

例如：JENSON
ORDER N0.325952065
LJCE766896505
CTN1-270

（1）此栏填写的唛头应与货物外包装上的唛头及发票上的唛头一致。

（2）唛头不得出现中国以外的国家或地区制造的字样，也不能出现中国香港、澳门、台湾地区原产地字样（如MADE IN MACAO）。

（3）如货物无唛头应填“无唛头”（N/M或NO MARK）。

（4）如唛头为图文等较复杂的内容，此栏打上“SEE ATTACHMENT”，申请单位用空白纸制作带图文的唛头附页，签证机构加盖签证印章。

（5）对于多页证书的情况，续页一律使用FORM E证书，不得用白纸作为证书续页。

8.第七栏：包装数量及种类，商品描述及H.S.编码

例如：SIX HUNDRED（600）CTNS OF SHRIMPS

H.S.：030613

****

（1）包装数量必须用英文和阿拉伯数字同时表示，填写货物的具体包装种类（如

CASE、CARTON、BAG等）。

（2）如果无包装，应填明货物出运时的状态，如NUDE CARGO（裸装货）、IN BULK（散装货）、HANGING GARMENTS（挂装）等。

（3）商品名称必须具体填明，应详细到可以准确判定该商品。如果信用证、合同中品名笼统或拼写错误，应在括号内加注具体描述或正确品名。商品名称后需填写商品的6位H.S.编码。

（4）商品名称及H.S.编码等项列完后，应在最后一行下方加上表示结束的符号（***），以防止加填伪造内容。

（5）国外信用证要求填具合同、信用证号码、转口商出具的发票号等，可加填在结束符下的空白处。

（6）出口至东盟成员方的货物在进口国海关报关时如使用第三方发票，应在本栏目空白处注明开具发票的公司名称及所在国家等信息。例如，THE THIRD PARTY：××× CO., LTD，INDONESIA。第三方必须为中国以外的第三方公司，不得为国内公司。

9.第八栏：原产地标准

此栏为原产地证书的核心栏目，填写要求如下：

（1）完全获得的，填写"WO"。

（2）在一方境内由取得原产资格的材料生产的，填写"PE"。

（3）由非原产材料生产：

a：符合区域价值成分标准的，即单一国家成分或中国-东盟自贸区累计成分大于等于产品离岸价40%的，应填写增值的百分比，如"40%"（同时第九栏需加注货物FOB值）；

b：符合税则归类改变标准的，填写"CTH"。

（4）符合特定产品规则的：

a：列入特定原产地规则清单，但采用完全获得原产地规则的，填写"WO"；

b：列入特定原产地规则清单，但采用区域价值成分原产地规则的，填写"PSR"（同时第九栏需加注货物FOB值）；

c：列入特定原产地规则清单，但采用除以上两种原产地规则外的，填写"PSR"。

10.第九栏：毛重、净重或其他数量及价格（FOB）（仅采用区域价值成分标准时填制价格）

例如：1 200KGS G.W.

（1）此栏应填写商品的正常计量单位，如"PCS""PAIRS""SETS"等。货物以重量计，填毛重或净重的，则需加注G.W.（GROSS WEIGHT）或N.W.（NET WEIGHT）。

（2）对于原产地标准采用区域价值成分标准的情况，此栏需显示产品FOB值，其余情况无须填写金额。

11.第十栏：发票号码及日期

例如：SDAKFO522

MAY 05，2021

（1）此栏不得留空，发票号码、日期必须与正式商业发票一致，月份一般用英文缩写JAN.，FEB.等表示。

（2）发票日期不能迟于提单日期和申报日期。

（3）涉及第三方的，应注明第三方发票号。

12.第十一栏：出口商声明

例如：Ningbo，China，OCT.26，2021 ×××

(1) 生产国国名应填写“CHINA”，进口国国名必须是东盟成员国，一般与最终收货人或目的港的国别一致。签证国家有文莱、柬埔寨、印度尼西亚、老挝、马来西亚、缅甸、菲律宾、新加坡、泰国、越南。

(2) 此栏填写申报地点、日期，申请单位应在此栏加盖印章并授权专人在此栏签字。生产企业（非出口商）作为申请单位时，此栏加盖生产企业印章。

13.第十二栏：签证机构证明

例如：Ningbo，China，OCT.28，2021 ×××

(1) 此栏填写签证机构签证地点、日期。

(2) 签证机构授权签证人员在此栏签字，在提供给申请单位的证书正本和副本上加盖中英文签证印章，印章应加盖清晰，不能与签名重叠。签证人员的手签笔迹必须经海关总署统一向东盟备案，签名必须清楚，且与备案笔迹保持一致。

(3) 如属重发证书，签证机构在此栏加“CERTIFIED TRUE COPY OF THE ORIGINAL CERTIFICATE OF ORIGIN NUMBER____DATED____”字样。

14.第十三栏：此栏为后发证书、流动证书、展览证书和第三方发票等四项内容的勾选项目

(1) 后发证书：申报日期迟于出运日期3天，勾选“Issued Retroactively”。

(2) 流动证书：勾选“Movement Certificate”。

(3) 展览证书：当产品由出口方运至另一方展览并在展览期间或展览后销售给一方时，勾选“Exhibition”。展览的名称及地址应在第二栏中注明。

(4) 第三方发票：当发票是由第三方开具时，勾选“Third Party Invoicing”。

其他说明：

1.凡申请办理中国-东盟优惠原产地证书的单位，须在当地海关备案。

2.如果签发的证书正本遗失或损毁，申请单位可向原签证机构申请重发，提供申请单位和丢证方书面说明及原证的复印件，经核实，予以重发。

3.FORM E证书内容需要更改时，需提供更改申请书，由签证人员审核后，将证书上错误项目以横线划去，在旁边空白处手写或打印正确的内容，在正确内容周围加“*”截止符，签证人员签字，加盖签证印章（本条不同关区适用情况不太一样）。

第三步 教师示范制作FORM E

27: SEQUENCE OF 1/1

40A: FORM OF DOC.: IRREVOCABLE

20: DOCUMENT CREDIT NO.: DK20160708-1

31C: DATE OF ISSUE: 21-04-25

31D: DATE OF EXPIRY: 21-07-30

50: APPLICANT:

MALAYSIA KUALA LUMPUR THIRD IMPORT AND EXPORT TRADING COMPANY
LOT 3008, 5TH FLOOR, MENARA, 2 FABER TOWER, TANAN, DESA 59100

KUALA LUMPUR，MALYASIA

59： BENEFICIARY：

GUANGXI WUZHOU RUNHONG TEXTILES IMPORT AND EXPORT COMPANY，18TH FLOOR，FOREIGN TRADING BUILDING，4HT DONGTI ROAD，WUZHOU，GUANGXI，CHINA.

32B： AMOUNT：USD150 000.00（US DOLLARS ONE HUNDRED AND FIFTY THOUSAND ONLY）

41D： AVAILABLE WITH/BY ANY BANK BY NEGOTIATION

42C： DRAFTS AT SIGHT

42A： DRAWEE：MAYBANK，PUBLIC BANK KUALA LUMPUR

43P： PARTIAL SHIPMENT：NOT ALLOWED

43T： TRANSSHIPMENT：NOT ALLOWED

44E： LOADING PORT：BEIHAI，GUANGXI，CHINA

44F： FOR TRANSPORTATION TO：PORT KELANG，MALAYSIA

44C： LATEST DATE：21-06-30

45A： DESCRIPTION OF GOODS AND/OR SERVICES：

100 PCT NYLON FABRICS 100 000 YARDS AT USD1.5/YARD

PRICE TERM：CFR PORT KELANG

PACKING：PACKED IN BUNDLES OF 1 000 YARDS EACH，10 BUNDLES TO A CARTONS

DETAILS AS PER CONTRACT NO. 99WS061

46A： DOCUMENTS REQUIRED：

（1）MANUALLY SIGNED COMMERCIAL INVOICE IN 5 FOLDS.

（2）FULL SET（3/3）OF CLEAN ON BOARD MARINE BILLS OF LADING MADE OUT TO ORDER AND BLANK ENDORSED，MARKED “FREIGHT PREPAID” AND NOTIFY THE APPLICANT.

（3）PACKING LIST IN 3 FOLDS.

（4）CERTIFICATE OF ORIGIN FORM E IN 2 FOLDS.

（5）SHIPPING ADVICE ADVISING NAME AND QUANTITY OF GOODS，L/C NO.，NAME OF VESSEL，INVOICE NO.，INVOICE VALUE，DATE OF SHIPMENT. SHIPPING MARKS，ETA AND ETD.

47A： ADDITIONAL CONDITIONS：

+ ALL DOCUMENTS MUST INDICATE THIS L/C NO.

48： PERIOD FOR PRESENTATION：

DOCUMENTS MUST BE PRESENTED WITHIN 15 DAYS AFTER THE DATE OF SHIPMENT BUT WITHIN THE VALIDITY OF THE CREDIT.

49： ONFIRMATION：WITHOUT

57D： “ADVISE THROUGH” BANK

BANK OF CHINA，WUZHOU BRANCH

72： SENDER TO RECEIVER INFORMATION：

PLS RELEASE THE L/C UPON RECEIPT OF ADVISING FEES.

补充信息：船名 LAUD DIRYJAR MALYASIA 08；船期 2021-06-22；货物数量共 10 箱；总体积 3.5 立方米；总重量 312 千克；货物产地广东省佛山市；H.S. 编码：631010；发票号码和日期自定；要求自行设计唛头。

ORIGINAL

1.Goods consigned from (Exporter's business name, address, country) GUANGXI WUZHOU RUNHONG TEXTILES IMPORT AND EXPORT COMPANY, 18TH FLOOR, FOREIGN TRADING BUILDING, 4HT DONGTI ROAD, WUZHOU, GUANGXI, CHINA			Reference No. E084401810440086 CHINA-ASEAN FREE TRADE AREA PREFERENTIAL TARIFF CERTIFICATE OF ORIGIN (Combined Declaration and Certificate) FROM E Issued in THE PEOPLE'S REPUBLIC OF CHINA (Country) See notes overleaf		
2.Goods consigned to (Consignee's name, address, country) MALAYSIA KUALA LUMPUR THIRD IMPORT AND EXPORT TRADING COMPANY LOT 3008, 5TH FLOOR, MENARA, 2 FABER TOWER , TANAN, DESA 59100 KUALA LUMPUR, MALAYSIA					
3.Means of transport and route (as far as known) BY VESSEL FROM BEIHAI, CHINA TO PORT KELANG, MALAYSIA Departure date : JUNE 22, 2021 Vessel's name/Aircraft etc.: LAUD DIRYJAR MALYASIA 08 Port of discharge : PORT KELANG, MALAYSIA			4.For official use ☐ Preferential Treatment Given under CHINA-ASEAN Free Trade Area Preferential Tariff ☐ Preferential Treatment not Given (Please state reason/s) Signature of Authorised Signatory of the Importing Country		
5.Item number	6.Marks and numbers on packages	7. Number and type of packages, description of goods (including quantity where appropriate and H. S. number of the importing Country)	8.Origin criterion (see notes overleaf)	9.Gross weight or other quantity and value (FOB)	10. Number and date of invoices
1	LUMPUR THIRD DK20160708-1 PORT KELANG C/NO.:1-10	TEN (10) CARTONS OF NYLON FABRICS H.S.: 631010 L/C NO.: DK20160708-1 *** *** ***	"WO"	G.W.: 312KGS FOB VALUE: USD135 000	LWT220618 JUNE 12, 2021
11.Declaration by the exporter The undersigned hereby declares that the above details and statements are correct, that all the goods were produced in CHINA (Country) and that they comply with the origin requirement specified for these products in the Rules of Origin of the ACFTA for the products exported to MALYASIA (Importing Country) WUZHOU, JUNE. 19, 2021 莫运天 Place and date, signature and stamp of certifying authority			12.Certification It is hereby certified, on the basis of control carried out, that the Declaration by the exporter is correct. WUZHOU, JUNE. 20, 2021 李顺民 Place and date, signature and stamp of certifying authority		
13. ☐ Issued Retroactively ☐ Exhibition ☐ Movement Certificate ☐ Third Party Invoicing					

第四步　学生制作东盟产地证

请各个学生小组根据下面的合同及附加信息，填写FORM E 产地证书纸质版。

SALES　CONTRACT

No.：DM11M033

Date：April 8，2021

Place：Nanning

The Seller：Guangxi Daguilin Chemicals Manufacturer

Address：233，Gucheng Road ，Nanning，Guangxi，P.R.C.

Fax：0086-771-5854×××

Tel：0086-771-5854×××

E-mail：daguilin @chemicals.com

****

The Buyer：UNIQUE GOODWILL CO.，LTD.

Address：898-900 SONGWAD ROAD，BANGKOK，THAILAND

Fax：0066-2-2234×××

Tel：0066-2-2234×××

E-mail：unique @goodwill.com

****

The Seller has agreed to sell while the Buyer has agreed to buy the following goods as per the terms and conditions listed below：

Name of Commodity	Quantity	Unit Price	Total Amount
Manganese dioxide powder	30 M/T （±5% at the seller's option）	USD985 per M/T CFR Bangkok	USD29 550.00

1.Packing：In plastic bags of 25 kgs net each，40 bags to a wooden pallet.

2.Shipment：Shipment from Nanning to Bangkok in June and July of 2021.

Partial shipment and transshipment are not allowed.

3.Insurance：To be covered by the buyer

4.Payment Terms：D/P at sight

5.Specification：MnO_2：70% min. Fe：0.3% max. P：0.15% max.S：0.15% max.

Fineness：325 mesh 98% min. passing through

6.Inspection

Both the sellers and the buyers mutually agreed that the Certificate of Quality and Weight and/or Quantity issued by related organizations at the port of shipment shall be part of the documents to be presented for negotiation under the relevant S/C. The buyers shall have the right to re-inspect the quality and weight and/or quantity of the cargo at the port of destination. However, the re-inspection fee shall be borne by the buyers.

7.Discrepancy and Claim

Should the quality and/or weight be found not in conformity with that of the contract, the buyers shall be entitled to lodge a claim with the sellers. Such claim should be supported by survey reports issued by a recognized surveyor approved by the sellers. The claim, if any, shall be filed within 30 days after arrival of the cargo at the port of destination specified in the relative Bill of Lading. If the goods have been processed, the buyers shall thereupon lose the right to claim. Claims in respect of matters within responsibility of insurance company and/or shipping company shall not be considered or entertained by the sellers.

8.Arbitration

All disputes arising out of the performance of, or relating to this contract, shall be settled friendly through negotiation. In case no settlement can be reached through negotiation, the case shall then be submitted to the China International Economic and Trade Arbitration Commission, Beijing, China, for arbitration in accordance with its provisional rules for arbitration. The arbitral award is final and binding upon both parties.

9.Force Majeure

In case the contracted goods are prevented or delayed in whole or in part by reason of war, earthquake, flood, fire, storm, heavy snow, tsunami or other causes of Force Majeure, the seller shall not be held responsible for non-shipment or late shipment of the goods under this contract. In that case, the seller shall notify the buyer by cable, fax or telephone and furnish the buyer within 20 days by registered airmail with a certificate issued by the China Council for the Promotion of International Trade attesting such event or events.

10. Remarks

This confirmation is written in English. Both the Seller and the Buyer shall hold one copy of the original. The Seller shall mail this confirmation to the Buyer as soon as possible for signature .The Buyer shall countersign them and return one copy of this confirmation to the Seller for his file.

Buyer's Signature :	Seller's Signature:
苏青江	莫少云
(Managing Director)	(Managing Director)

补充资料：锰粉包装为编织袋；每袋净重25千克；每个编织袋重0.5千克；40只包装于一个木制托盘，一个木制托盘自重25千克；完全国产，不含进口成分；发票号码和日期自编。

ORIGINAL

1.Goods consigned from (Exporter's business name, address, country)	Reference No. E084401810440086 CHINA-ASEAN FREE TRADE AREA PREFERENTIAL TARIFF CERTIFICATE OF ORIGIN (Combined Declaration and Certificate) FROM E Issued in THE PEOPLE'S REPUBLIC OF CHINA (Country) See notes overleaf
2.Goods consigned to (Consignee's name, address, country)	
3.Means of transport and route (as far as known) BY VESSEL FROM　　　TO Departure date Vessel's name/Aircraft etc. Port of discharge	4.For official use ☐ Preferential Treatment Given Under CHINA-ASEAN Free Trade Area Preferential Tariff ☐ Preferential Treatment Not Given (Please state reason/s) Signature of Authorised Signatory of the Importing Country

5. Item number	6. Marks and numbers on packages	7. Number and type of packages, description of goods (including quantity where appropriate and H. S. number of the importing Country)	8. Origin criterion (see notes overleaf)	9. Gross weight or other quantity and value (FOB)	10. Number and date of invoices

11.Declaration by the exporter The undersigned hereby declares that the above details and statements are correct, that all the goods were produced in CHINA (Country) and that they comply with the origin requirement specified for these products in the Rules of Origin of the ACFTA for the products exported to (Importing Country) Place and date, signature and stamp of certifying authority	12.Certification It is hereby certified, on the basis of control carried out, that the Declaration by the exporter is correct. Place and date, signature and stamp of certifying authority
13. ☐ Issued Retroactively　☐ Exhibition ☐ Movement Certificate　☐ Third Party Invoicing	

第五步　课后训练

请各个学生小组根据下面的合同及附加信息，填写FORM E 产地证书电子版，并发到教师电子邮箱中。

SALES　CONTRACT

No.：DM20M038

Date：May 18，2021

Place：Nanning

The Seller：Guangxi Daguilin Chemicals Manufacturer

Address：233，Gucheng Road，Nanning，Guangxi，P.R.C.

Fax：0086-771-585××××

Tel：0086-771-585××××

E-mail：daguilin @chemicals.com

****

The Buyer：UNIQUE GOODWILL CO.，LTD.

Address：898-900 SONGWAD ROAD，BANGKOK，THAILAND

Fax：0066-2-223××××

Tel：0066-2-223××××

E-mail：unique @goodwill.com

****

The Seller has agreed to sell while the Buyer has agreed to buy the following goods as per the terms and conditions listed below：

Name of Commodity	Quantity	Unit Price	Total Amount
"RECONSTRUCTION" brand hydrated lime in powder	260M/T (±5% at the seller's option)	USD128.00 per M/T CIF Bangkok	USD33 280.00

1.Packing：In outer plastic woven bags with inner 4-ply kraft paper bags of 25 kgs net each，40 bags to a wooden pallet.

2.Shipment：Shipment from Nanning to Bangkok in August of 2021.

Partial shipment and transshipment are not allowed.

3.Insurance：To be covered by the buyer.

4.Payment Terms：D/P at sight.

5.Specification：Ca（OH）$_2$：85% min. MgO：4% max.

Whiteness：90%min.

Fineness：100 mesh 95% min. passing through.

6.Inspection

Both the sellers and the buyers mutually agreed that the Certificate of Quality and Weight and/or Quantity issued by related organizations at the port of shipment shall be part of the documents to be presented for negotiation under the relevant S/C. The buyers shall have the right to re-inspect the quality and weight and/or quantity of the cargo at the port of destination. However, the re-inspection fee shall be borne by the buyers.

7. Discrepancy and Claim

Should the quality and/or weight be found not in conformity with that of the contract, the buyers shall be entitled to lodge a claim with the sellers. Such claim should be supported by survey reports issued by a recognized surveyor approved by the sellers. The claim, if any, shall be filed within 30 days after arrival of the cargo at the port of destination specified in the relative Bill of Lading. If the goods have been processed, the buyers shall thereupon lose the right to claim. Claims in respect of matters within responsibility of insurance company and/or shipping company shall not be considered or entertained by the sellers.

8. Arbitration

All disputes arising out of the performance of, or relating to this contract, shall be settled friendly through negotiation. In case no settlement can be reached through negotiation, the case shall then be submitted to the China International Economic and Trade Arbitration Commission, Beijing, China, for arbitration in accordance with its provisional rules for arbitration. The arbitral award is final and binding upon both parties.

9. Force Majeure

In case the contracted goods are prevented or delayed in whole or in part by reason of war、earthquake, flood, fire, storm, heavy snow, tsunami or other causes of Force Majeure, the seller shall not be held responsible for non-shipment or late shipment of the goods under this contract.In that case, the seller shall notify the buyer by cable, fax or telephone and furnish the buyer within 20 days by registered airmail with a certificate issued by the China Council for the Promotion of International Trade attesting such event or events.

10.Remarks

This confirmation is written in English. Both the Seller and the Buyer shall hold one copy of the original. The Seller shall mail this confirmation to the Buyer as soon as possible for signature.The Buyer shall countersign them and return one copy of this confirmation to the Seller for his file.

Buyer's Signature：	Seller's Signature：
苏青江	莫少云
(Managing Director)	(Managing Director)

补充资料：熟石灰粉包装为编织袋；每袋净重25千克；每个编织袋重0.5千克；40只包装于一个木制托盘；一个木托盘自重25千克；发票号码和日期视合同情况自编。

ORIGINAL

1.Goods consigned from (Exporter's business name,address,country)

Reference No. E084401810440086

CHINA-ASEAN FREE TRADE AREA
PREFERENTIAL TARIFF
CERTIFICATE OF ORIGIN
(Combined Declaration and Certificate)
FROM E

Issued in THE PEOPLE'S REPUBLIC OF CHINA
(Country)
See Notes Overleaf

2.Goods consigned to(Consignee's name,address,country)

3.Means of transport and route(as far as known)

BY VESSEL FROM TO

Departure date

Vessel's name/Aircraft etc.

Port of discharge

4.For official use

☐ Preferential Treatment Given under CHINA-ASEAN Free Trade Area Preferential Tariff

☐ Preferential Treatment not Given(Please state reason/s)

Signature of Authorised Signatory of the Importing Country

5. Item number	6. Marks and numbers on packages	7. Number and type of packages, description of goods (including quantity where appropriate and H.S. number of the importing Country)	8. Origin criterion (see notes overleaf)	9.Gross weight or other quantity and value(FOB)	10. Number and date of invoices

11.Declaration by the exporter

The undersigned hereby declares that the above details and statements are correct, that all the goods were produced in

CHINA
(Country)

and that they comply with the origin requirement specified for these products in the Rules of Origin of the ACFTA for the products exported to

(Importing Country)

Place and date,signature and stamp of certifying authority

12.Certification

It is hereby certified, on the basis of control carried out, that the Declaration by the exporter is correct.

Place and date,signature and stamp of certifying authority

13.

☐ Issued Retroactively ☐ Exhibition

☐ Movement Certificate ☐ Third Party Invoicing

任务九　受益人证明

情境导入

2021年1月下旬，广西梧州春江五金矿产进出口有限公司拟向加拿大出口100公吨特级金属硅。1月28日下午，货物已经装船并且取得了提单。实习单证员谭雅梅所在的出口部经理王瑞荣要求她抓紧时间制作和办理所有议付单据，并按照信用证的要求，在货物装船后一周内将一套副本单据邮寄给客户。

第一步　学生学

一、受益人证明的含义

受益人证明（Beneficiary's Certifcate）是由受益人按合同、信用证和有关规定对外出具的说明其已履行了某项义务、完成了某项工作或行为符合进口商和进口国要求的各种书面证明文件，如证明所交货物的品质、证明运输包装的处理、证明按要求寄单寄样等。

二、受益人证明的格式

受益人证明属于非要式单据，一般无固定格式，内容多种多样，多以英文制作，通常签发一份。

第二步　教师教

一、受益人证明的内容

1.寄单证明

寄单证明是受益人证明中最常见的一种，通常由受益人根据信用证的规定，在货物装运后一定时期内，邮寄/传真/快递给规定的收受人全套或部分副本单据，并将该证明作为一种议付单据交议付银行。

例如：Certificate from the beneficiary stating that one copy of the documents called for under the letter of credit has been dispatched by courier service directly to the applicant within 3 days after shipment has been effected.

受益人证明证实一套本信用证要求的单据的副本已用快件形式在装船后3天内直接邮寄给了开证申请人。

2.寄样证明

寄样证明通常是指受益人根据信用证的规定或装船指令，在一定时期内，将货物样品邮寄或快递给规定的收受人。

例如：Certificate from the beneficiary to show that the required shipment samples have been sent by DHL to the applicant 15 days before shipment.

受益人证明证实所要求的货物样品已经在装船前15日用敦豪快递直接寄送给开证申请人。

3.包装和标签证明

包装和标签证明通常用以证明受益人已根据信用证或合同的规定，按照要求做好包装或贴扎好标签。

例1：A certificate from the beneficiary to the effect that one set of invoice and packing list has been placed on the inner side of the door of each container in case of FCL cargo or attached to the goods or packages at an obvious place in case of LCL cargo.

受益人应证明已把一套发票和装箱单贴在集装箱箱门内侧（整箱货）或拼箱货的显眼的地方。

例2：Beneficiary certificate in triplicate stating the shipment does not include non-manufactured wood dunnage，pallets，crating or other packaging materials；the shipment is completely free of wood bark，visible pests and signs of living pests.

受益人证明一式三份，证明货物不携带未加工的木垫板、托盘、藤条或其他包装材料。货物完全无树皮、无肉眼可见虫害、无活虫。

例3：Certificate confirming that all goods are labelled in English.

受益人证明证实货物加贴英文标签。

例4：Beneficiary's certificate stating original B/L of 1 set carried by the captain of the vessel.

受益人证明证实一套正本提单已交由船长携带。

例5：A statement from the beneficary evidencing that packing effected in 25 kgs ctn。

受益人证明证实货物25千克箱装。

例6：Beneficiary's certificate confirming their acceptance of the amendment dated 10/09/2021 made under this credit quoting the relevant amendment number.

受益人证明证实他们接受2021年10月9日所作的本信用证项下的修改，注明有关修改书号码。

例7：Certificate to show goods are not of Israeli origin and do not contain any Israeli material.

货物需保证非以色列产并且不含以色列的材料。

二、受益人证明的要求

（1）单据名称。受益人证明的名称因所证明事项的不同而略异，可能是寄单证明、寄样证明（船样、样卡和码样等）、取样证明，或货物产地、品质、唛头、包装和标签情况证明，电抄形式的装运通知，产品生产过程的证明，商品业已检验的证明，或环保卫生、非使用童工、非狱犯制造等方面的证明。

（2）证明上通常会显示发票号、合同号或信用证号，以表明与其他单据的关系。

（3）证明的内容应严格与合同或信用证规定相符。

（4）因属于证明性质，按有关规定证明人（受益人）必须签字。

（5）单据一般都应在规定的时间内做出。

三、受益人证明的制作方法

（1）要证明的内容必须准确，而且是正面证明，不要反证。一般的行文规则是以所提要求为准，直接照搬照抄，有时也应做必要的修改。

例如：Beneficiary's certificate evidencing that two copies of non-negotiable B/L will be despatched to applicant within two days after shipment.

在具体制作证明的时候，应将要求中的“will be despatched”改为“have been despatched”。

又如：Beneficiary's certificate stating that the production date of this shipment not to be earlier than half month than the date of shipment.

在制作证明文句时，应写成：

This is to certify that the production date of this shipment is not earlier than half month than the date of shipment.

不要在证明文句中写上具体的生产日期，说明这天距离装船日期不超过半个月。这种做法属于反证。

（2）格式上常用“This is to certify”（或 declare，state，evidence 等）或“We hereby certify”等习惯性证明文句。

（3）由于受益人证明也是一种议付单据，如果信用证中有特约事项，也要在受益人证明中显示，这样才能做到单证一致、单单一致。

第三步　教师制作受益人证明

根据下面给出的信用证和补充资料，开具受益人证明。

27：　SEQUENCE OF TOTAL：1/1
40A：FORM OF DOCUMENTARY CREDIT：IRREVOCABLE
20：　DOCUMENTARY CREDIT NUMBER：EXP2021-1207
31C：DATE OF ISSUE：21-12-07
40E：APPLICABLE RULES：UCP LATEST VERSION
31D：DATE AND PLACE OF EXPIRY：
22-02-15 IN BENEFICIARY'S COUNTRY
50：　APPLICANT：
GOOD BROTHER RESOURCES CO.，LTD.，2950 HIGHWAY DRIVE TRAIL
BRITISH COLOMBIA，CANADA
59：　BENEFICIARY：
GUANGXI WUZHOU XINDASHUN TRADING CORP.
555，WEST XINXING ROAD，WUZHOU，GUANGXI，P.R.C.
32B：CURRENCY CODE，AMOUNT
CURRENCY：USD（US DOLLAR）
AMOUNT：# 165 000.00 #
41D：AVAILABLE WITH...BY...
ANY BANK IN BENEFICIARY'S COUNTRY
BY NEGOTIATION
42C：DRAFTS AT：
SIGHT FOR 100% OF INVOICE VALUE
42A：DRAWEE：NORTHEAST AMERICA BANK OF CANADA.
43P：PARTIAL SHIPMENTS：
ALLOWED
43T：TRANSSHIPMENT：

ALLOWED

44E：PORT OF LOADING：

GUANGZHOU，CHINA

44F：PORT OF DISCHARGE：

MONTREAL，CANADA

44C：LATEST DATE OF SHIPMENT：

22-01-31

45A：DESCRIPTION OF GOODS &/OR SERVICES

100M/T/100BAGS OF SILICON METAL

Si：99% MIN. Fe：0.4% MAX.

Al：0.4% MAX. Ca：0.1% MAX.

SIZE：10-100 MM 90% MIN.

UNIT PRICE：USD1 650/MT CIF MONTREAL，CANADA

AS PER SALES CONTRACT NO.APE101208.

PACKED IN PLASTIC WOVEN BAGS OF ABOUT 1 000KGS NET EACH

46A：DOCUMENTS REQUIRED

（1）SIGNED COMMERCIAL INVOICE IN DUPLICATE.

（2）FULL SET OF CLEAN ON BOARD MARINE BILLS OF LADING IN TWO ORIGINALS AND 3 COPIES，MADE OUT TO ORDER，ENDORSED IN BLANK，MARKED FREIGHT PREPAID，NOTIFYING APPLICANT EVIDENCING SHIPMENT FROM GUANGZHOU TO MONTREAL BY VESSEL.

（3）INSPECTION CERTIFICATE OF QUALITY AND WEIGHT IN DUPLICATE.

（4）PACKING LIST IN TRIPLICATE.

（5）CERTIFICATE OF ORIGIN GSP FORM A IN 1 ORIGINAL AND 2 COPIES ISSUED BY CORRESPONDING AUTHORITY.

（6）INSURANCE POLICY OR CERTIFICATE ENDORSED IN BLANK WITH CLAIMS PAYABLE AT THE DESTINATION WITH THE SAME CURRENCY OF DRAFT AGAINST ALL RISKS AND WAR RISK OF C.I.C. FOR 110% OF INVOICE VALUE.

（7）BENEFICIARY'S CERTIFICATE CERTIFYING THAT ONE SET OF NON-NEGOTIABLE SHIPPING DOCUMENTS HAS BEEN SENT TO APPLICANT BY EMS WITHIN 7 DAYS AFTER SHIPMENT HAS BEEN EFFECTED.

47A：ADDITIONAL CONDITIONS

（1）ALL DOCUMENTS MUST BEAR THIS CREDIT NUMBER.

（2）SHIPMENT DATE PRIOR TO L/C'S ISSUING DATE IS PROHIBITED.

（3）5% MORE OR LESS IN QUANTITY AND AMOUNT ARE ACCEPTABLE.

（4）GOODS COVERING FREE OF CHARGE ARE ACCEPTABLE.

（5）IF DOCUMENTS PRESENTED UNDER THIS L/C ARE FOUND TO BE DISCREPANT，WE SHALL GIVE ITS NOTICE OF REFUSAL AND SHALL HOLD DOCUMENTS AT YOUR DISPOSAL SUBJECT TO THE FOLLOWING CONDITION：“IF WE HAVE NOT RECEIVED

YOUR DISPOSAL INSTRUCTIONS FOR THE DISCREPANT DOCUMENTS PRIOR TO RECEIPT OF THE APPLICANT'S WAIVER OF DISCREPANCIES, WE WILL RELEASE DOCUMENTS TO APPLICANT WITHOUT NOTICE TO YOU."

71B：CHARGES

ALL BANKING CHARGES OUTSIDE CANADA, IF ANY, ARE FOR ACCOUNT OF BENEFICIARY.

48：PERIOD FOR PRESENTATION

DOCUMENTS PRESENTED WITHIN 15 DAYS AFTER SHIPMENT BUT WITHIN THE VALIDITY OF THE CREDIT.

49：CONFIRMATION INSTRUCTIONS

WITHOUT

78：INSTR TO PAYG/ACCPTG/NEGOTG BANK

（1）ALL DOCUMENTS MUST BE SENT TO US IN ONE LOT, OUR ADDRESS:

NORTHEAST AMERICA BANK OF CANADA, 238 #, BEIXALU, GM, MONTREAL, CANADA

（2）A DISCREPANCY FEE OF USD60.00 SHOULD BE DEDUCTED FROM NEGOTIATION AMOUNT FOR EACH PRESENTATION IF DOCUMENTS DO NOT COMPLY WITH L/C TERMS AND CONDITIONS.

（3）UPON RECEIPT OF DOCUMENTS ALONG WITH DRAFT（S）STRICTLY COMPLYING WITH TERMS AND CONDITIONS OF THIS CREDIT, WE WILL REMIT PROCEEDS LESS OUR HANDLING CHARGES TO YOU AS INSTRUCTED.

（4）ONE COPY OF BILL OF LADING AND COMMERCIAL INVOICE IS REQUIRED FOR ISSUING BANK'S FILE. USD10.00 WILL BE CHARGED IF THESE COPIES ARE NOT PRESENTED.

57D：ADVISE THROUGH BANK

BANK OF CHINA WUZHOU BRANCH

72：SENDER TO RECEIVER INFORMATION

PLS. RELEASE THE L/C UPON RECEIPT OF ADVISING FEES.

END OF MESSAGE

补充信息：船名：KUIBEIQUE 12WV；船期：2022-01-28；实装货物数量：100包；净重100M/T；毛重：100.8M/T；体积：40M³；货物存放地点：广州黄埔码头2号仓库。

BENEFICIARY'S CERTIFICATE

JAN.28, 2022

TO：GOOD BROTHER RESOURCES CO., LTD.

2950 HIGHWAY DRIVE TRAIL BRITISH COLOMBIA, CANADA

RE：100 BAGS（100M/T）SILICON METAL UNDER L/C NO.EXP2021-1207 AND INVOICE NO. CF006.

THIS IS TO CERTIFY THAT ONE SET OF NON-NEGOTIABLE SHIPPING DOCUMENTS HAS

BEEN SENT TO APPLICANT BY EMS WITHIN 7 DAYS AFTER SHIPMENT HAS BEEN EFFECTED.

L/C NO.：EXP2021-1207

GUANGXI WUZHOU XINDASHUN TRADING CORP.

莫运金

第四步 学生制作受益人证明

请根据下面给出的信用证及相关补充资料，制作受益人证明。

SEQUENCE OF TOTAL：27：1/1

FORM OF DOC.CREDIT：40A：IRREVOCABLE

DOC.CREDIT NUMBER：20：EX1070/2021

DATE OF ISSUE 31C：21-07-30

EXPIRY DATE AND PLACE 31D：21-09-15 PLACE IN CHINA

APPLICANT 50： NORTHEAST INTERNATIONAL RESOURCES COMPANY，
BG STREET，W.BOX 178，NEW YORK，U.S.A.

BENEFICIARY 59：GUANGXI WUZHOU GUANGDA METALS EXPORT GROUP COMPANY，
235 WEST XINXING ROAD，WUZHOU，CHINA

AMOUNT：32B： CURRENCY USD AMOUNT 800 000.00

POS./NEG.TOL.（%）39A：5/5

AVAILABLE WITH/BY：41D：ANY BANK IN CHINA BY NEGOTIATION

DRAFTS AT 42C：SIGHT

DRAWEE 42A：IMPORT-EXPORT BANK OF NEW YORK

PARTIAL SHIPMENT 43P：NOT ALLOWED

TRANSSHIPMENT 43T： NOT ALLOWED

LOADING IN CHARGES 44E：GUANGZHOU，CHINA

FOR TRANSPORT TO 44F：NEW YORK，U.S.A.

LATEST DATE OF SHIPMENT 44C：21-08-30

DESCRIPT. OF GOODS 45A：50M/T TIN INGOT

SPECIFICATION：Sn：99.90% MIN.

PACKING：IN BUNDLES OF ABOUT 1 000KGS NET EACH

UNIT PRICE AT USD 16 000.00

PRICE TERM：PER M/T CIF NEW YORK

AS PER SALES CONTRACT NO. WLE1008

DOCUMENTS REQUIRED：46A：

+ SIGNED COMMERCIAL INVOICE IN SEXTUPLICATE，SHOWING PRICE CIF NEW YORK.

+ FULL SET OF CLEAN ON BOARD OCEAN BILL OF LADING，IN DUPLICATE，PLUS 5 NON-NEGOTIABLE，MADE OUT TO ORDER OF IMPORT-EXPORT BANK OF NEW YORK，EVIDENCING SHIPMENT FROM GUANGZHOU TO NEW YORK.MARKED FREIGHT PREPAID AND NOTIFY APPLICANT.

+ SIGNED PACKING LIST IN TRIPLICATE.

+ CERTIFICATE OF ORIGIN IN 1 SET.

+ INSURANCE POLICY OR CERTIFICATE ENDORSED IN BLANK FOR 110 PCT OF INVOICE VALUE WITH CLAIMS PAYABLE AT DESTINATION IN CURRENCY OF DRAFT COVERING C.I.C. ALL RISKS AND WAR RISK.

+ INSPECTION CERTIFICATE OF QUALITY ISSUED BY CORRESPONDING AUTHORITY.

+ BENEFICIARY'S CERTIFICATE CERTIFYING THAT ONE SET OF NON-NEGOTIABLE SHIPPING DOCUMENTS HAS BEEN SENT VIA COURIER AND VIA FAX NO：(001) -203-785-1879 DIRECTLY TO APPLICANT WITHIN 7 DAYS AFTER SHIPMENT.

ADDITIONAL CONDITION 47A：

+ ALL DOCUMENTS PRESENTED FOR NEGOTIATION SHALL BEAR NO.OF THIS CREDIT.

+ 5 PCT MORE OR LESS IN QUANTITY AND AMOUNT ARE ACCEPTABLE.

DETAILS OF CHARGES

71B：ALL BANK CHARGES OUTSIDE THE U.S. ARE FOR THE BENEFICIARY'S ACCOUNT.

CONFIRMATION 49：WITHOUT

INSTRUCTIONS 78：

+ THE NEGOTIATING BANK MUST FORWARD THE DRAFTS AND ALL DOCUMENTS IN 1 LOT TO IMPORT-EXPORT BANK OF NEW YORK，MAMA2 BRANCH，111/917-919 MOO. RAMA 2 RD.SAMAEDUN，NEW YORK，U.S.A.

+ UPON RECEIPT OF COMMERCIAL DOCUMENTS，WE SHALL REMIT THE PROCEEDS AS PER THE NEGOTIATING BANK'S INSTRUCTIONS.

+ A DISCREPANCY FEE OF USD50.00 WILL BE DEDUCTED FROM PROCEEDS IF DISCREPANT DOCUMENTS ARE PRESENTED.

+ THE AMOUNT OF ANY DRAFT DRAWN UNDER THIS CREDIT MUST BE ENDORSED ON THE REVERSE OF THE ORIGINAL CREDIT. ALL DRAFTS MUST MARK DRAWN UNDER THIS DOCUMENTARY CREDIT AND BEARING ITS NUMBER AND DATE.

SEND.TO REC.INFO.72：

+ PLS ACKNOWLEDGE RECEIPT AND ADVISE BENEFICIARY UNGENTLY.

货物原始资料如下：

唛头：NORTHEAST INTL.

L/C NO.：EX1070/2021

NEW YORK

C/NO.1-50

发票号码：M2010087；提单编号：WLY10021；提单日期：2021-08-16；货存地点：广州黄埔码头1号仓库；净重：50M/T；毛重：50.1M/T；体积：30M³；产地：贺州市钟山县冶炼厂；运输工具：DONGFENG 001；发货日期：2021-08-16；锡锭 H.S. 编码：80011000.00；订舱联系人：莫小梅，电话：0774-20003788。

第五步　课后训练

广西梧州星河纺织品进出口公司2021年6月向英国某公司出口毛巾360打。信用证号码为LX201106229E，合同号为WZ0021，发票号为LM0012。信用证要求受益人出具一份证明，证明每打包装上都捆扎有布条标签。请你代为写作此受益人证明。

任务十　船东证明

情境导入

在信用证付款方式下，有时候会要求受益人出具船东证明并且作为一种议付单据。那么什么是船东证明？它包含哪些内容？怎样出具这类证明？有哪些应该注意的问题？

第一步　学生学

一、船东证明的含义

船东证明（Certificate of Ownership）就是承载货物运输的船方出具的证明文件。

二、船东证明的类型

1.船级证明（Confirmation of Vessel’s Class）

有的信用证规定要提供劳合社船级证明。劳合社的船级符号为LR，标志为100A1，100A表示该船的船体和机器设备是根据劳氏规范和规定建造的，1表示船舶的装备如船锚、锚链和绳索等处于良好和有效的状态。通常，对这样的要求应予以满足。国际上著名的船级社有英国劳合社、德国船级社（GL）、挪威船级社（DNV）、法国船级社（BV）、日本海事协会（NK）、美国船级社（ABS）等。

例如：Class certificate certifying that the shipment is made by a seaworthy vessel which are classified 100A1 issued by Lloyds or equivalent classification society.

船级证明证实所装货物使用劳埃德船级社或其他等同船级社分类的100A1船级的船只运输。

2.船龄证明（Certificate of Vessel Age）

船龄证明是指船方出具的证明承载货物的船只的年龄的文件。

例如：Vessel should not be more than 15 years of age and is subject to Institute Classfications Clauses. A certificate to this effect from the shipping company/agent must accopmany documents presented for negotiation.

根据（伦敦保险）协会船级条款，船只不应该超过15年船龄，船公司/代理出具的这样的证明在议付时应随同单据一起提交。

3.停靠港口证明

例如：A certificate from the shipping company or their agents or from owner/master of the vessel is to be presented stating：To whom it may concern. We certify that the vessel is allowed to call at any Arab ports in accordance with the rules and regulations of Arab authorities.（not applicable in case shipment is effected by United Arab Shipping Company Vessel.）

由船公司或它们的代理或船东出具的证明，写有“呈递给有关人员”“兹证明该船只可以停靠在符合阿拉伯国家规定的任何港口”（该条款不适用于阿拉伯联合船运公司的船只）。

4.船籍证明（Certificate of Registry）

船籍证明是指船方出具的用于证明船舶所属国籍的文件。其要求运输船只必须是哪个国家的船或者不是哪个国家的船。这种要求一般在审证时候提出修改或删除。

5.航程证明（Certificate of Itinerary）

航程证明主要用来说明航程中船舶停靠的港口。例如，一些阿拉伯国家开来的信用证中往往要求在提单上随附声明一份，明确船籍、船名、船东及途中所经港口顺序，出口方需按要求签发此类证明并按证明中所述行驶、操作船舶。

6.转船证明书（Certificate of Transshipment）

出口方出具转船证明书，说明出口货物将在中途转船且已联系妥当，并由托运人负责将有关转船事项通知收货人。

7.货装具名船舶证明

例如：A certificate from the shipping company or its agent stating that goods are shipped by APL.（出口方）应提供由船公司或其代理出具的货装美国总统轮船公司的证明。

第二步　教师教

一、船东证明示范

CERTIFICATE OF VESSEL AGE

JAN.28，2021

TO WHOM IT MAY CONCERN，

THIS IS TO CERTIFY THAT VESSEL LYODDONGFENG 002E IS NOT MORE THAN 15 YEARS OF AGE AND IS SUBJECT TO INSTITUTE CLASSFICATIONS CLAUSES.

L/C NO.：EXP2020-1207

GUANGDONG BEIMEI SHIPPING CO.，LTD.

黄少聪

二、船东证明出具的注意事项

1.证明抬头要紧跟信用证所用的单据名字。

2.证明的内容要开门见山、直截了当，即要证明什么就证明什么，不绕弯，不反证。

3.此类证明一般无固定格式要求，出口人可以自己写好，让船东盖章；也可以直接将内容告知船方，让船方出具并盖章。

4.由于此类证明也是一种议付单据，信用证如有特约事项，也要在此证明中处理。

任务十一　汇票

情境导入

2021年1月下旬，广西梧州春江五金矿产进出口有限公司拟向加拿大某公司出口100公吨特级金属硅。1月28日下午，货物已经装船并且取得了提单。实习单证员谭雅梅所在的出口部经理王瑞荣要求她在制作和办理所有议付单据后，按照信用证的要求，制作汇票，然后准备交单议付。

第一步　学生学

一、汇票的含义

汇票（Bill of Exchange/Draft）是出票人签发的，委托付款人在见票时或在指定日期无条件支付确定的金额给收款人或者持票人的票据。

二、汇票的结构

汇票是一种要式票据，不仅有固定格式，还有规定的内容要求，出口人不能自行设计和填写。

三、汇票的作用

出口商以逆汇方式（如托收、信用证）结算货款时，需要出具一种书面凭证，作为向进口商索取款项的依据。在信用证付款方式下，汇票不是一种议付单据。现在一般使用托收付款方式付款，议付单据中也不用提供汇票了。

四、汇票的内容

根据我国《票据法》的规定，汇票必须记载下列事项：

1.表明“汇票”的字样。

2.无条件支付的委托。其应理解成汇票上不能记载支付条件。

3.确定的金额。

4.付款人名称。在国际贸易中，通常是进口方或其指定银行。

5.收款人名称。在国际贸易中，通常是出口方或其指定银行。

6.出票日期。

7.出票人签章。

汇票上未记载上述规定事项之一的，汇票无效。实际业务中，汇票上尚需列明付款日期、付款地点和出票地点。如未列明，可根据《票据法》予以确定。

五、汇票样本

汇 票

凭
Drawn under ______________________________
信用证　　　　　　第　　　　　　号
L/C NO. ______________________________
日期　　　　　年　　　　　月　　　　　日
Dated ______________________________

按　　　　　　　　　息　　　　　　　　　付　款
Payable with interest @　　　　　　% per annum
号码　　　　　　汇票金额　　　　　　　中国，　　　年　　月　　日
NO. ...　　　　.........Exchange for　　　　　　China.
见票　　　　　　　　　　　　　　　　　　日后（本汇票之复本未付）付
At ......　　　　......sight of this FIRST of Exchange（Second of exchange being unpaid）
Pay to the order of ______________________________ 或其指定人
金 额
The sum of ______________________________
此致
To: ______________________________

____
×××

六、汇票的填写

1.Drawn under：填写信用证开证银行的名称。

2.L/C NO.：填写信用证号码。

3. 日期：填写信用证开证日期。

4. 按……息：不填，通常由议付银行定。

5. 号码：填写发票号码。

6. 汇票金额：填写发票金额（小写）。

7. 出票地点、时间：出口人所在地；时间按照实际填写，可填写交单日期或提单日期。

8. 见票：即期填写六个黑圆点（……），远期按实际填写。

9.Pay to the order of：填写议付银行的名称。

10. 金额：大写，将上面小写的汇票金额用英文表达出来。

11.To：填写信用证的受票人，即信用证中的42A。

12. 签名、盖章：在汇票右下角，出票人签名盖章。

第二步　教师填写汇票

根据以下所给资料，填写汇票。

微课2-8

汇票的制作

27：　SEQUENCE OF TOTAL：1/1

40A：FORM OF DOCUMENTARY CREDIT：IRREVOCABLE

20：　DOCUMENTARY CREDIT NUMBER：EXP2021-1207

31C：DATE OF ISSUE：21-12-07

40E：APPLICABLE RULES：UCP LATEST VERSION

31D：DATE AND PLACE OF EXPIRY：22-02-15 IN BENEFICIARY'S COUNTRY

50：　APPLICANT：
GOOD BROTHER RESOURCES CO.，LTD.
2950 HIGHWAY DRIVE TRAIL BRITISH COLOMBIA，CANADA

59：　BENEFICIARY：
GUANGXI WUZHOU XINDASHUN TRADING CORP.
555，WEST XINXING ROAD，WUZHOU，GUANGXI，P.R.C.

32B：CURRENCY CODE，AMOUNT
CURRENCY：USD（US DOLLAR）
AMOUNT：#165 000.00#

41D：AVAILABLE WITH... BY...
ANY BANK IN BENEFICIARY'S COUNTRY
BY NEGOTIATION

42C：DRAFTS AT：
SIGHT FOR 100% OF INVOICE VALUE

42A：DRAWEE：NORTHEAST AMERICA BANK OF CANADA

43P：PARTIAL SHIPMENTS：ALLOWED

43T：TRANSSHIPMENT：ALLOWED

44E：PORT OF LOADING：GUANGZHOU，CHINA

44F：PORT OF DISCHARGE：MONTREAL，CANADA

44C：LATEST DATE OF SHIPMENT：22-01-31

45A：DESCRIPTION OF GOODS &/OR SERVICES

100M/T/100BAGS OF SILICON METAL

Si：99% MIN.　　Fe：0.4% MAX.

Al：0.4% MAX.　　Ca：0.1% MAX.

SIZE：10-100 MM 90% MIN.

UNIT PRICE：USD1 650M/T CIF MONTREAL，CANADA

AS PER SALES CONTRACT NO.GBR10086

PACKED IN PLASTIC WOVEN BAGS OF ABOUT 1 000KGS NET EACH

46A：DOCUMENTS REQUIRED

（1）SIGNED COMMERCIAL INVOICE IN DUPLICATE.

（2）FULL SET OF CLEAN ON BOARD MARINE BILLS OF LADING IN TWO ORIGINALS AND 3 COPIES，MADE OUT TO ORDER，ENDORSED IN BLANK，MARKED FREIGHT PREPAID，NOTIFYING APPLICANT EVIDENCING SHIPMENT FROM GUANGZHOU TO MONTREAL BY VESSEL.

（3）INSPECTION CERTIFICATE OF QUALITY AND WEIGHT IN DUPLICATE.

（4）PACKING LIST IN TRIPLICATE.

（5）CERTIFICATE OF ORIGIN GSP FORM A IN 1 ORIGINAL AND 2 COPIES ISSUED BY CORRESPONDING AUTHORITY.

（6）INSURANCE POLICY OR CERTIFICATE ENDORSED IN BLANK WITH CLAIMS PAYABLE AT THE DESTINATION WITH THE SAME CURRENCY OF DRAFT AGAINST ALL RISKS AND WAR RISK OF C.I.C. FOR 110% OF INVOICE VALUE.

（7）BENEFICIARY'S CERTIFICATE CERTIFYING THAT ONE SET OF NON-NEGOTIABLE SHIPPING DOCUMENTS HAS BEEN SENT TO APPLICANT BY EMS WITHIN 7 DAYS AFTER SHIPMENT HAS BEEN EFFECTED.

47A：ADDITIONAL CONDITIONS

（1）ALL DOCUMENTS MUST BEAR THIS CREDIT NUMBER.

（2）SHIPMENT DATE PRIOR TO L/C'S ISSUING DATE IS PROHIBITED.

（3）5% MORE OR LESS IN QUANTITY AND AMOUNT ARE ACCEPTABLE.

（4）GOODS COVERING FREE OF CHARGE ARE ACCEPTABLE.

（5）IF DOCUMENTS PRESENTED UNDER THIS L/C ARE FOUND TO BE DISCREPANT，WE SHALL GIVE ITS NOTICE OF REFUSAL AND SHALL HOLD DOCUMENTS AT YOUR DISPOSAL SUBJECT TO THE FOLLOWING CONDITION："IF WE HAVE NOT RECEIVED YOUR DISPOSAL INSTRUCTIONS FOR THE DISCREPANT DOCUMENTS PRIOR TO RECEIPT OF THE APPLICANT'S WAIVER OF DISCREPANCIES，WE WILL RELEASE DOCUMENTS TO APPLICANT WITHOUT NOTICE TO YOU."

71B：CHARGES

ALL BANKING CHARGES OUTSIDE CANADA，IF ANY，ARE FOR ACCOUNT OF BENEFICIARY.

48：PERIOD FOR PRESENTATION

DOCUMENTS PRESENTED WITHIN 15 DAYS AFTER SHIPMENT BUT WITHIN THE

VALIDITY OF THE CREDIT.

49：CONFIRMATION INSTRUCTIONS

WITHOUT

78：INSTR TO PAYG/ACCPTG/NEGOTG BANK

（1）ALL DOCUMENTS MUST BE SENT TO US IN ONE LOT，OUR ADDRESS：

NORTHEAST AMERICA BANK OF CANADA，238 #，BEIXALU，GM，MONTREAL，CANADA

（2）A DISCREPANCY FEE OF USD60.00 SHOULD BE DEDUCTED FROM NEGOTIATION AMOUNT FOR EACH PRESENTATION IF DOCUMENTS DO NOT COMPLY WITH L/C TERMS AND CONDITIONS.

（3）UPON RECEIPT OF DOCUMENTS ALONG WITH DRAFT（S）STRICTLY COMPLYING WITH TERMS AND CONDITIONS OF THIS CREDIT，WE WILL REMIT PROCEEDS LESS OUR HANDLING CHARGES TO YOU AS INSTRUCTED.

（4）ONE COPY OF BILL OF LADING AND COMMERCIAL INVOICE IS REQUIRED FOR ISSUING BANK'S FILE. USD10.00 WILL BE CHARGED IF THESE COPIES ARE NOT PRESENTED.

57D：ADVISE THROUGH BANK

BANK OF CHINA WUZHOU BRANCH

72：SENDER TO RECEIVER INFORMATION

PLS. RELEASE THE L/C UPON RECEIPT OF ADVISING FEES.

END OF MESSAGE

补充信息：船名：KUIBEIQUE 12W V；船期：2022-01-28；实装货物数量：100包；净重100M/T；毛重：100.8M/T；体积：40M³；货物存放地点：广州黄埔码头2号仓库。

汇　票

凭
Drawn under NORTHEAST AMERICA BANK OF CANADA
信用证　　第　　号
L/C NO. EXP2021-1207
日期　　年　　月　　日
Dated DEC.07,2021

按　　息　　付 款
Payable with interest @　　% per annum
号码　　汇票金额　　中国，　年　月　日
NO. CF006　......... Exchange for USD165 000.00　　WUZHOU，CHINA. JAN.28，2022
见票　　日后（本汇票之复本未付）付
At ......　......sight of this FIRST of Exchange（Second of exchange being unpaid）
Pay to the order of BANK OF CHINA WUZHOU BRANCH　　或其指定人
金 额
The sum of US DOLLARS ONE HUNDRED AND SIXTY FIVE THOUSAND ONLY
此致
To: NORTHEAST AMERICA BANK OF CANADA

GUANGXI WUZHOU XINDASHUN TRADING CORP.

莫大君

第三步　学生做

请根据下面给出的信用证及相关补充资料，制作汇票。

SEQUENCE OF TOTAL：27：1/1

FORM OF DOC. CREDIT：40A：IRREVOCABLE

DOC. CREDIT NUMBER：20：EX1070/2010

DATE OF ISSUE　　　31C：21-07-30

EXPIRY DATE AND PLACE：31D 21-09-15 PLACE IN CHINA

APPLICANT 50：　NORTHEAST INTERNATIONAL RESOURCES COMPANY，

BG STREET，W.BOX 178，NEW YORK，U.S.A.

BENEFICIARY 59：GUANGXI WUZHOU GUANGFA METALS EXPORT GROUP COMPANY，

235 WEST XINXING ROAD，WUZHOU，CHINA

AMOUNT：32B：　CURRENCY USD AMOUNT 800 000.00

POS./NEG. TOL.（%）39A：5/5

AVAILABLE WITH/BY：41D：ANY BANK IN CHINA BY NEGOTIATION

DRAFTS AT 42C：SIGHT

DRAWEE 42A ：IMPORT-EXPORT BANK OF NEW YORK

PARTIAL SHIPMENT 43P：NOT ALLOWED

TRANSSHIPMENT 43T：NOT ALLOWED

LOADING PORT 44E：GUANGZHOU，CHINA

FOR TRANSPORT TO 44F：NEW YORK，THE U.S.

LATEST DATE OF SHIPMENT 44C：21-08-30

DESCRIPT. OF GOODS 45A：50M/T TIN INGOT

SPECIFICATION：Sn：99.90% MIN.

PACKING：IN BUNDLES OF ABOUT 1 000KGS NET EACH.

UNIT PRICE AT USD 16 000.00

PRICE TERM：PER M/T CIF NEW YORK.

AS PER SALES CONTRACT NO. WLE1008.

DOCUMENTS REQUIRED：46A：

+ SIGNED COMMERCIAL INVOICE IN SEXTUPLICATE，SHOWING PRICE CIF NEW YORK.

+ FULL SET OF CLEAN ON BOARD OCEAN BILLS OF LADING，IN DUPLICATE，PLUS 5 NON-NEGOTIABLE，MADE OUT TO ORDER OF IMPORT-EXPORT BANK OF NEW YORK，EVIDENCING SHIPMENT FROM GUANGZHOU TO NEW YORK.MARKED FREIGHT PREPAID AND NOTIFY APPLICANT.

+ SIGNED PACKING LIST IN TRIPLICATE.

+ CERTIFICATE OF ORIGIN IN 1 SET.

+ INSURANCE POLICY OR CERTIFICATE ENDORSED IN BLANK FOR 110 PCT OF INVOICE VALUE WITH CLAIMS PAYABLE AT DESTINATION IN CURRENCY OF DRAFT

COVERING C.I.C.ALL RISKS AND WAR RISK.

+ INSPECTION CERTIFICATE OF QUALITY ISSUED BY CORRESPONDING AUTHORITY.

+ BENEFICIARY'S CERTIFICATE CERTIFYING THAT ONE SET OF NON-NEGOTIABLE SHIPPING DOCUMENTS HAS BEEN SENT VIA COURIER AND VIA FAX NO.:（001）-203-785-1879 DIRECTLY TO APPLICANT WITHIN 7 DAYS AFTER SHIPMENT.

ADDITIONAL CONDITION 47A:

+ 5 PCT MORE OR LESS IN QUANTITY AND AMOUNT ARE ACCEPTABLE.

DETAILS OF CHARGES

71B: ALL BANK CHARGES OUTSIDE THE U.S.A. ARE FOR THE BENEFICIARY'S ACCOUNT.

CONFIRMATION 49: WITHOUT

INSTRUCTIONS 78:

+ THE NEGOTIATING BANK MUST FORWARD THE DRAFTS AND ALL DOCUMENTS IN 1 LOT TO IMPORT-EXPORT BANK OF NEW YORK，MAMA2 BRANCH，111/917-919 MOO. RAMA 2 RD.SAMAEDUN，NEW YORK，THE U.S.

+ UPON RECEIPT OF COMMERCIAL DOCUMENTS，WE SHALL REMIT THE PROCEEDS AS PER THE NEGOTIATING BANK'S INSTRUCTIONS.

+ A DISCREPANCY FEE OF USD50.00 WILL BE DEDUCTED FROM PROCEEDS IF DISCREPANT DOCUMENTS ARE PRESENTED.

+ ALL DOCUMENTS PRESENTED FOR NEGOTIATION SHALL BEAR NO. OF THIS CREDIT AND NAME OF ISSUING BANK.

+ THE AMOUNT OF ANY DRAFT DRAWN UNDER THIS CREDIT MUST BE ENDORSED ON THE REVERSE OF THE ORIGINAL CREDIT. ALL DRAFTS MUST MARK DRAWN UNDER THIS DOCUMENTARY CREDIT AND BEARING ITS NUMBER AND DATE.

+ PLS. ACKNOWLEDGE RECEIPT AND ADVISE BENEFICIARY UNGENTLY.

唛头：NORTHEAST INTL.
EX1070/2010
NEW YORK
C/NO.1-50

发票号码：M2010087；提单编号：WLY10021；提单日期：2021-08-16；货存地点：广州黄埔码头1号仓库；净重：50M/T；毛重：50.1M/T；体积：30M³；产地：贺州市钟山县冶炼厂；运输工具：DONGFENG 001；发货日期：2021-08-16；锡锭 H.S. 编码：80011000.00；订舱联系人：莫小梅，电话：0774-20003788。

汇票

凭
Drawn under ____________________
信用证 第 号
L/C NO. ____________________
日期 年 月 日
Dated ____________________

按 息 付 款
Payable with interest @ % per annum
号码 汇票金额 中国， 年 月 日
NO. ... .Exchange for China.
见票 日后（本汇票之复本未付）付
At ....sight of this FIRST of Exchange（Second of exchange being unpaid）
Pay to the order of ____________________ 或其指定人
金 额
The sum of ____________________
此致
To: ____________________

____
×××

第四步 课后训练

课后由各个学生小组根据下面的资料制作汇票。

SEQUENCE OF TOTAL 27：1/1

FORM OF DOC. CREDIT 40A：IRREVOCABLE

DOC. CREDIT NUMBER 20：MCBB61561

DATE OF ISSUE 31C：21-12-15

EXPIRY 31D：DATE 22-02-15 PLACE AT OUR COUNTRY（IN CHINA）

APPLICANT 50：SHUNDA DEVELOPMENT LTD.
UNIT10-6，15/F MENAL ASIA GRANITE，34 WAI YIP STREET，KOWLOON，
HONG KONG

BENEFICIARY 59：PUFA TEXTILE AND LIGHT INDUSTRY CO.，LTD.
120 TAIPING ROAD，NANJING，CHINA

AMOUNT 32B：CURRENCY USD AMOUNT 155 000.00

POS./NEG.TOL.（%） 39A：10/10

AVAILABLE WITH/BY 41D：ANY BANK IN CHINA
BY NEGOTIATION

DRAFTS AT... 42C：AT SIGHT

DRAWEE 42A：SHANGHAI COMMERCIAL BANK LTD.
HONG KONG FOR FULL INVOICE VALUE

PARTIAL SHIPMENTS 43P：ALLOWED

TRANSSHIPMENT 43T：ALLOWED

LATEST DATE OF SHIPMENT：44C：22-01-31

LOADING PORT　　44E：ANY PORT IN CHINA
FOR TRANSPORT TO　44F：COPENHAGEN，DENMARK
DESCRIPTION OF GOODS 45A：
FABRIC CRUSHED VELOUR，11 000M，AT USD15.5/M
AS PER S/C NO. 2K11121，JSL ORDER NO.2010500
ART. 5360004/10，2 500M VANILLA
ART. 5360025/30，3 500M BURGUNDY
ART. 5360029/40，5 000M HUNTER GREEN
ALL CIF COPENHAGEN，DENMARK
DOCUMENTS REQUIRED 46A：

+ SIGNED COMMERCIAL INVOICE IN TRIPLICATE.

+ FULL SET OF CLEAN ON BOARD OCEAN VESSEL BILL OF LADING ISSUED TO ORDER AND BLANK ENDORSED NOTIFYING APPLICANT AND MARKED FREIGHT PREPAID SHOWING NAME AND ADDRESS OF SHIPPING COMPANY ' S AGENT AT DESTINATION.

+ PACKING LISTS IN TRIPLICATE.

+ INSPECTION CERTIFICATE OF QUALITY AND WEIGHT ISSUED BY COMPETENT AUTHORITY IN CHINA.

+ CERTIFICATE OF ORIGIN G.S.P. FORM A IN DUPLICATE ISSUED BY COMPETENT AUTHORITY OF THE P.R.C.

+ INSURANCE POLICY OR CERTIFICATE IN ASSIGNABLE FORM AND ENDORSED IN BLANK FOR 110% OF INVOICE VALUE AGAINST ALL RISKS AND WAR RISK OF C.I.C. WITH CLAIM PAYABLE AT DESTINATION IN THE SAME CURRENCY OF DRAFT.

+ ONE SET OF NON - NEGOTIABLE SHIPPING DOCUMENTS SHALL BE SENT TO APPLICANT WITHIN 7 DAYS AFTER SHIPMENT HAS BEEN EFFECTED. A BENEFICIARY'S CERTIFICATE TO THIS EFFECT IS REQUIRED.

ADDITIONAL COND. 47A：

+ ALL DOCUMENTS TO PRESENTED FOR NEGOTIATION SHALL INDICATE THIS CREDIT NUMBER AND DATE AS WELL AS THE NAME OF ISSUING BANK.

+ CHARGES INCURRED IN RESPECT OF ANY TELEGRAPHIC TRANSFER/CHARTS PAYMENT/PAYMENT ADVICE BY SWIFT/TELEX ARE FOR ACCOUNT OF BENEFICIARY.

+ A HANDLING COMMISSION OF USD50.00 OR EQUIVALENT，PLUS TELEX CHARGES，IF ANY，WILL BE DEDUCTED FROM THE PROCEEDS FOR EACH SET OF DOCUMENTS WITH DISCREPANCIES PRESENTED UNDER THIS LETTER OF CREDIT.

+ ALL DOCUMENTS MUST BE PRESENTED THROUGH BENEFICIARY ' S BANKER AND EXTRA COPY OF INVOICE AND TRANSPORT DOCUMENT FOR L/C ISSUING BANK'S FILE REQUIRED.

WE HEREBY ENGAGE WITH THE DRAWERS，ENDORSERS AND BONA FIDE HOLDERS THAT DRAFTS DRAWN AND NEGOTIATED IN COMPLIANCE WITH THE

TERMS AND CONDITIONS OF THIS CREDIT WILL BE DULY HONOURED ON PRESENTATION.

THIS DOCUMENTARY CREDIT IS SUBJECT TO THE UNIFORM CUSTOMS AND PRACTICE FOR DOCUMENTARY CREDITS（2007）REVISION，INTERNATIONAL CHAMBER OF COMMERCE，PUBLICATION NO.600.

DETAILS OF CHARGES 71B：ALL BANKING CHARGES OUTSIDE U.K. ARE FOR ACCOUNT OF BENEFICIARY .

PRESENTATION PERIOD 48 ：ALL DOCUMENTS MUST BE PRESENTED TO AND REACH OUR COUNTER IN HONG KONG WITHIN 7 DAYS AFTER B/L DATE.

CONFIRMATION 49 ：WITHOUT

INSTRUCTIONS 78：

+ PLS FORWARD AT BENEFICIARY'S EXPENSES THE WHOLE SET OF DOCUMENTS IN ONE LOT TO OUR BILLS PROCESSING CENTRE AT 190#，GREAT BRITISH NEW STREET，LONDON，THE UNITED KINGDOM，FAX：0044-20-2763-2133，TEL：0044-20-2767-2132.

+ IN REIMBURSEMENT，WE SHALL REMIT PROCEEDS IN ACCORDANCE WITH YOUR INSTRUCTIONS UPON RECEIPT OF THE DOCUMENTS.

ADVISE THROUGH 57D：BANK OF CHINA NANJING BRANCH

附加信息：货物的包装皮重为一个双层牛皮袋重0.5千克；发票号码：MJ110608；提单日期：2021-06-18；装运港：Shanghai；目的港：Copenhagen。

汇票 1

凭
Drawn under ____

信用证 第 号
L/C NO. ____

日期 年 月 日
Dated ____

按 息 付 款
Payable with interest @ % per annum

号码 汇票金额 中国， 年 月 日
NO. ... .Exchange for China.

见票 日后（本汇票之复本未付）付
At ....sight of this FIRST of Exchange（Second of exchange being unpaid）

Pay to the order of ______________________________________ 或其指定人

金 额
The sum of ____

此致
To: ____

____

×××

综合训练

一、判断题

（1）我国原产地证书的官方发证机构是各地的海关。（ ）

（2）根据我国的相关规定，出口企业向签发机构申请办理原产地证的最迟时间是货物出运前3天。（ ）

（3）若信用证要求受益人提供保险单，则受益人既可以提供保险单，也可以提供保险凭证，有权在二者中任选其一。（ ）

随堂测2

（4）承运人在海运提单上加注任何批注，都使此海运提单构成不清洁提单。（ ）

（5）Drawee是指汇票的出票人，一般是开证行，有时也可能是偿付行。（ ）

（6）根据《UCP600》的规定，在信用证付款方式下，汇票的付款人应该是议付行。（ ）

（7）装船通知是在货物装船后发出的，因此其日期一定会晚于提单日期。（ ）

（8）商业发票是要式单据，受益人不能自己设计、制作和签发。（ ）

（9）在信用证方式下，原产地证明中的货物描述必须与发票的货物描述一致，不得使用统称。（ ）

（10）货物的体积、毛重、净重、包装方法以及单价可以不在装箱单中列明。（ ）

（11）在信用证业务中，各有关当事人处理的是单据而不是实际货物，即使受益人出口的货物是垃圾，只要其提交的单证完全符合信用证的要求，开证银行就必须付款。（ ）

（12）信用证规定的最迟装运期是2021年6月30日，有效期是2021年7月15日，若实际装船日期是2021年6月30日，则受益人可以于2021年7月16日交单。（ ）

（13）合同规定装运时间为2021年5月和6月，则卖方应该在5月和6月各交一批货物，且这两批货物要求数量相等。（ ）

（14）按照有关惯例的规定，受益人对信用证修改书的内容既可以全部接受，也可以部分接受。（ ）

（15）一切险就是保一切。（ ）

二、简答题

（1）在制作产地证时，使用结束符号的作用是什么？

（2）海运提单的收货人抬头栏目一般有多少种表示方法？

（3）最晚装船期和船期有什么不同？

（4）为什么在CFR术语成交条件下，卖方装船后及时发出装船通知尤为重要？

（5）商业发票应该包括哪些内容？

（6）如果信用证不指定出具原产地证的机构，通常由什么机构出具？

（7）在制作受益人证明时，通常用来表示“兹证明”意思的英文句子是什么？

（8）外贸单证的制作有什么要求？

（9）交单时应注意哪些问题？

（10）为什么说商业发票是基本单证，起核心和统帅作用？

三、手工操作题

请根据下面的信用证制作商业发票、装箱单、产地证和汇票，并发出装船通知。

21: SEQUENCE OF 1/1

40A: FORM OF DOC.CREDIT: IRREVOCABLE

20: DOCUMENT CREDIT NO.: DK20160708-1

31C: DATE OF ISSUE: 21-06-25

31D: DATE OF EXPIRY: 21-08-30

50: APPLICANT: GUODONGYOU TRADING CO., LTD.,
1008 WHITE QUEENS ROAD, DUNKERQUE, FRANCE

59: BENEFICIARY: KUNSHANG HUACHENG WEAVING AND DYEING CO., LTD,
HUANGLONG RD., LIUJIA ZHEN, FOSHAN CITY, GUANGDONG PROVINCE, P.R.C.

32B: AMOUNT: USD150 000.00 (US DOLLARS ONE HUNDRED AND FIFTY THOUSAND ONLY)

41D: AVAILABLE WITH/BY: ANY BANK BY NEGOTIATION

42C: DRAFTS AT SIGHT FOR 100% OF INVOICE VALUE

42A: DRAWEE: UNITED OVERSEAS BANK OF FRANCE

43P: PARTIAL SHIPMENT: NOT ALLOWED

43T: TRANSSHIPMENT: NOT ALLOWED

44E: LOADING PORT: YANTIAN, SHENZHEN

44F: FOR TRANSPORTATION TO: DUNKERQUE

44C: LATEST DATE OF SHIPMENT: 21-07-30

45A: DESCRIPTION OF GOODS AND/OR SERVICES:

100 PCT NYLON FABRICS 100 000 YARDS AT USD1.5/YARD

PRICE TERM: CFR DUNKERQUE

PACKING: PACKED IN BUNDLES OF 1 000 YARDS EACH, 10 BUNDLES TO A CARTON

DETAILS AS PER CONTRACT NO.99WS061

46A: DOCUMENTS REQUIRED:

(1) MANUALLY SIGNED COMMERCIAL INVOICE IN 5 FOLDS.

(2) FULL SET (3/3) OF CLEAN ON BOARD MARINE BILLS OF LADING MADE OUT TO ORDER AND BLANK ENDORSED, MARKED FREIGHT PREPAID AND NOTIFY THE APPLICANT.

(3) PACKING LIST IN 3 FOLDS.

(4) CERTIFICATE OF ORIGIN FORM A IN 2 FOLDS.

(5) SHIPPING ADVICE ADVISING NAME AND QUANTITY OF GOODS, L/C NO., NAME OF VESSEL, INVOICE NO., INVOICE VALUE, DATE OF SHIPMENT, SHIPPING MARKS, ETA AND ETD.

47A: ADDITIONAL CONDITIONS:

+ ALL DOCUMENTS MUST INDICATE THIS L/C NO.

48: PERIOD FOR PRESENTATION:

DOCUMENTS MUST BE PRESENTED WITHIN 15 DAYS AFTER THE DATE OF

SHIPMENT BUT WITHIN THE VALIDITY OF THE CREDIT.

49：CONFIRMATION：WITHOUT

…

补充信息：船名：PRINCE 018；船期：2021-07-22；货物数量10箱；总体积3.5M³；总重312千克；货物产地广东省佛山市；H.S.编码：631010；发票号码和日期自定。

四、案例分析

（1）中国某国际贸易公司对国外乔治公司出口500吨花生。买方申请开来的信用证规定："分5个月装运，3月份装80吨；4月份装120吨；5月份装140吨；6月份装110吨；7月份装50吨。每月不许分批装运；从中国港口至伦敦。"

该贸易公司接到信用证后，根据信用证的规定于3月15日在青岛港装运了80吨花生；于4月20日在青岛港又装运了120吨花生，均顺利收回了货款。

该贸易公司后因货源不足于5月20日在青岛港只装了70.5吨。经联系得知烟台某公司有一部分同样规格的货物，所以该贸易公司要求"HULIN"轮再驶往烟台港继续装其不足数量。船方考虑到目前船舱空载，所以同意在烟台港装64.1吨花生。该贸易公司向银行提交了两套单据：一套是在青岛港于5月20日签发的提单，其货量为70.5吨；另一套是在烟台港于5月28日签发的提单，货量为64.1吨。银行认为单据有两处不符点：①在青岛和烟台分批装运货物；②短量。

请问：不符点是否成立？

（2）2021年5月，广西梧州某进出口公司出口价值5万美元的软锰粉到中东某国，凭即期不可撤销信用证付款。货物于12月中旬报关装船出运。根据信用证的规定，卖方在货物装船后15天内制单交单，但不能超过信用证有效期。由于单证员是位大学毕业不久的新人，没有制单交单经验。她在货物装船出运后第二周过半时间才将全套议付单据备齐，并向梧州的议付银行递交了单据。该银行收到单据后，经审查发现所交全套单据的特约事项条款均处理不当。信用证规定"ALL SHIPPING DOCUMENTS MUST BEAR THIS CREDIT NUMBER AND DATE."，单证员在每种单据上只是机械地抄录信用证特约事项条款这句英文，没有进行具体的灵活化处理。此外，信用证对商业发票还有一个特别要求，即"SHOWING FREIGHT CHARGES、INSURANCE PREMIUM AND FOB VALUE SEPERATELY AND CERTIFYING THE GOODS ARE OF CHINESE ORIGIN."，单证员也没有进行相关处理。这样的单据与信用证严重不符，被梧州的议付银行断然拒绝议付，要求其重做。而此时信用证规定的交单期还剩下仅仅两天。一般来说，中东国家开来的信用证对议付单据的要求多而复杂。该进出口公司要在短短的两天时间内补齐包括产地证在内的全套议付单据而后二次提交给议付银行非常困难。

请问：该出口公司该如何处理？

（3）2021年10月中旬，法国Montpellier Calmetter Altert Co.，Ltd向加利进出口贸易有限公司开来一份购买200吨金属硅即期付款的信用证。

加利进出口贸易有限公司接到信用证后，立即着手备货、包装、检验、配船。由于单证员过期申请产地证FORM A而被海关拒绝，后经过多次紧急磋商，海关才同意出具后发证书，但是要缴纳5万元人民币作为保证金。该贸易公司最终错过了交单期，银行拒绝付款，建议其改为证下托收。加利进出口贸易有限公司致电法国公司，对方的答复是：涉及的当事人较多，要好好考虑一下再定。中国银行梧州分行也联系了国外开证行，得到的答复是：由于采用信用证方式付款，超过了交单期，信用证失效了。加利公司多次用传真与开证申请人协商，并同意降价20%，恳请法国客户接单接货。法国客户看到有利可图，才勉强同意赎单，还附加条件要求加利公司在下次交易时提供优惠价格。此单生意给加利公司造成了18万元的损失，不可谓不严重。

请问：证下托收如何操作？

项目三

综合制单

能力目标

1. 能正确制作信用证付款方式下的全套议付单据；
2. 能正确制作托收和汇付方式下的全套议付单据。

知识目标

1. 掌握信用证付款方式下发票、包装单、提单、保险单、G. S. P. FORM A、C. O.、装船通知、受益人证明等议付单据的制作。

2. 掌握托收和汇付方式下发票、包装单、提单、保险单、G. S. P. FORM A、C. O.、装船通知、受益人证明等议付单据的制作。

思政目标

通过全套外贸单据的制作，认识到外贸单证在整个进出口业务中的重要作用，培养学生诚实、认真、严谨、一丝不苟的工作作风和勇于开拓、精益求精的工匠精神。

项目引例

单证不一致导致无法收款

2021年6月，广州A出口公司对美国B贸易公司出口女士短裙1 000件，合同规定蓝色和黑色按4 6的比例搭配，即蓝色400件、黑色600件。而国外来证上黑色和蓝色的比例是4∶6。A公司按合同规定的颜色比例装船出口，货物、发票、装箱单、提单、原产地证书等单据都与合同一致，去银行办理议付时，遭到银行拒付。

引例评析：信用证下单据的制作应严格遵守“单单相符、单证相符”的原则。本案例属于单证不符的情形，故银行有理由拒付。本案例告诉我们，在综合制单环节，一定要做到认真细致，具有高度的责任心。

情境导入

2021年5月8日，广东省广州市春常在进出口公司与英国伦敦一家经营化工品的公司签订了合同，出口250吨钛白粉，即期信用证付款。5月中旬信用证按时到达。经审查信用证没有问题，6月18日货物顺利装船。出口部经理王瑞荣要求实习单证员覃芳芳负责该份信用证项下全套单据的制作。

任务一　信用证项下的综合制单

第一步　教师教

一、分项制单与综合制单的区分

微课3

分项制单和综合制单

在现实工作中，当收到客户的信用证后，受益人往往要对信用证进行全面细致的审查；审查出问题的，还要改证。只有确保信用证没有问题了，才会按照信用证的要求制作各种单据。单据制作分为分项制单和综合制单。

分项制单又叫一次制单，指在货物装船前的各个出口环节中，制作一个个单据，要什么单据就制作什么单据。这个时候制作的单据还不是议付单据，因为还不是拿去银行办理议付手续用的，而是拿去办理货物出口前的各种手续，如报检和报关、保险等。

综合制单又叫二次制单，指受益人取得提单后，一次性集中时间高标准重新制作信用证所要求的全部议付单据，审查合格后交给议付银行，办理议付手续。

这前后两次制单，其作用和要求有所不同。二次制单往往是在一次制单的基础上修改完成的。

1.用途不同

一次制单一般是用于办理商检、报关、保险和其他手续，二次制单的目的是议付货款。通常，外贸公司在取得提单前，不会一开始就按照议付单据的标准和要求来制作各种单据，都是在不同环节制作不同的单据。

例如，一家外贸公司在3月份开出商业发票、包装单等单据，提交办理商检手续，由于种种原因，货物暂停出口，或5月中旬才出口，则办理议付手续时用的发票和包装单，绝对不会是原来3月份所制作的发票和包装单，一般都是重新制作或稍加修改后再使用。

2.要求不同

由于分项制单的目的和用途不同，要求也不同。一次制单时所制作的单据一般比较随意、松散，不会用议付单据的标准来要求。取得了提单之后的二次制单的目的是办理议付货款手续。议付单据的制作必须遵循“单证相符、单单一致”的原则，只有这样才能保证安全收汇。

3.时间不同

很多外贸单证的初学者对各种单据制作时间的先后顺序弄不懂，不知如何处理和安排，这里有个很好的方法：

如果是一次制单，什么时候用到什么单据，就什么时候制作，单据上就显示制单时的具体时间；如果是二次制单，各种单据上显示的时间，都可以瞄准提单的日期，即与提单日期保持一致（注：海关出具的各种证书的出单日期会比提单日期早一些）。

4.前提和基础

分项制单是综合制单的前提和基础。只要完全掌握了分项制单的技能，综合制单也就没有什么大困难了。综合制单要用到分项制单的各种技能和知识。

二、单据制作时间

（1）一次制单时间：什么时候用到，就什么时候制作，显示制单的真实时间。

（2）二次制单时间：受益人取得提单后，一般有15天时间用来办理制单、交单、结汇。业务熟练的制单者一般用第一周时间来制单、审单，第二周时间用来交单议付。即使单据有错误被银行退单，也有足够的时间修改处理后再交单。

三、二次制单原则

（1）单证一致：各种单据要符合信用证的规定和要求。

（2）单单一致：各种单据之间要协调一致，不要矛盾。

（3）时间协调：除海关出具的证书外，所有单据的时间都可瞄准提单日期。

（4）以信用证为准：一切以信用证为准，一切服从信用证，合同起辅助作用。

（5）在信用证付款方式下，开证银行对单据质量的要求非常严格。因为信用证付款方式属于银行信用，开证银行是付款人，合同买方不是付款人。开证银行只看单据表面质量决定是否付款。只要卖方做到了单据与信用证严格一致，开证银行就得无条件付款；相反，如果单据与信用证不一致，开证银行就有权拒付。

第二步　学生做

一、制作信用证项下的全套单据

请根据下面给出的合同、信用证及后面的附加信息，制作全套议付单据。

1.合同

SALES　CONTRACT

No.：ES202080

Date：May 9，2021

Place：Guangzhou

The Seller：Guangzhou Everspring Import & Export Co.，Ltd.

Address：383，Sijiangsi Road，Guangzhou，Guangdong，P.R.C.

Fax：0086-20-8420 8688

Tel：0086-20-8420 8838

E-mail：everspring@com.cn

****

The Buyer：London Chemicals Sourcing Co.，Ltd.

Address：22#，Great British Street，London，The United Kingdom

Fax：0044-20-2663-1133

Tel：0044-20-2667-1132

E-mail：Lchemicals@com.un

****

The Seller has agreed to sell and the Buyer has agreed to buy the following goods as per the terms and conditions listed below：

Name of Commodity	Quantity	Unit Price	Total Amount
TITANIUM DIOXIDE （钛白粉样图如图 3-1 所示）	90M/T	USD1 980.00M/T CIF London	USD178 200.00

1.Packing：In two-ply craft paper bags of 25 kgs net each，40 bags to a wooden pallet（木制托盘样图如图3-2所示）.

2.Shipment：Shipment from Guangzhou to London in May and June of 2021. Partial shipment and transshipment are not allowed.

3.Insurance：To be covered by the Seller for 110% of invoice value against All Risks and War Risk of C.I.C. with payable claim at destination in the same currency of credit.

4.Payment Terms：L/C at sight to reach the seller not later than May 20，2021.

5.Specification：TiO_2: 98% min.

Whiteness：97% min.

Oil Absorption：20 ~ 30kgs

pH Value：6.5 ~ 8

Water Soluble Objects：0.4% max.

6.Inspection

Both the sellers and the buyers mutually agreed that the Certificate of Quality and Weight and/or Quantity issued by related organizations at the port of shipment shall be part of the documents to be presented for negotiation under the relevant L/C. The buyers shall have the right to reinspect the quality and weight and/or quantity of the cargo at the port of destination. However，the reinspection fee shall be borne by the buyers.

7.Discrepancy and Claim

Should the quality and/or weight be found not in conformity with that of the contract，the buyers shall be entitled to lodge a claim with the sellers. Such claim should be supported by survey reports issued by a recognized surveyor approved by the sellers. The claim，if any，shall be filed within 30 days after arrival of the cargo at the port of destination specified in the relative Bill of Lading. If the goods have been processed，the buyers shall thereupon lose the right to claim. Claims in respect of matters within responsibility of insurance company and/or shipping company shall not be considered or entertained by the sellers.

8.Arbitration

All disputes arising out of the performance of，or relating to this contract，shall be settled friendly through negotiation. In case no settlement can be reached through negotiation，the case shall then be submitted to the China International Economic and Trade Arbitration Commission，Beijing，China，for arbitration in accordance with its provisional rules. The arbitral award is final and binding upon both parties.

9.Force Majeure

In case the contracted goods are prevented or delayed in whole or in part by reason of war, earthquake, flood, fire, storm, heavy snow, tsunami or other causes of Force Majeure, the seller shall not be held responsible for non-shipment or late shipment of the goods under this contract. In that case, the seller shall notify the buyer by cable, fax or telephone and furnish the buyer within 20 days by registered airmail with a certificate issued by the China Council for the Promotion of International Trade attesting such event or events.

10.Remarks

This confirmation is written in English. Both the Seller and the Buyer shall hold one copy of the original. The Seller shall mail this confirmation to the Buyer for signature as soon as possible. The Buyer shall countersign them and return one copy of this confirmation to the Seller for his file.

Buyer's Signature :	Seller's Signature:
Terry Smith	Lihang
(Managing Director)	(Managing Director)

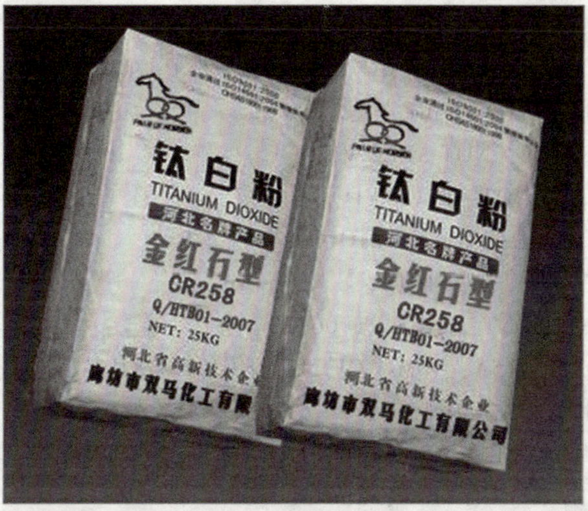

图3-1　钛白粉

图3-2　木制托盘

2.信用证

SEQUENCE OF TOTAL 27：1/1

FORM OF DOC. CREDIT 40A：IRREVOCABLE

DOC. CREDIT NUMBER 20：ESP200562

DATE OF ISSUE 31C：21-05-16

EXPIRY 31D：DATE 21-07-15 PLACE IN CHINA

APPLICANT 50：LONDON CHEMICALS SOURCING CO.，LTD.
22#，GREAT BRITISH STREET，LONDON，THE UNITED KINGDOM

BENEFICIARY 59：GUANGZHOU EVERSPRING IMPORT & EXPORT CO.，LTD.
383，SIJIANGSI ROAD，GUANGZHOU，GUANGDONG，P.R.C.

AMOUNT 32B：CURRENCY USD AMOUNT 178 200.00

POS./NEG.TOL.（%）39 A：10/10

AVAILABLE WITH/BY 41D：ANY BANK IN CHINA
BY NEGOTIATION

DRAFTS AT... 42C：AT SIGHT

DRAWEE 42D：BRITISH COMMERCIAL BANK LIMITED LONDON
FOR FULL INVOICE VALUE

PARTIAL SHIPMENTS 43P：NOT ALLOWED

TRANSSHIPMENT 43T：NOT ALLOWED

LOADING PORT 44E：GUANGZHOU

FOR TRANSPORT TO...44F：LONDON，U.K.

LATEST DATE OF SHIPMENT：44C：21-06-30

DESCRIPTION OF GOODS 45A：90M/T OF TITANIUM DIOXIDE

SPECIFICATION：TiO_2：98% MIN.
WHITENESS：97% MIN.
OIL ABSORPTION：20 ~ 30 KGS
pH VALUE：6.5 ~ 8
WATER SOLUBLE OBJECTS：0.4% MAX.
PACKED IN TWO-PLY CRAFT PAPER BAGS OF 25 KGS NET EACH，40 BAGS TO A WOODEN PALLET.
AS PER SALES CONTRACT NO.ES202080
PRICE TERM：USD1 980.00M/T CIF LONDON

DOCUMENTS REQUIRED 46A：

+ SIGNED COMMERCIAL INVOICE IN TRIPLICATE.

+ FULL SET OF CLEAN ‘ON BOARD OCEAN VESSEL’ BILL OF LADING MADE OUT TO ORDER AND BLANK ENDORSED NOTIFYING APPLICANT AND MARKED ‘FREIGHT PREPAID’ SHOWING NAME AND ADDRESS OF SHIPPING COMPANY ’S AGENT AT DESTINATION.

+ PACKING LIST IN TRIPLICATE.

+ INSPECTION CERTIFICATE OF QUALITY AND WEIGHT ISSUED BY CORRESPONDING AUTHORITY IN CHINA.

+ CERTIFICATE OF ORIGIN G.S.P.FORM A IN DUPLICATE ISSUED BY CORRESPONDING AUTHORITY OF P.R.C.

+ INSURANCE POLICY OR CERTIFICATE IN ASSIGNABLE FORM AND ENDORSED IN BLANK FOR 110% OF INVOICE VALUE AGAINST ALL RISKS AND WAR RISK OF C.I.C. CLAUSE WITH CLAIM PAYABLE AT DESTINATION IN THE SAME CURRENCY OF DRAFT.

+ ONE SET OF NON-NEGOTIABLE SHIPPING DOCUMENTS SHALL BE SENT TO APPLICANT WITHIN 7 DAYS AFTER SHIPMENT HAS BEEN EFFECTED. A BENEFICIARY'S CERTIFICATE TO THIS EFFECT IS REQUIRED.

ADDITIONAL COND. 47A:

+ ALL DOCUMENTS TO PRESENTED FOR NEGOTIATION SHALL INDICATE THIS CREDIT.

+ CHARGES INCURRED IN RESPECT OF ANY TELEGRAPHIC TRANSFER/CHARTS PAYMENT/PAYMENT ADVICE BY SWIFT/TELEX ARE FOR ACCOUNT OF BENEFICIARY.

+ A HANDLING COMMISSION OF USD50.00 OR EQUIVALENT, PLUS TELEX CHARGES, IF ANY, WILL BE DEDUCTED FROM THE PROCEEDS FOR EACH SET OF DOCUMENTS WITH DISCREPANCIES PRESENTED UNDER THIS LETTER OF CREDIT.

+ ALL DOCUMENTS MUST BE PRESENTED THROUGH BENEFICIARY'S BANKER AND EXTRA COPY OF INVOICE AND TRANSPORT DOCUMENT FOR L/C ISSUING BANK'S FILE REQUIRED.

WE HEREBY ENGAGE WITH THE DRAWERS, ENDORSERS AND BONA FIDE HOLDERS THAT DRAFTS DRAWN AND NEGOTIATED IN COMPLIANCE WITH THE TERMS AND CONDITIONS OF THIS CREDIT WILL BE DULY HONOURED ON PRESENTATION.

THIS DOCUMENTARY CREDIT IS SUBJECT TO THE UNIFORM CUSTOMS AND PRACTICE FOR DOCUMENTARY CREDITS (2007) REVISION, INTERNATIONAL CHAMBER OF COMMERCE, PUBLICATION NO.600.

DETAILS OF CHARGES 71B: ALL BANKING CHARGES OUTSIDE U. K. ARE FOR ACCOUNT OF BENEFICIARY.

PRESENTATION PERIOD 48: ALL DOCUMENTS MUST BE PRESENTED TO NEGOTIATING BANK WITHIN 15 DAYS AFTER B/L DATE.

CONFIRMATION 49: WITHOUT

INSTRUCTIONS 78:

+ PLS FORWARD AT BENEFICIARY'S EXPENSES THE WHOLE SET OF DOCUMENTS

IN ONE LOT TO OUR BILLS PROCESSING CENTRE（KOWLOON）AT 190#，GREAT BRITISH NEW STREET，LONDON，THE UNITED KINGDOM，FAX：0044-20-2763-2133，TEL：0044-20-2767-2132.

+ IN REIMBURSEMENT，WE SHALL REMIT PROCEEDS IN ACCORDANCE WITH YOUR INSTRUCTIONS UPON RECEIPT OF THE DOCUMENTS.

ADVISE THROUGH 57D：BANK OF CHINA GUANGZHOU BRANCH

197 WEST DONGFENG ROAD，GUANGZHOU，P.R.C.

附加信息：货物的包装皮重为一个双层牛皮袋重0.5千克，一个木托盘重25千克；发票号码：MYJ200608；提单日期：2021-06-18；装运港：广州；目的港：伦敦；船名：ELIES 028T；提单编号：WSI200821H。

二、制作完成的单据示例

1.商业发票

COMMERCIAL INVOICE

DATE：JUNE 18，2021

NO.：MYJ200608

TO：LONDON CHEMICALS SOURCING CO.，LTD.

22#，GREAT BRITISH STREET，LONDON，THE UNITED KINGDOM

SHIPMENT FROM GUANGZHOU TO LONDON BY VESSEL

NAME OF GOODS	SPECIFICATION	QUANTITY	MARKS & NOS.	N.W./G.W.	UNIT PRICE
TITANIUM DIOXIDE	TiO_2:98% MIN. WHITENESS：97% MIN. OIL ABSORPTION: 20 ~ 30KGS pH VALUE:6.5 ~ 8 WATER SOLUBLE OBJECTS:0.4% MAX.	90 PALLETS （90M/T）	CHEMICALS ESP200562 LONDON C/NO.1-90	90M/T/ 94.05M/T	USD1 980.00 M/T CIF LONDON TOTAL: USD178 200.00

SAY US DOLLARS ONE HUNDRED AND SEVENTY EIGHT THOUSAND AND TWO HUNDRED ONLY

NO.OF L/C：ESP200562

GUANGZHOU EVERSPRING IMPORT & EXPORT CO.，LTD.

覃芳芳

2. 提单

BILL OF LADING

Shipper GUANGZHOU EVERSPRING IMPORT & EXPORT CO., LTD. 383,SIJIANGSI ROAD,GUANGZHOU,GUANGDONG,P.R.C.			B/L NO. WSI200821H	
Consignee TO ORDER			Ocean Transport BILL OF LADING	
Notify Party LONDON CHEMICALS SOURCING CO.,LTD. 22#,GREAT BRITISH STREET,LONDON,THE UNITED KINGDOM			For delivery of goods please apply to: NAME AND ADDRESS OF SHIPPING COMPANY'S AGENT IN LONDON: LONDON SHIPPING AGENT, 29#,HONOUR OLIVE STREET,LONDON, THE UNITED KINGDOM, FAX:0044-20-3663-1138 TEL:0044-20-2667-1139	
Pre-carriage by	Place of Receipt GUANGZHOU			
Ocean Vessel Voy. No. ELIES 028T	Port of Loading GUANGZHOU			
Port of Discharge LONDON	Place of Delivery LONDON		Final Destination for the Merchant's Reference only	
Container,Seal No. & Marks & Nos. CHEMICALS ESP200562 LONDON C/NO.1-90	No.of Package & Description of Goods 90 PALLETS(90M/T) OF TITANIUM DIOXIDE NO.OF L/C:ESP200562 SAY:NINETY PALLETS ONLY		Gross Weight (Kgs) 94 050	Measurement (M^3) 50
FREIGHT & CHARGES	Revenue Tons	Rate Per	Prepaid ✓	Collect
Ex. Rate:	Prepaid at GUANGZHOU	Payable at GUANGZHOU	Place and Date of Issue:GUANGZHOU	
	Total Prepaid	No.of Original B(s)/L TWO	Stamp & Signature ×××	
Date: JUNE 18, 2021	LADEN ON BOARD THE VESSEL BY			

3. 装箱单

PACKING LSIT

NO.MYJ200608

DATE: JUNE 18, 2021

TO: LONDON CHEMICALS SOURCING CO., LTD.

22#, GREAT BRITISH STREET, LONDON, THE UNITED KINGDOM

SHIPMENT FROM GUANGZHOU TO LONDON BY VESSEL

NAME OF GOODS	WAY OF PACKING	QUANTITY	MARK & NOS.	N.W./G.W.
TITANIUM DIOXIDE	IN TWO-PLY CRAFT PAPER BAGS OF 25 KGS NET EACH, 40 BAGS TO A WOODEN PALLET	90 PALLETS (90M/T)	CHEMICALS ESP200562 LONDON C/NO.1-90	90M/T/ 94.05M/T

SAY: NINETY PALLETS ONLY

NO.OF L/C: ESP200562

GUANGZHOU EVERSPRING IMPORT & EXPORT CO., LTD.

覃芳芳

4.产地证

ORIGINAL

1. Goods consigned from (Exporter's business name, address, country)
GUANGZHOU EVERSPRING IMPORT & EXPORT CO., LTD.
383, SIJIANGSI ROAD, GUANGZHOU, GUANGDONG, P.R.C.

Reference No.
GENERALIZED SYSTEM OF PREFERENCES
CERTIFICATE OF ORIGIN
(Combined declaration and certificate)
FORM A
Issued in THE PEOPLE'S REPUBLIC OF CHINA
(country)
See notes overleaf

2. Goods consigned to (Consignee's name, address, country)
LONDON CHEMICALS SOURCING CO., LTD.
22#, GREAT BRITISH STREET, LONDON, THE UNITED KINGDOM

3. Means of transport and route (as for as known)
FROM GUANGZHOU TO LONDON BY VESSEL

4. For official use

5. Item number	6. Marks and numbers of packages	7. Number and kind of packages; Description of goods	8. Origin criterion (see notes overleaf)	9. Gross weight or other quantity	10. Number and date of Invoice
1	CHEMICALS ESP200562 LONDON C/NO.1-90	90(NINETY) PALLETS OF TITANIUM DIOXIDE NO.OF L/C: ESP200562 *** *** *** *** ***	"P"	G.W.: 94.05M/T	MYJ200608 JUNE 18, 2021

11. Certification
It is hereby certified, on the basis of control carried out, that the declaration by the exporter is correct.

GUANGZHOU: JUNE 16, 2021 汤静静

Place and date, signature and stamp of certifying authority

12. Declaration by the exporter
The undersigned hereby declares that the above details and statements are correct; that all the goods were Produced in
CHINA
(country)
And that they comply with the origin requirements specified for those goods in the Generalized System of preferences for goods exported to
U.K.
(importing country)

GUAGNZHOU: JUNE 15, 2021 覃芳芳

place and date, signature of authorized signatory

5.保险单

海洋货物运输保险单

MARINE CARGO TRANSPORTATION INSURANCE POLICY

NUMBER OF ORIGINAL I/P：TWO

发票号码　　　　　　　　　　　　　　　　　　　　保险单号次

Invoice No. MYJ200608　　　　　　　　　　　　　Policy No.01

中国人民保险公司根据 GUANGZHOU EVERSPRING IMPORT & EXPORT CO.，LTD.（被保险人）的要求，由被保险人向本公司缴付约定的保险费，按照本保险单承担的险别和背后所载条款与下列条款承担下述货物运输保险，特立本保险单。

标记 Marks & Nos.	包装及数量 Packing & Quantity	保险货物项目 Description of Goods	保险金额 Amount Insured
CHEMICALS ESP200562 LONDON C/NO.1–90	IN TWO - PLY CRAFT PAPER BAGS OF 25 KGS NET EACH,40 BAGS TO A WOODEN PALLET 90 PALLETS（90M/T）	TITANIUM DIOXIDE NO.OF L/C：ESP200562	USD196 020.00

总保险金额：

Total Amount Insured：US DOLLARS ONE HUNDRED NINETY SIX THOUSAND AND TWENTY ONLY

保费　　　　　　　　　　费率　　　　　　　　装载工具

Premium as arranged______ Rate as arranged______ per conveyance S.S. ELIES 028T

开航日期　　　　　　　　自　　　　　　　　　　至

Slg.on or abt. JUNE 18，2021 from GUANGZHOU to LONDON

承保险别：

Conditions

（注：险别条款由保险公司加盖险别章）

所保货物，如遇风险，本公司凭本保险单及有关证件给付赔款。

Claims，if any，payable on surrender of this Policy together with other relevant documents.

所保货物，如发生保险单项下负责赔偿的损失或事故，应立即通知本公司下述代理人查勘。

In the event of accident whereby loss or damage may result in a claim under this Policy immediate notice applying for survey must be given to Company's Agent as mentioned hereunder.

中国人民保险公司

THE PEOPLE'S INSURANCE CO. OF CHINA

赔款偿付地点

Claim payable at LONDON

出单公司地址　　　　　　　　　　　　　　　　　　日期

Add. of Issuing Office　　　　　　　　　　　　Date：JUNE 18，2021

6.受益人证明

BENEFICIARY'S CERTIFICATE

DATE：JUNE 18，2021

TO：LONDON CHEMICALS SOURCING CO.，LTD.
22#，GREAT BRITISH STREET，LONDON，THE UNITED KINGDOM

RE：90 PALLETS（90M/T）OF TITANIUM DIOXIDE UNDER L/C NO.ESP200562 AND B/L NO. WSI200821H AND INVOICE NO.MYJ200608

WE HEREBY CERTIFY THAT ONE SET OF NON-NEGOTIABLE SHIPPING DOCUMENTS HAS BEEN SENT TO APPLICANT WITHIN 7 DAYS AFTER SHIPMENT HAS BEEN EFFECTED.

CHEMICALS
ESP200562
LONDON
C/NO.1-90

NO. OF L/C：ESP200562

GUANGZHOU EVERSPRING IMPORT & EXPORT CO.，LTD.
覃芳芳

7.汇票

汇 票　　1

凭
Drawn under BRITISH COMMERCIAL BANK LIMITED LONDON

信用证　第　号
L/C NO.ESP200562

日期　年　月　日
Dated MAY 16，2021

按　息　付款
Payable with interest @　% per annum

号码　汇票金额　中国，广州　年　月　日
NO. ... MYJ200608 ....Exchange for USD178 200.00 GUANGZHOU China. JUNE 18，2021

见票　日后（本汇票之复本未付）付
At ....sight of this FIRST of Exchange（Second of exchange being unpaid）

Pay to the order of BANK OF CHINA GUANGZHOU BRANCH 或其指定人

金 额
The sum of US DOLLARS ONE HUNDRED AND SEVENTY EIGHT THOUSAND AND TWO HUNDRED ONLY

此致
To：BRITISH COMMERCIAL BANK LIMITED LONDON

GUANGZHOU EVERSPRING IMPORT & EXPORT CO.，LTD.
覃芳芳

任务二 托收和汇付项下综合制单

第一步 教师教

一、方法技巧

托收和汇付付款方式下综合制单的方法和技巧与信用证项下的综合制单大同小异。如果掌握了信用证项下分项和综合制单的方法和技巧，那么托收和汇付项下的综合制单问题就迎刃而解了。两种情况下的单据制作方法是一样的。

二、注意事项

（1）虽然托收和汇付项下的单据制作不像信用证项下的单据制作要求得那么严格，但也要力求完全正确无误，以免影响公司形象和安全收汇。

（2）信用证付款方式是银行信用，开证银行是第一付款人，对议付单据质量的要求非常严格，开证银行凭单据付款。托收和汇付付款方式是商业信用，买方是付款人，对单据质量的要求略低，付不付款主要看买方信誉、经济实力、市场前景以及利润高低，而不仅仅看单据质量。

出口方交单前，要密切注意国际市场的变化以及买方的情况。如果市场变化太大，买方的情况太糟糕，出口方可暂不交单以规避买方赖账的风险。

（3）托收和汇付项下，制单的依据是合同、装船指令及商品资料。买方对制单和交单时间没有明确规定。但从减少费用支出、加快货款回笼的角度出发，取得提单后，出口人还是要尽快制单和交单，办理议付手续。

第二步 学生做

学生小组根据下面的合同等资料，制作全套议付单据。

2021年4月26日，广西梧州春江五金矿产进出口有限公司李彪彪总经理参加了当年的春交会，与澳大利亚国际采购公司签订了一份20公吨金属硅的出口合同。回到梧州后，李彪彪总经理将合同交给出口部门执行。货物装船后，部门经理要求单证员制作全套议付单据。

SALES CONTRACT

No.: CJ2020E88

Date: April 26, 2021

Place: Wuzhou

The Seller: Guangxi Wuzhou Chunjiang Metals and Minerals Import and Export Co., Ltd.

Address: 21, Sijiangwu Road, Wuzhou, Guangxi, P.R.C.

Fax: 0086-774-8421 8687

Tel: 0086-774-8421 8689

E-mail: chunjiang@chemicals.com

The Buyer: International Sourcing Company

Address: 358, 29#, New Street, Northbridge, Sydney, Australia

Fax: 0061-2-5653-1170

Tel: 0061-2-5657-1171

E-mail: int'lsource@northbridge.com

The seller has agreed to sell and the buyer has agreed to buy the following goods as per the terms and conditions listed below:

Name of Commodity	Quantity	Unit Price	Total Amount
Silicon Metal	20 M/T (±5% at the seller's option)	USD9 655.00 per M/T CFR Sydney	USD193 100.00

1.Way of Packing: In plastic woven bags of about 1 000 kgs net each.

2.Time of Shipment: Shipment from Wuzhou to Sydney via Hong Kong in May and June of 2021. Partial shipment and transshipment are allowed.

3.Insurance: To be covered by the buyer.

4.Payment Terms: D/P at sight.

5.Specification: Si: 99.9% min; Fe: 0.4% max; Al: 0.4% max;
Ca: 0.1% max; Size: 10-100mm 90% min.

6.Documents required by the buyer:

(1) Commercial Invoice in six copies.

(2) Packing List in triplicate.

(3) Full set of ocean bills of lading made out to order, endorsed in blank, marked freight prepaid and notify the full name and address of the contract buyer.

(4) Certificate of Origin G.S.P. Form A issued by corresponding authority in duplicate.

(5) Inspection Certificate issued by corresponding authority in duplicate.

(6) Beneficiary's Certificate certifying that one set of non-negotiable shipping documents has been sent to us by EMS within 7 days after shipment.

7.Buyer's banker's materials: International Private Group Banker, W. box 2578, 53#, New Street, Northbridge, Sydney, Australia, fax: 0061-02-7663-3871.

8.Inspection: Both the sellers and the buyers mutually agreed that the Certificate of Quality and Weight and/or Quantity issued by related organization at the port of shipment shall be part of the documents to be presented for negotiation under the relevant S/C. The buyers shall have the right to re-inspect the quality and weight and/or quantity of the cargo at the port of destination. However, the re-inspection fee shall be borne by the buyers.

9.Discrepancy and Claim: Should the quality and/or weight be found not in conformity with that of the contract, the buyers shall be entitled to lodge a claim with the sellers. Such claim should be supported by survey reports issued by a recognized surveyor approved by the sellers. The claim, if any, shall be filed within 30 days after arrival of the cargo at the port of destination specified in the relative Bill of Lading. If the goods have been processed , the buyers shall thereupon lose the right to claim. Claims in respect of matters within responsibility of insurance company and/or shipping company shall not be considered or entertained by the sellers.

10. Arbitration: All disputes arising out of the performance of, or relating to this contract, shall be settled friendly through negotiation. In case no settlement can be reached through negotiation, the case shall then be submitted to the China International Economic and Trade Arbitration Commission, Beijing, China, for arbitration in accordance with its provisional rules for arbitration. The arbitral award is final and binding upon both parties.

11. Force Majeure: In case the contracted goods are prevented or delayed in whole or in part by reason of war, earthquake, flood, fire, storm, heavy snow, tsunami or other causes of Force Majeure, the seller shall not be held responsible for non-shipment or late shipment of the goods under this contract. In that case, the seller shall notify the buyer by cable, fax or telephone and furnish the buyer within 20 days by registered airmail with a certificate issued by the China Council for the Promotion of International Trade attesting such event or events.

12. Remarks: This confirmation is written in English. Both the Seller and the Buyer shall hold one copy of the original. The Seller shall mail this confirmation to the Buyer as soon as possible for signature .The Buyer shall countersign them and return one copy of this confirmation to the Seller for his file.

Buyer's Signature:	Seller's Signature:
Bob Covery	Li Biaobiao
(Managing Director)	(Managing Director)

综合训练

一、根据信用证及补充信息，课后制作全套议付单据

SEQUENCE OF TOTAL 27: 1/1

FORM OF DOC. CREDIT 40A: IRREVOCABLE

DOC. CREDIT NUMBER 20: MCBB61561

DATE OF ISSUE 31C: 21-12-15

EXPIRY 31D: DATE 22-02-15 PLACE IN CHINA

APPLICANT 50: SHUNDA DEVELOPMENT LTD.
UNIT 10-6, 15/F MENAL ASIA GRANITE
34 WAI YIP STREET, KOWLOON HONG KONG

BENEFICIARY 59: PUFA TEXTILE AND LIGHT INDUSTRY CO., LTD.
120 TAIPING ROAD, NANJING, CHINA

AMOUNT 32B: CURRENCY USD AMOUNT 155 000.00

随堂测3

POS./NEG.TOL.（%）39A：10/10

AVAILABLE WITH/BY 41D：ANY BANK IN CHINA
BY NEGOTIATION

DRAFTS AT...42C：AT SIGHT

DRAWEE 42A：SHANGHAI COMMERCIAL BANK LTD.
HONGKONG FOR FULL INVOICE VALUE

PARTIAL SHIPMENTS 43P：ALLOWED

TRANSSHIPMENT 43T：ALLOWED

LOADING IN CHARGE 44E：ANY PORT IN CHINA

FOR TRANSPORT TO...44F：COPENHAGEN，DENMARK

LATEST DATE OF SHIPMENT：44C：22-01-31

DESCRIPTION OF GOODS 45A：FABRIC CRUSHED VELOUR，10 000M，AT USD15.5/M
AS PER S/C NO. 2K11121，JSL ORDER NO.2020500
ART. 5360004/10，2 500M VANILLA
ART. 5360025/30，2 500M BURGUNDY
ART. 5360029/40，5 000M HUNTER GREEN
ALL CIF COPENHAGEN，DENMARK

DOCUMENTS REQUIRED 46 A：

（1）SIGNED COMMERCIAL INVOICES IN TRIPLICATE SHOWING CIF VALUE OF THE MENTIONED GOODS AND STATING ‘WE HEREBY CERTIFY THAT THE GOODS HEREIN INVOICED CONFIRM WITH P/O NO. 2K11121.

（2）FULL SET OF CLEAN ON BOARD OCEAN VESSEL BILL OF LADING MADE OUT TO ORDER AND BLANK ENDORSED NOTIFYING JYSK CO.，LTD.，AND MARKED “FREIGHT PREPAID” SHOWING NAME AND ADDRESS OF SHIPPING COMPANY’S AGENT AT DESTINATION.

（3）PACKING LISTS IN TRIPLICATE SHOWING NUMBER OF CARTONS，GROSS WEIGHT，NET WEIGHT AND SPECIFIED PER CONTAINER.

（4）CERTIFICATE OF ORIGIN G.S.P. FORM A IN DUPLICATE ISSUED BY CORRESPONDING AUTHORITY OF P.R. CHINA.

（5）INSURANCE POLICY OR CERTIFICATE IN ASSIGNABLE FORM AND ENDORSED IN BLANK FOR 110 PCT OF INVOICE VALUE WITH CLAIMS PAYABLE AT DESTINATION IN CURRENCY OF DRAFT COVERING ICC（A），INSTITUTE WAR CLAUSES（CARGO），INSTITUTE STRIKES CLAUSES（CARGO），WAREHOUSE TO WAREHOUSE CLAUSES AND SHOWING NO. OF ORIGINALS ISSUED.

ADDITIONAL COND. 47A：

（1）CHARGES INCURRED IN RESPECT OF ANY TELEGRAPHIC TRANSFER/CHARTS PAYMENT/PAYMENT ADVICE BY SWIFT/TELEX ARE FOR ACCOUNT OF BENEFICIARY.

（2）A HANDLING COMMISSION OF USD50.00 OR EQUIVALENT，PLUS TELEX

CHARGES, IF ANY, WILL BE DEDUCTED FROM THE PROCEEDS FOR EACH SET OF DOCUMENTS WITH DISCREPANCIES PRESENTED UNDER THIS LETTER OF CREDIT.

(3) ALL DOCUMENTS MUST BE PRESENTED THROUGH BENEFICIARY'S BANK AND EXTRA COPY OF INVOICE AND TRANSPORT DOCUMENT FOR L/C ISSUING BANK'S FILE REQUIRED.

WE HEREBY ENGAGE WITH THE DRAWERS, ENDORSERS AND BONA FIDE HOLDERS THAT DRAFTS DRAWN AND NEGOTIATED IN COMPLIANCE WITH THE TERMS AND CONDITIONS OF THIS CREDIT WILL BE DULY HONOURED ON PRESENTATION.

THIS DOCUMENTARY CREDIT IS SUBJECT TO THE UNIFORM CUSTOMS AND PRACTICE FOR DOCUMENTARY CREDITS (2007) REVISION, INTERNATIONAL CHAMBER OF COMMERCE, PUBLICATION NO.600.

DETAILS OF CHARGES 71B: ALL BANKING CHARGES OUTSIDE HONG KONG ARE FOR ACCOUNT OF BENEFICIARY.

CONFIRMATION 49: WITHOUT

INSTRUCTIONS 78:

(1) PLS FORWARD THE WHOLE SET OF DOCUMENTS IN ONE LOT TO OUR BILLS PROCESSING CENTRE (KOWLOON) AT 2/F., 666 NATHAN ROAD, KOWLOON, HONG KONG VIA COURIER SERVICE AT BENEFICIARY'S EXPENSES.

(2) IN REIMBURSEMENT, WE SHALL REMIT PROCEEDS IN ACCORDANCE WITH YOUR INSTRUCTIONS UPON RECEIPT OF THE DOCUMENTS.

ADVISE THROUGH 57D: YOUR JIANGSU BRANCH,
148 ZHONGSHAN SOUTH ROAD, NANJING, CHINA

补充信息：船期为2021-01-28；船名为DAWEI201W；提单编号为JWY1101280；毛重2 000千克；净重1 950千克；发票编号为LM210128。

二、根据下面的合同、装船指令及补充资料，制作全套议付单据

1.销售合同

SALES CONTRACT

No.: EX09M088

Date: April 22, 2021

Place: Wuzhou

The Seller: Guangxi Wuzhou Chunwang Chemicals Manufacturer

Address: 2233, Sijiangsi Road, Wuzhou, Guangxi, P.R.C.

Fax: 0086-774-84208688　　Tel: 0086-774-84208838

E-mail: chunwang@chemicals.com

****

The Buyer: International Sourcing Company

Address: W.box 3578, 23#, New Street, Northbridge, Sydney, Australia

Fax: 0061-2-5663-1879　Tel: 0061-2-5667-1122

E-mail：int'lsource@northbridge.com

****

The seller has agreed to sell and the buyer has agreed to buy the following goods as per the terms and conditions listed below：

Name of Commodity	Quantity	Unit Price	Total Amount
Manganese Dioxide Powder	20M/T (±5% at the seller's option)	USD1 125.00 per M/T CFR Sydney	USD22 500.00

1.Packing： In plastic bags of 25 kgs net each，40 bags to a wooden pallet.

2.Shipment：Shipment from Wuzhou to Sydney via Hong Kong in June and July of 2021. Partial shipment and transshipment are not allowed.

3.Insurance：To be covered by the buyer.

4.Payment Terms：D/P at sight.

5.Specification：MnO_2：75% min. Fe：0.3% max. P：0.15% max. S：0.15% max.
Fineness：325 mesh 98% min.passing through.

6.Inspection：Both the sellers and the buyers mutually agreed that the Certificate of Quality and Weight and/or Quantity issued by related organizations at the port of shipment shall be part of the documents to be presented for negotiation under the relevant S/C. The buyers shall have the right to re-inspect the quality and weight and/or quantity of the cargo at the port of destination. However，the re-inspection fee shall be borne by the buyers.

7.Discrepancy and Claim：Should the quality and/or weight be found not in conformity with that of the contract，the buyers shall be entitled to lodge a claim with the sellers. Such claim should be supported by survey reports issued by a recognized surveyor approved by the sellers. The claim，if any，shall be filed within 30 days after arrival of the cargo at the port of destination specified in the relative Bill of Lading. If the goods have been processed，the buyers shall thereupon lose the right to claim. Claims in respect of matters within responsibility of insurance company and/or shipping company shall not be considered or entertained by the sellers.

8.Arbitration：All disputes arising out of the performance of，or relating to this contract，shall be settled friendly through negotiation. In case no settlement can be reached through negotiation，the case shall then be submitted to the China International Economic and Trade Arbitration Commission，Beijing，China，for arbitration in accordance with its provisional rules for arbitration. The arbitral award is final and binding upon both parties.

9.Force Majeure：In case the contracted goods are prevented or delayed in whole or in part by reason of war，earthquake，flood，fire，storm，heavy snow，tsunami or other causes of

Force Majeure, the seller shall not be held responsible for non-shipment or late shipment of the goods under this contract. In that case, the seller shall notify the buyer by cable, fax or telephone and furnish the buyer within 20 days by registered airmail with a certificate issued by the China Council for the Promotion of International Trade attesting such event or events.

10.Remarks: This confirmation is written in English. Both the seller and the buyer shall hold one copy of the original. The seller shall mail this confirmation to the buyer as soon as possible for signature. The buyer shall countersign them and return one copy of this confirmation to the seller for his file.

Buyer's Signature: Seller's Signature:

Bob Percy Li Faxiao

(Managing Director) (Managing Director)

2.装船指令

SHIPPING INSTRUCTION

To: Guangxi Wuzhou Chunwang Chemicals Manufacturer
2233, Sijiangsi Road, Wuzhou, Guangxi, P.R.C.
Fax: 0086-774-84208688 E-mail: chunwang@chemicals.com

From: International Sourcing Company
W.box 3578, 23#, New Street, Northbridge, Sydney, Australia
Fax: 0061-02-5663-1879 E-mail: int'lsource@northbridge.com

Date: May 15, 2021

Attn: Li Faxiao

Dear Sirs,

We were very happy to have met you in the Spring Guangzhou Fair last month and signed contract No. EX09M088 with your company for 20 M/T of Manganese Dioxide Powder. To tell you the truth, we are in urgent need of this product. In order to help you execute the contract, we fax you the following details of shipping instructions. Please effect shipment as soon as possible.

The followings are the documents we require. You are requested to send us the full set of original shipping documents through your bank. Upon receipt of them, we shall remit the proceeds by telegraphic transfer.

1.Name and address of our banker:

International Private Group Banker, W. box 2578, 53#, New Street, Northbridge, Sydney, Australia, Fax: 0061-02-7663-3871.

2.Details of goods:

20 M/T Manganese Dioxide Powder

3.Loading port and destination:

Wuzhou; Sydney.

4.Shipment in June and July, 2021.

5.Documents required:

(1) Commercial Invoice in six copies;

(2) Packing List in triplicate;

(3) Full set of Ocean Bills of Lading made out to order, endorsed in blank, notifying the full name and address of the contract buyer;

(4) Certificate of Origin G.S.P. Form A issued by corresponding authority in duplicate;

(5) Inspection Certificate issued by corresponding authority in duplicate;

(6) Beneficiary's Certificate certifying that one set of non-negotiable shipping documents has been sent to us by EMS within 7 days after shipment.

Best regards.

Bob Percy

Managing Director

补充信息：发票编号为MH100211U；船期为2021-07-23；船名为GUIBO006；提单编号为TYU20100176；毛重20.1公吨；净重20公吨；货物体积13M³。

三、手工操作题

根据下面的信用证及补充信息，制作全套或部分议付单据。

（一）信用证1

27: SEQUENCE OF TOTAL
1/1

40A: FORM OF DOCUMENTARY CREDIT
IRREVOCABLE

20: DOCUMENTARY CREDIT NUMBER
2021FTCL06-1403

31C: DATE OF ISSUE
21-06-15

40E: APPLICABLE RULES
UCP LATEST VERSION

31D: DATE AND PLACE OF EXPIRY
21-08-30 IN BENEFICIARY'S COUNTRY

50: APPLICANT
FIREBIRD TRADING CO., LTD. (CANADA)
280, BRIGHTWAY AVENUE, BRITISH COLOMBIA

59: BENEFICIARY
GUANGXI WUZHOU SENGONG IMPORT AND EXPORT CO., LTD.
20, EAST QIXING ROAD, WUZHOU, GUANGXI, P.R.C.

32B: CURRENCY CODE, AMOUNT

CURRENCY：USD（US DOLLAR）

AMOUNT：# USD345 000.00 #

41D：AVAILABLE WITH... BY...

ANY BANK IN BENEFICIARY'S COUNTRY

BY NEGOTIATION

42C：DRAFTS AT...

SIGHT

FOR 100% INVOICE VALUE

42A：DRAWEE

NORTHEAST AMERICA BANK OF CANADA

43P：PARTIAL SHIPMENTS

ALLOWED

43T：TRANSSHIPMENT

ALLOWED

44E：PORT OF LOADING

GUANGZHOU，CHINA

44F：PORT OF DISCHARGE

MONTREAL，CANADA

44C：LATEST DATE OF SHIPMENT

21-07-30

45A：DESCRIPTION OF GOODS AND/OR SERVICES

250 M/T OF MANGANESE DIOXIDE POWDER

MnO_2：86% MIN.　Fe：5% MAX.　AlO：4% MAX.　SiO_2：10% MAX.

H_2O：4% MAX.　FINESS：400. MESH 90% MIN. PASSING THROUGH

UNIT PRICE：USD1 380/MT CIF MONTREAL，CANADA

PACKED IN WOODEN PALLETS OF ABOUT 1 000 KGS EACH.

AS PER SALES CONFIRMATION NO.MHT202106E01

46A：DOCUMENTS REQUIRED

+ SIGNED COMMERCIAL INVOICE IN THREE COPIES.

+ FULL SET OF CLEAN ON BOARD MARINE BILLS OF LADING IN TWO ORIGINALS AND 3 COPIES，MADE OUT TO ORDER，ENDORSED IN BLANK，FREIGHT PREPAID，AND NOTIFY APPLICANT EVIDENCING SHIPMENT FROM GUANGZHOU TO MONTREAL.

+ CERTIFICATE OF ORIGIN ISSUED BY CORRESPONDING AUTHORITY IN DUPLICATE.

...

47A：ADDITIONAL CONDITIONS

+ ALL DOCUMENTS MUST BEAR THIS CREDIT NUMBER.

+ SHIPMENT DATE PRIOR TO L/C'S ISSUING DATE IS PROHIBITED.

+5 PCT MORE OR LESS IN QUANTITY AND AMOUNT ARE ACCEPTABLE.

...

71B：CHARGES

ALL BANKING CHARGES OUTSIDE CANADA，IF ANY，ARE FOR ACCOUNT OF BENEFICIARY.

48：PERIOD FOR PRESENTATION

DOCUMENTS PRESENTED WITHIN 15 DAYS AFTER SHIPMENT BUT WITHIN THE VALIDITY OF THE CREDIT.

49：CONFIRMATION INSTRUCTIONS

WITHOUT

...

补充信息：实际出口软锰粉250公吨（250托盘）；船期：2021-07-22；船名：PRINCE CHALIES 087；要求自行设计唛头，发票日期和号码自定；软锰粉的H.S.编码是85062090。

（1）根据上面提供的信用证，制作商业发票。

（2）根据上面提供的信用证，填写提单相关栏目。

（3）根据上面提供的信用证，填写原产地证书相关栏目。

制作好的相关单据（一）（参考答案）

COMMERCIAL INVOICE

DATE：JULY 10，2021

NO.：M18008

TO：FIREBIRD TRADING CO.，LTD.（CANADA）

280，BRIGHTWAY AVENUE，BRITISH COLOMBIA

SHIPMENT BY VESSEL FROM GUANGZHOU TO MONTREAL

MARKS & NUMBERS	QUANTITY	NAME OF GOODS	SPEC.	UNIT PRICE
FIREBIRD 2021FTCL06-1403 MONTREAL C/NO. 1-250	250 M/T	MANGANESE DIOXIDE POWDER	MnO_2:86% MIN Fe:5% MAX. AlO:4% MAX SiO_2:10% MAX. H_2O:4% MAX FINESS:400 MESH 90% MIN. PASSING THROUGH	USD1 380/MT CIF MONTREAl TOTAL AMOUNT: USD345 000.00

SAY：US DOLLARS THREE HUNDRED AND FORTY FIVE THOUSAND ONLY.

L/C NO.：2021FTCL06-1403

GUANGXI WUZHOU SENGONG IMPORT AND EXPORT CO.，LTD.

谢国诚

1.Shipper
GUANGXI WUZHOU SENGONG IMPORT AND EXPORT CO.，LTD.
20，EAST QIXING ROAD，WUZHOU，GUANGXI，P.R.C.

中远集装箱运输有限公司
COSCO CONTAINER LINES

Port-to-Port or Combine Transport
BILL OF LADING

ORITNAL

2.Consignee
TO ORDER

3.Notify Party
FIREBIRD TRADING CO.，LTD.（CANADA）
280，BRIGHTWAY AVENUE，BRITISH COLOMBIA
CERTIFICATE OF ORIGIN

Marks and numbers	Number and kind of packages; description of goods	H.S. Code	Quantity	Number and Date of Invoice
FIREBIRD 2021FTCL06-1403 MONTREAL C/NO.1-250	250（TWO HUNDRED AND FIFTY）PALLETS OF MANGANESE DIOXIDE POWDER L/C NO.: 2021FTCL06-1403 *** *** *** *** *** *** ***	85062090	250 M/T	M18008 JULY 10,2021

（二）信用证 2

27:　SEQUENCE OF TOTAL：1/1
40A：FORM OF DOCUMENTARY CREDIT：IRREVOCABLE
20:　DOCUMENTARY CREDIT NUMBER：CTHW2021-0415
31C：DATE OF ISSUE：21-04-15
40E：APPLICABLE RULES：ICC UCP LATEST VERSION
31D：DATE AND PLACE OF EXPIRY：
21-07-30 IN BENEFICIARY'S COUNTRY
50：APPLICANT
XIHANOOK INTERNATIONAL CO.，LTD.，136# BRIGHT STREET，
BANGKOK，THAILAND
59：BENEFICIARY
NO.1 FOSHAN NANHAI NON-FERROUS METAL MANUFACTURER
288#，PINGTAN INDUSTRIAL ZONE，NANHAI CITY，FOSHAN，GUANGDONG，CHINA.
32B：CURRENCY CODE，AMOUNT
CURRENCY：USD（US DOLLAR）
AMOUNT：# 120 000.00 #（ONE HUNDRED AND TWENTY THOUSAND ONLY）
41D：AVAILABLE WITH... BY...
ANY BANK IN BENEFICIARY'S COUNTRY
BY NEGOTIATION
42C：DRAFTS AT

SIGHT FOR 100% OF INVOICE VALUE

42A: DRAWEE

HUGE STANDARD CHARTERED BANK BANGKOK

43P: PARTIAL SHIPMENTS

NOT ALLOWED

43T: TRANSSHIPMENT

ALLOWED

44E: PORT OF LOADING

NANHAI，FOSHAN，CHINA

44F: PORT OF DISCHARGE

BANGKOK，THAILAND

44C: LATEST DATE OF SHIPMENT

21-06-30

45A: DESCRIPTION OF GOODS AND/OR SERVICES

10 000 KGS OF BRASS ELECTRODE WIRE TRIANGLE BRAND

Cu：90% MIN. SIZE：Φ0.5 MM.

UNIT PRICE：USD12 PER KG CIF BANGKOK，THAILAND

AS PER SALES CONTRACT NO.XHB1803008

PACKED IN STRONG EXPORT CARTONS OF ABOUT 50 KGS NET EACH.

46A: DOCUMENTS REQUIRED

…

（4）PACKING LIST IN TWO COPIES.

（5）INSURANCE POLICY OR CERTIFICATE ENDORSED IN BLANK WITH CLAIM PAYABLE AT DESTINATION WITH THE SAME CURRENCY OF DRAFT AGAINST ALL RISKS OF C.I.C. FOR 120% OF INVOICE VALUE.

47A: ADDITIONAL CONDITIONS

（1）ALL DOCUMENTS MUST BEAR THIS CREDIT NUMBER.

（2）SHIPMENT DATE PRIOR TO L/C'S ISSUING DATE IS NOT ACCEPTABLE.

（3）5% MORE OR LESS IN QUANTITY AND AMOUNT ARE BOTH ACCEPTABLE.

…

ALL BANKING CHARGES OUTSIDE THAILAND，IF ANY，ARE FOR ACCOUNT OF BENEFICIARY.

48: PERIOD FOR PRESENTATION

DOCUMENTS MUST BE PRESENTED WITHIN 15 DAYS AFTER SHIPMENT BUT WITHIN THE VALIDITY OF THE CREDIT.

49: CONFIRMATION INSTRUCTIONS：

WITHOUT

…

补充信息：船名 GREAT PRINCE 2090；船期 2021-06-18；货物数量共 200 箱；净重

共10 000千克；毛重共10 400千克；体积共25立方米；货物存放地点为佛山南海金山港8号仓；要求卖方设计唛头；发票号MYJ908；发票日期2021-06-10；黄铜电极线H.S.编码为740819。

（1）根据以上提供的信用证，制作装箱单。

（2）根据以上提供的信用证，填写给出的保险单相关栏目。

（3）根据以上给出的信用证，填写汇票。

制作好的相关单据（二）（参考答案）

PACKING LIST

DATE：JUNE 10，2021
NO.：MYJ908

TO：XIHANOOK INTERNATIONAL CO.，LTD. 136# BRIGHT STREET，BANGKOK THAILAND

SHIPMENT FROM FOSHAN TO BANGKOK BY VESSEL

MARKS & NOS.	NAME OF GOODS	WAY OF PACKING	QUANTITY	N.W./G.W.	MEASUREMENT
XIHANOOK GTHW2021-0415 BANGKOK C/NO.1-200	BRASS ELECTRODE WIRE TRIANGLE BRAND	PACKED IN STRONG EXPORT CARTONS OF ABOUT 50 KGS NET EACH.	10 000 KGS / 200 CARTONS	G.W.:10 400 KGS	25 CBM

SAY：TWO HUNDRED CARTONS ONLY

NO. OF L/C：GTHW2021-0415

NO.1 FOSHAN NANHAI NON-FERROUS METAL MANUFACTURER
杨柳青

唛头及标记 Marks & Nos.	包装及数量 Packing & Quantity	保险货物项目 Description of Goods	保险金额 Amount Insured
XIHANOOK GTHW2021-0415 BANGKOK C/NO.1-200	10 000 KGS/200 CARTONS PACKED IN STRONG EXPORT CARTONS OF ABOUT 50 KGS NET EACH.	BRASS ELECTRODE WIRE TRIANGLE BRAND NO.OF L/C:GTHW2021-0415	USD144 000.00

总保险金额：
Total Amount Insured：US DOLLARS ONE HUNDRED AND FORTY FOUR THOUSAND ONLY

汇 票

凭

Drawn under HUGE STANDARD CHARTERED BANK BANGKOK

信用证 第 号

L/C NO. GTHW2021-0415

日期 年 月 日

Dated APRIL 15,2021

按 息 付 款

Payable with interest @ % per annum

号码 汇票金额 中国，佛山 年 月 日

NO. ... MYJ908 ....Exchange for USD120 000.00 FOSHAN China. JUNE 10，2021

见票 日后（本汇票之复本未付）付

At ....sight of this FIRST of Exchange（Second of exchange being unpaid）

Pay to the order of BANK OF CHINA FOSHAN BRANCH 或其指定人

金 额

The sum of US DOLLARS ONE HUNDRED AND TWENTY THOUSAND ONLY

此致

To: HUGE STANDARD CHARTERED BANK BANGKOK

NO.1 FOSHAN NANHAI NON-FERROUS METAL MANUFACTURER

杨柳青

（三）信用证3

27：SEQUENCE OF TOTAL

1/1

40A：FORM OF DOCUMENTARY CREDIT

IRREVOCABLE

20：DOCUMENTARY CREDIT NUMBER

21CDRLC2057

31C：DATE OF ISSUE

21-05-10

40E：APPLICABLE RULES

UCP LATEST VERSION

31D：DATE AND PLACE OF EXPIRY

21-08-15 IN BENEFICIARY'S COUNTRY

50：APPLICANT

DAIMMEI INTERNATIONAL CO.，LTD.NO.808 LANE 63 ZHONG QING SOUTH ROAD，TA-YA TAICHUNG，TAIWAN，CHINA

59：BENEFICIARY

JUNXIONG IMPORT AND EXPORT CO.，LTD. YONGHAO BUILDING

XIABEI ROAD，3225 COUNTRY WAY，JUJAN TOWN，NANHAI，FOSHAN，GUANGDONG，CHINA

32B：CURRENCY CODE，AMOUNT
CURRENCY：USD（US DOLLAR）
AMOUNT：# 27 300.00#（US DOLLARS TWENTY SEVEN THOUSAND AND THREE HUNDRED ONLY）

41D：AVAILABLE WITH... BY...-NAME&ADDR.
ANY BANK IN BENEFICIARY'S COUNTRY
BY NEGOTIATION

42C：DRAFTS AT...
SIGHT FOR FULL INVOICE VALUE

42A：DRAWEE
TAIWAN COOPERATIVE BANK，TAICHUNG BRANCH

43P：PARTIAL SHIPMENTS
ALLOWED

43T：TRANSSHIPMENT
ALLOWED

44E：PORT OF LOADING.
SHENZHEN，CHINA

44F：PORT OF DISCHARGE
TAICHUNG，TAIWAN，CHINA

44C：LATEST DATE OF SHIPMENT
21-06-30

45A：DESCRIPTION OF GOODS AND/OR SERVICES
TV.STAND　　B-M-TV054　　350 PCS
USD78/PC　　FOB　SHENZHEN，CHINA
PACKED IN CARTONS OF 1 PIECE EACH.

46A：DOCUMENTS REQUIRED

（1）SIGNED COMMERCIAL INVOICE IN THREE COPIES.

（2）FULL SET OF CLEAN ON BOARD MARINE BILLS OF LADING MADE OUT TO ORDER OF TAIWAN COOPERATIVE BANK，NOTIFY APPLICANT.

（3）PACKING LIST IN THREE COPIES.

47A：ADDITIONAL CONDITIONS

（1）ALL DOCUMENTS MUST BEAR THIS CREDIT NUMBER.

（2）SHIPMENT DATE PRIOR TO L/C'S ISSUING DATE IS PROHIBITED.

（3）5 PCT MORE OR LESS IN QUANTITY AND AMOUNT ARE ACCEPTABLE.

...

71B：CHARGES
ALL BANKING CHARGES OUTSIDE TAIWAN，IF ANY，ARE ACCOUNT OF BENEFICIARY.

48：PERIOD FOR PRESENTATION
DOCUMENTS PRESENTED WITHIN 14 DAYS AFTER SHIPMENT BUT WITHIN THE

VALIDITY OF THE CREDIT.

49: CONFIRMATION INSTRUCTIONS

WITHOUT

补充信息：共出口350件（350箱）电视机；船期：2021-06-12。要求自行设计唛头，发票日期和号码自定。

（1）根据以上给出的信用证，制作商业发票。

（2）根据以上给出的信用证，填写给出的提单相关栏目。

（3）根据以上给出的信用证，制作汇票。

制作好的相关单据（三）（参考答案）

COMMERCIAL INVOICE

DATE: JUNE 2，2021

NO.: MYJ210602

TO: DAIMMEI INTERNATIONAL CO.，LTD.NO.808 LANE 63
ZHONG QING SOUTH ROAD，TA-YA TAICHUNG，TAIWAN，CHINA
SHIPMENT BY VESSEL FROM SHENZHEN，CHINA TO TAICHUNG，TAIWAN，CHINA

MARKS & NUMBERS	QUANTITY	NAME OF GOODS	SPEC.	UNIT PRICE
DAIMMEI 21CDRLC2057 TAICHUNG C/NO.1-350	350 PCS	TV.STAND	B-M-TV054	USD78/PC FOB SHENZHEN
				TOTAL: USD27 300.00

SAY: US DOLLARS TWENTY SEVEN THOUSAND AND THREE HUNDRED ONLY

L/C NO.: 21CDRLC2057

JUNXIONG IMPORT AND EXPORT CO.，LTD.
江伟鸿

1.Shipper JUNXIONG IMPORT AND EXPORT CO.，LTD. YONGHAO BUILDING XIABEI ROAD，3225 COUNTRY WAY，JUJAN TOWN，NANHAI，FOSHAN，GUANGDONG，CHINA	中远集装箱运输有限公司 COSCO COSCO CONTAINER LINES Port-to-Port or Combine Transport BILL OF LADING ORIGINAL
2.Consignee TO ORDER OF TAIWAN COOPERATIVE BANK	
3.Notify Party DAIMMEI INTERNATIONAL CO.，LTD.NO.808 LANE 63 ZHONG QING SOUTH ROAD，TA-YA TAICHUNG，TAIWAN，CHINA	

汇 票

凭

Drawn under TAIWAN COOPERATIVE BANK, TAICHUNG BRANCH

信用证 第 号

L/C .NO. 21CDRLC2057

日期 年 月 日

Dated MAY 10,2021

按 息 付 款

Payable with interest @ % per annum

号码 汇票金额 中国， 佛山 年 月 日

NO. ... MYJ210602 ....Exchange for USD27 300.00 FOSHAN CHINA JUNE 12,2021

见票 日后（本汇票之复本未付）付

At ....sight of this FIRST of Exchange（Second of exchange being unpaid）

Pay to the order of BANK OF CHINA FOSHAN BRANCH 或其指定人

金 额

The sum of US DOLLARS TWENTY SEVEN THOUSAND AND THREE HUNDRED ONLY

此致

To: TAIWAN COOPERATIVE BANK, TAICHUNG BRANCH

JUNXIONG IMPORT AND EXPORT CO., LTD.

江伟鸿

（四）信用证 4

27: SEQUENCE OF TOTAL: 1/1

40A: FORM OF DOCUMENTARY CREDIT: IRREVOCABLE

20: DOCUMENTARY CREDIT NUMBER: EXP2021-1207

31C: DATE OF ISSUE : 21-12-07

40E: APPLICABLE RULES : UCP LATEST VERSION

31D: DATE AND PLACE OF EXPIRY :
22-02-15 IN BENEFICIARY'S COUNTRY

50: APPLICANT:
GOOD BROTHER RESOURCES CO., LTD. 2950 HIGHWAY DRIVE TRAIL
BRITISH COLOMBIA, CANADA

59: BENEFICIARY:
GUANGXI WUZHOU XINDASHUN TRADING CORP.
555, WEST XINXING ROAD, WUZHOU, GUANGXI, P.R.C.

32B: CURRENCY CODE, AMOUNT
CURRENCY: USD（US DOLLAR）
AMOUNT: # 165 000.00 #

41D: AVAILABLE WITH... BY...
ANY BANK IN BENEFICIARY'S COUNTRY

BY NEGOTIATION

42C：DRAFTS AT：

SIGHT FOR 100% OF INVOICE VALUE

42A：DRAWEE：NORTHEAST AMERICA BANK OF CANADA

43P：PARTIAL SHIPMENTS：

ALLOWED

43T：TRANSSHIPMENT：

ALLOWED

44E：PORT OF LOADING：

GUANGZHOU，CHINA

44F：PORT OF DISCHARGE：

MONTREAL，CANADA

44C：LATEST DATE OF SHIPMENT：

22-01-31

45A：DESCRIPTION OF GOODS AND/OR SERVICES

100 M/T/100 BAGS OF SILICON METAL

Si：99% MIN.　　Fe：0.4% MAX.

Al：0.4% MAX.　　Ca：0.1% MAX.

SIZE：10-100 MM 90% MIN.

UNIT PRICE：USD1 650/MT CIF MONTREAL，CANADA

AS PER SALES CONTRACT NO.GBR10086

PACKED IN PLASTIC WOVEN BAGS OF ABOUT 1 000 KGS NET EACH.

46A：DOCUMENTS REQUIRED

（1）SIGNED COMMERCIAL INVOICE IN DUPLICATE.

（2）FULL SET OF CLEAN ON BOARD MARINE BILLS OF LADING IN TWO ORIGINALS AND THREE COPIES，MADE OUT TO ORDER AND ENDORSED IN BLANK，MARKED FREIGHT PREPAID AND NOTIFY APPLICANT EVIDENCING SHIPMENT FROM GUANGZHOU TO MONTREAL BY VESSEL.

（3）INSPECTION CERTIFICATE OF QUALITY AND WEIGHT IN DUPLICATE.

（4）PACKING LIST IN TRIPLICATE.

（5）CERTIFICATE OF ORIGIN G.S.P. FORM A IN 1 ORIGINAL AND 2 COPIES ISSUED BY CORRESPONDING AUTHORITY.

（6）INSURANCE POLICY OR CERTIFICATE ENDORSED IN BLANK WITH CLAIMS PAYABLE AT THE DESTINATION WITH THE SAME CURRENCY OF DRAFT AGAINST ALL RISKS AND WAR RISK OF C.I.C. FOR 110% OF INVOICE VALUE.

（7）BENEFICIARY'S CERTIFICATE CERTIFYING THAT ONE SET OF NON-NEGOTIABLE SHIPPING DOCUMENTS HAS BEEN SENT TO APPLICANT BY EMS WITHIN 7 DAYS AFTER SHIPMENT HAS BEEN EFFECTED.

47A：ADDITIONAL CONDITIONS

（1）ALL DOCUMENTS MUST BEAR THIS CREDIT NUMBER.

（2）SHIPMENT DATE PRIOR TO L/C'S ISSUING DATE IS PROHIBITED.

（3）5% MORE OR LESS IN QUANTITY AND AMOUNT ARE ACCEPTABLE.

（4）GOODS COVERING FREE OF CHARGE ARE ACCEPTABLE.

（5）IF DOCUMENTS PRESENTED UNDER THIS L/C ARE FOUND TO BE DISCREPANT, WE SHALL GIVE ITS NOTICE OF REFUSAL AND SHALL HOLD DOCUMENTS AT YOUR DISPOSAL SUBJECT TO THE FOLLOWING CONDITION："IF WE HAVE NOT RECEIVED YOUR DISPOSAL INSTRUCTIONS FOR THE DISCREPANT DOCUMENTS PRIOR TO RECEIPT OF THE APPLICANT'S WAIVER OF DISCREPANCIES，WE WILL RELEASE DOCUMENTS TO APPLICANT WITHOUT NOTICE TO YOU."

71B：CHARGES

ALL BANKING CHARGES OUTSIDE CANADA，IF ANY，ARE FOR ACCOUNT OF BENEFICIARY.

48：PERIOD FOR PRESENTATION

DOCUMENTS PRESENTED WITHIN 15 DAYS AFTER SHIPMENT BUT WITHIN THE VALIDITY OF THE CREDIT.

49：CONFIRMATION INSTRUCTIONS

WITHOUT

78：INSTR TO PAYG/ACCPTG/NEGOTG BANK

（1）ALL DOCUMENTS MUST BE SENT TO US IN ONE LOT，OUR ADDRESS: NORTHEAST AMERICA BANK OF CANADA，238#，BEIXALU，GM，MONTREAL，CANADA.

（2）A DISCREPANCY FEE OF USD60.00 SHOULD BE DEDUCTED FROM NEGOTIATION AMOUNT FOR EACH PRESENTATION IF DOCUMENTS DO NOT COMPLY WITH L/C TERMS AND CONDITIONS.

（3）UPON RECEIPT OF DOCUMENTS ALONG WITH DRAFT(S) STRICTLY COMPLYING WITH TERMS AND CONDITIONS OF THIS CREDIT，WE WILL REMIT REOCEEDS LESS OUR HANDLING CHARGES TO YOU AS INSTRUCTED.

（4）ONE COPY OF BILL OF LADING AND COMMERCIAL INVOICE IS REQUIRED FOR ISSUING BANK'S FILE. USD10.00 WILL BE CHARGED IF THESE COPIES ARE NOT PRESENTED.

57D："ADVISE THROUGH" BANK：BANK OF CHINA WUZHOU BRANCH

72：SENDER TO RECEIVER INFORMATION

PLS RELEASE THE L/C UPON RECEIPT OF ADVISING FEES.

END OF MESSAGE

补充信息：船名KUIBEIQUE 12WV；船期2022-01-28；提单编号QW001100；实装货物数量100包；净重100 M/T；毛重100.8 M/T；体积40 M^3；货物存放地点为广州黄埔码头2号仓库；要求自行设计唛头；发票编号为LK110026。

（五）信用证 5

Sequence of Total	27：	1/1
Doc. Credit Number	20：	64251EIUR554
Date of Issue	31C：	MAR.10，2021
Expiry	31D：	Date MAY 30，2021 Place CHINA
Applicant	50：	DEXICA SUPERMARK S.A. BOULEVARD PACHECO 44 B-1000，BRUSSELS，BELGIUM
Beneficiary	59：	NANJING ANGEL TEXTILE CO.，LTD. UNIT A 18/F，ANGEL BUILDING，NO.118， XINGMING ROAD，NANJING，CHINA
Amount	32B：	Currency EUR Amount 54 000.00，CIF BRUSSELS
Pos./Neg.Tol.（%）	39A：	5/5
Available...by...Name/Addr.	41D：	CONSTRUCTION BANK OF CHINA NEGOTIATION
Drafts at	42C：	SIGHT
Drawee	42A：	KBC GROUP，BRUSSELS，BELGIUM
Partial Shipments	43P：	ALLOWED
Transshipment	43T：	ALLOWED
Loading in Charge	44E：	NANJING PORT
For Transport to...	44F：	BRUSSELS，BELGIUM
Latest Date of Ship.	44C：	MAY 15，2021
Descript. of Goods	45A：	LADIES GARMENTS 10 800 PCS PACKED IN ONE HUNDRED AND EIGHT CARTONS ONLY
Documents Required	46A：	

+ SIGNED COMMERCIAL INVOICE IN TRIPLICATE.

+ PACKING LIST IN DUPLICATE.

+ 3/3 CLEAN ON BOARD OCEAN BILL OF LADING MADE TO ORDER.ENDORSED IN BLANK，MARKED FREIGHT PREPAID NOTIFYING APPLICANT EVIDENCING SHIPMENT FROM NANJING PORT TO BRUSSELS NOT LATER THAN MAY 2，2021.

+ 1 ORIGINAL（S）OF CERTIFICATE OF ORIGIN，ISSUED BY AUTHORITIES OF COUNTRY OF ORIGIN OF GOODS，ATTESTING ORIGIN OF GOODS.

+ 2 INSURANCE POLICY/CERTIFICATE ENDORSED IN BLANK FOR 110% INVOICE VALUE，COVERING ALL RISKS AND WAR RISK OF PICC（1/1/1981）INCL. WAREHOUSE TO WAREHOUSE AND SHOWING THE CLAIMING CURRENCY IS THE SAME AS THE CURRENCY OF CREDIT.

Additional Cond. 47A：

+ ALL DOCUMENTS MUST INDICATE THE NUMBER.

+ SHIPPING MARK DEXICA

S/C NJT120212
BRUSSELS
C/NO. 1-UP

+ 5 PCT MORE OR LESS IN QUANTITY AND AMOUNT ARE ACCEPTABLE.

Details of Charges 71B：ALL BANK CHARGES OUTSIDE BELGIUM ARE FOR THE BENEFICIARY'S ACCOUNT.

Confirmation 49：WITHOUT

Instructions 78：

+ UPON RECEIPT OF COMMERCIAL DOCUMENTS，WE SHALL REMIT THE PROCEEDS AS PER THE NEGOTIATING BANK'S INSTRUCTIONS.

+ A DISCREPANCY FEE OF USD 50.00 WILL BE DEDUCTED FROM PROCEEDS IF DISCREPANT DOCUMENTS ARE PRESENTED.

+ PLEASE ACKNOWLEDGE RECEIPT AND ADVISE BENEFICIARY UNGENTLY.

补充信息：发票编号为NJT120212；H.S.编码为6204430090；装船日期为2021-05-01；船名为HONGCANG NO.098；净重16.2M/T；毛重16.5M/T；体积25m^3。

项目四

审单和交单

能力目标

能审查信用证、托收、汇付付款方式下全套议付单据，然后按照一定顺序将单据装订好，在规定时间内交给议付银行签收。

知识目标

审单技巧和方法、单据装订方法、交单时间和方法。

思政目标

通过对实际案例的分析和对外贸单据的审核，学生能够深刻体会单据出错给企业带来的损失，从而进一步培养良好的思想政治素质、职业道德和工匠精神，在实践中感悟和践行社会主义核心价值观。

项目引例

遵循“四个一致”原则顺利结汇

2021年10月，广州A出口公司与韩国B贸易公司在中国进出口商品交易会上达成协议，订立了一份陶瓷产品出口贸易合同，采用信用证支付，合同规定交货数量为“ABOUT 8 000 SETS”。A公司原打算备货7 100套，外贸单证员认真查阅了《UCP600》对“ABOUT”的规定：凡“约”“大约”“大概”或类似的词语用于信用证规定的金额、数量和单价时，应解释为有关金额、数量或单价不超过10%的增减幅度。因此，A公司的交货数量应在7 200～8 800套之间。A公司及时调整了备货数量，增加到7 200套，商业发票、装箱单和提单中的交货数量都是“7 200 SETS”，在银行交单时，顺利结汇。

引例评析：本案例告诉我们，单据的审核要遵循“四个一致”原则：单证一致、单单一致、单约一致、货证一致。这就要求我们必须仔细对照合同、信用证、货物情况，严格审查每一份单据。在工作中，要保持高度的责任感和爱岗敬业、乐于奉献的职业精神，树立团队协作意识，做好本职工作，增强为中国特色社会主义共同理想奋斗的信念和信心。

任务一　审单

情境导入

2021年5月8日，广东省广州市春常在进出口公司与英国伦敦一家经营化工商品的公司签订了合同，出口250吨钛白粉，即期信用证付款。5月中旬信用证按时到达，经审查信用证没有问题。6月18日货物装船后，实习单证员覃芳芳用几天时间就把全套议付单据制作或办理好。部门经理小莫要求她抓紧时间审查单据，然后在信用证规定时间内交给议付银行办理议付货款手续。

第一步　教师教

一、审单的含义

对制作好的全套议付单据进行交单前审查核对，以保证单据准确无误。

微课4-1

审单

二、审单的依据

审单依据包括以下六点：

①合同；②信用证；③《UCP600》《URC522》等国际贸易惯例；④商品实际资料；⑤装船指令；⑥国家有关法律、法规。

三、审单方法

1.对制作好的单据一一检查，以保证单据种类足够。

2.对制作好的单据，一一对照信用证各个条款，逐字、逐句、逐段审查；字母、单词、标点符号都要与信用证一致；不符之处要改过来，确保单证相符。

3.审查表达方法，特别是关于信用证要求受益人如何做的文句表达，重点审查受益人是否按照要求完成。

4.审查单据之间的共通性，保证单单相符，不要相互矛盾。

5.遵循“四个一致”原则：单证一致、单单一致、单约一致、货证一致。

第二步　学生做

一、审单练习1

请各个学生小组审查本书项目四任务一第一步教师所做的全套单据，如有问题，则提出来并讨论改正。

二、审单练习2

请各个学生小组审查本书项目四任务三能力训练项目一、二、三所做的全套议付单据，如有问题，则提出来并讨论改正。

三、审单练习3

请各位学生对自己本学期针对某份信用证所制作的全套议付单据进行审查。

任务二 单据装订

情境导入

2021年5月8日，广东省广州市春常在进出口公司与英国伦敦一家经营化工商品的公司签订了合同，出口250吨钛白粉，信用证付款。5月中旬信用证按时到达，经审查信用证没有问题。6月18日货物装船后，实习单证员覃芳芳用几天时间就把全套议付单据制作或办理好，部门经理小莫要求她抓紧时间将全套议付单据装订好。

第一步 教师教

一、单据装订的含义

将制作好的全套议付单据用一定方法按一定顺序收集叠放，加上封面——银行的客户交单联系单，装订成套，以免散乱。

二、单据装订的方法

1.先按照信用证或装船指令单据要求的顺序，找齐各个议付单据种类，备足份数，叠放在一起；

2.封面为客户交单联系单，要填写好；

3.封底为汇票，也要填写好；

4.将三指宽A4白纸剪下，对折，又对折，用以盖住单据的顶头，用订书机钉牢；

5.装订纸不能遮挡交单联系单头部。

三、交单联系单填写

客户交单联系单样本

致：××银行

<table>
<tr><td colspan="16">兹随附下列出口单据一套，信用证业务请按国际商会现行《跟单信用证统一惯例》办理，跟单托收业务请按国际商会现行《托收统一规则》办理。</td></tr>
<tr><td rowspan="2">信用证</td><td colspan="8">开证行：</td><td colspan="7">信用证号：</td></tr>
<tr><td colspan="4">通知行号：</td><td colspan="3">提单日期：</td><td colspan="4">效期：</td><td colspan="4">交单期限：</td></tr>
<tr><td rowspan="3">无证托收</td><td colspan="15">付款人全名及详址：</td></tr>
<tr><td colspan="15">托收行外文名称及详址（供参考）：</td></tr>
<tr><td colspan="8">交单方式：（ ）D/P （ ）D/A</td><td colspan="7">付款期限：</td></tr>
<tr><td colspan="6">发票编号：</td><td colspan="5">核销单编号：</td><td colspan="5">金额：</td></tr>
<tr><td rowspan="2">单据</td><td>名称</td><td>汇票</td><td>发票</td><td>海关发票</td><td>装箱/重量单</td><td>产地证</td><td>G.S.P FORM A</td><td>数量/质量/重量证书</td><td>检验分析证</td><td>出口许可证</td><td>保险单</td><td>运输单据</td><td>电抄</td><td>受益人证明</td><td>船公司证明</td></tr>
<tr><td>份数</td><td></td><td></td><td></td><td></td><td></td><td></td><td></td><td></td><td></td><td></td><td></td><td></td><td></td><td></td><td></td></tr>
</table>

续表

<table>
<tr><td colspan="4">委办事项：（打“×”者）
（　　）上述单据请按我司与贵行签订之总质押书办理押汇。
（　　）上述单据系代理出口项下业务，收妥后请原币划＿＿＿＿开户行：＿＿＿＿＿＿＿＿＿＿＿，账号：＿＿＿＿＿＿＿＿＿＿＿＿＿＿＿＿＿＿＿＿＿＿
（　　）若付款人拒绝付款/承兑，不必做成拒绝证书，但须以电传通知我司。
（　　）附信用证及修改书共＿＿纸。
（　　）单据中有下列不符点：
　　（　　）请向开证行寄单，我司承担一切责任。
　　（　　）请电询开证行同意后再寄单。
　　（　　）＿＿＿＿＿＿＿＿＿＿＿＿＿＿＿＿＿＿＿＿＿＿＿＿＿
　　公司联系人：　　　　　　　联系电话：　　　　　　公司公章：</td></tr>
<tr><td rowspan="10">银行审单记录：</td><td colspan="3">银行接单日期：</td></tr>
<tr><td colspan="2">索汇金额：</td><td>BP NO.</td></tr>
<tr><td colspan="2">寄单日期：</td><td>OC NO.</td></tr>
<tr><td rowspan="6">银行费用</td><td>通知/保兑：</td><td rowspan="3">索汇方式：</td></tr>
<tr><td>议/承付：</td></tr>
<tr><td>邮费：</td></tr>
<tr><td>电传：</td><td rowspan="3">寄单方式：</td></tr>
<tr><td></td></tr>
<tr><td>小计：</td></tr>
<tr><td colspan="2">费用由　　　　　　　　承担</td><td></td></tr>
<tr><td>退单记录：</td><td colspan="2">银行经办：</td><td>银行复核：</td></tr>
</table>

第二步　学生做

一、单据装订练习1

请各个学生小组将本书项目四任务二第一步教师所做的全套单据打印出来，然后按照一定顺序装订好。

二、单据装订练习2

请各位学生将自己本学期针对某份信用证所制作的全套议付单据，按照一定顺序装订好。

客户交单联系单样本

致：中国银行

兹随附下列出口单据一套，信用证业务请按国际商会现行《跟单信用证统一惯例》办理，跟单托收业务请按国际商会现行《托收统一规则》办理。

信用证	开证行：		信用证号：	
	通知行号：	提单日期：	效期：	交单期限：
无证托收	付款人全名及详址：			
	托收行外文名称及详址（供参考）：			
	交单方式：（ ）D/P （ ）D/A		付款期限：	
发票编号：		核销单编号：	金额：	

单据	名称	汇票	发票	海关发票	装箱/重量单	产地证	G.S.P FORM A	数量/质量/重量证书	检验分析证	出口许可证	保险单	运输单据	电抄	受益人证明	船公司证明
	份数	1	3		3	2			2	1		2		2	

委办事项：（打“×”者）

（ ）上述单据请按我司与贵行签订之总质押书办理押汇。

（×）上述单据系代理出口项下业务，收妥后请原币划________开户行：广州中行新窖分行，账号：________________

（×）若付款人拒绝付款/承兑，不必做成拒绝证书，但须以电传通知我司。

（×）附信用证及修改书共 1 纸。

（×）单据中有下列不符点：（×）请向开证行寄单，我司承担一切责任。

（×）请电询开证行同意后再寄单。

（ ）________________

（ ）________________

公司联系人： 联系电话： 公司公章：

银行审单记录：	银行接单日期：		
	索汇金额：		BP NO.
	寄单日期：		OC NO.
	银行费用	通知/保兑：	索汇方式：
		议/承付：	
		邮费：	
		电传：	寄单方式：
		小计：	
	费用由 承担		
退单记录：	银行经办：		银行复核：

任务三　交单

情境导入

2021年5月8日，广东省广州市春常在进出口公司与英国伦敦一家经营化工商品的公司签订了合同，出口250吨钛白粉，信用证付款。5月中旬信用证按时到达，经审查信用证没有问题。6月18日货物装船后，实习单证员覃芳芳用几天时间就把全套议付单据制作或办理好。部门经理小莫要求她在信用证规定时间内交给议付银行办理议付货款手续。

第一步　教师教

一、交单的含义

出口人将全套议付单据在一定时间内交给议付银行签收。

微课4-2

交单

二、交单时间

1.在信用证付款方式下，如果信用证规定了交单期限，则在规定交单期限内交单。

2.在信用证付款方式下，如果信用证没规定交单期，则在提单日期后21日内交单，但不能超过信用证有效期。

3.在信用证付款方式下，一般规定提单日期后15日（两周）内交单。出口人可用第一周集中时间二次做单，在第二周交单。

4.在托收或汇付付款方式下，虽然没有规定明确的交单期限，但出口人在制作好单据后也应尽早交单，尽早回笼货款，减少利息支出。

5.在时间上，出口人要比规定的交单时间稍微提前交单，以保证单据不合格被议付银行退单时还有足够时间修改处理或补单。

三、交单方法

1.将全套议付单据收齐装订好。

2.将信用证原件或修改书找出，放在全套单据上面。

3.将以上资料全部送交议付银行签收，取得回执，完成交单义务。

第二步　学生做

一、交单练习1

请各个学生小组将本书项目四任务三第一步教师所做的全套单据打印出来，然后按照一定顺序装订好，不同小组模拟交单。一组扮演出口人交单，另一小组扮演议付银行签收。

二、交单练习2

请各位学生将自己本学期针对某份信用证所制作的全部议付单据审查装订好，交给老师。

请对照所给的信用证，审查单据。

27： SEQUENCE OF TOTAL：1/1

40A： FORM OF DOCUMENTARY CREDIT：IRREVOCABLE

20： DOCUMENTARY CREDIT NUMBER：GTHW2012-0331E

31C： DATE OF ISSUE：21-03-16

40E： APPLICABLE RULES：ICC UCP LATEST VERSION

31D： DATE AND PLACE OF EXPIRY：
21-05-30 IN BENEFICIARY'S COUNTRY

50： APPLICANT：
XIHANOOK INTERNATIONAL CO.，LTD.，136# BRIGHT STREET，BANGKOK THAILAND

59： BENEFICIARY：
NO.1 FOSHAN NANHAI NON-FERROUS METAL MANUFACTURER
288#，PINGTAN INDUSTRIAL ZONE，NANHAI CITY，FOSHAN，GUANGDONG，CHINA.

32B： CURRENCY CODE，AMOUNT
CURRENCY：USD（US DOLLAR）
AMOUNT：# 54 400 #（FIFTY FOUR THOUSAND FOUR HUNDRED ONLY）

41D： AVAILABLE WITH...BY... NAME & ADDR.
ANY BANK IN BENEFICIARY'S COUNTRY
BY NEGOTIATION

42C： DRAFTS AT：
SIGHT FOR 100% OF INVOICE VALUE

42A： DRAWEE：HUGE STANDARD CHARTERED BANK BANGKOK

43P： PARTIAL SHIPMENTS：
NOT ALLOWED

43T： TRANSSHIPMENT：
ALLOWED

44E： PORT OF LOADING：
NANHAI，FOSHAN，CHINA

44F： PORT OF DISCHARGE：
BANGKOK，THAILAND

44C： LATEST DATE OF SHIPMENT：
21-05-15

45A： DESCRIPTION OF GOODS AND/OR SERVICES
5 000 KGS OF BRASS ELECTRODE WIRE TRIANGLE BRAND
CU：90% MIN.
SIZE：Φ0.5 MM.
UNIT PRICE：USD10.88 PER KG CIF BANGKOK，THAILAND
AS PER SALES CONTRACT NO.XHB1203008
PACKED IN STRONG EXPORT CARTONS OF ABOUT 50 KGS NET EACH

46A： DOCUMENTS REQUIRED

(1) SIGNED COMMERCIAL INVOICE IN TRIPLICATE.

(2) FULL SET OF CLEAN ON BOARD MARINE BILLS OF LADING IN TWO ORIGINALS AND 3 COPIES, MADE OUT TO ORDER BLANK ENDORSED MARKED FREIGHT PREPAID, NOTIFYING APPLICANT EVIDENCING SHIPMENT FROM FOSHAN TO BANGKOK.

(3) INSPECTION CERTIFICATE OF QUALITY AND WEIGHT ISSUED BY CIQ.

(4) PACKING LIST IN TWO COPIES.

(5) CERTIFICATE OF ORIGIN FORM E ISSUED BY CORRESPONDING AUTHORITY IN DUPLICATE.

(6) INSURANCE POLICY OR CERTIFICATE ENDORSED IN BLANK WITH CLAIM PAYALBE AT DFESTINATION WITH THE SAME CURRENCY OF DRAFT AGAINST ALL RISKS OF C.I.C. FOR 120% OF INVOICE VALUE.

(7) BENEFICIARY'S CERTIFICATE CERTIFYING THAT ONE SET OF NON-NEGOTIABLE SHIPPING DOCUMENT HAS BEEN SENT TO APPLICANT BY EMS WITHIN 7 DAYS AFTER SHIPMENT HAS BEEN EFFECTED.

47A: ADDITIONAL CONDITIONS

(1) ALL DOCUMENTS MUST BEAR THIS CREDIT NUMBER.

(2) SHIPMENT DATE PRIOR TO L/C'S ISSUING DATE IS NOT ACCEPTABLE.

(3) 5% MORE OR LESS IN QUANTITY AND AMOUNT ARE BOTH ACCEPTABLE.

(4) IF DOCUMENTS PRESENTED UNDER THIS L/C ARE FOUND TO BE DISCREPANT, WE SHALL GIVE ITS NOTICE OF REFUSAL AND SHALL HOLD DOCUMENTS AT YOUR DISPOSAL SUBJECT TO THE FOLLOWING CONDITION: "IF WE HAVE NOT RECEIVED YOUR DISPOSAL INSTRUCTIONS FOR THE DISCREPANT DOCUMENTS PRIOR TO RECEIPT OF THE APPLICANT'S WAIVER OF DISCREPANCIES, WE WILL RELEASE DOCUMENTS TO APPLICANT WITHOUT NOTICE TO YOU."

71B: CHARGES

ALL BANKING CHARGES OUTSIDE THAILAND, IF ANY, ARE FOR ACCOUNT OF BENEFICIARY.

48: PERIOD FOR PRESENTATION

DOCUMENTS MUST BE PRESENTED WITHIN 15 DAYS AFTER SHIPMENT BUT WITHIN THE VALIDITY OF THE CREDIT.

49: CONFIRMATION INSTRUCTIONS:

WITHOUT

78: INSTR TO PAYG/ACCPTG/NGGOTG BANK

(1) ALL DOCUMENTS MUST BE SENT TO US BY EMS IN ONE LOT, OUR ADDRESS:

HUGE STANDARD CHARTERED BANK BANGKOK, 238#, GATEWAY AVENUE, BANGKOK, THAILAND.

(2) A DISCREPANCY FEE OF USD60.00 SHOULD BE DEDUCTED FROM NEGOTIATION AMOUNT FOR EACH PRESENTATION IF DOCUMENTS DO NOT COMPLY WITH L/C

TERMS AND CONDITIONS.

（3）UPON RECEIPT OF DOCUMENTS ALONG WITH DRAFT（S）STRICTLY COMPLYING WITH TERMS AND CONDITIONS OF THIS CREDIT，WE WILL REMIT PROCEEDS LESS OUR HANDLING CHARGES TO YOU AS INSTRUCTED.

（4）ONE COPY OF BILL OF LADING AND COMMERCIAL INVOICE IS REQUIRED FOR ISSUING BANK'S FILE. USD10.00 WILL BE CHARGED IF THESE COPIES ARE NOT PRESENTED.

57D：ADVISE THROUGHBANK

BANK OF CHINA，FOSHAN NANHAI BRANCH

72：SENDER TO RECEIVER INFORMATION

PLS RELEASE THE L/C UPON RECEIPT OF ADVISING FEES.

END OF MESSAGE

补充信息：船名：GREATPRINCE 3090V；船期：2021-05-13；货物数量：100箱；净重：5 000KGS；毛重：5 300KGS；体积：15 M^3；货物存放地点：佛山南海金山港5号仓。要求卖方设计唛头。

COMMERCIAL INVOICE

DATE：MAY 3，2021

NO.：20211011

TO：XIHANOOK INTERNATIONAL CO.，LTD.，136# BRIGHT STREET，BANGKOK THAILAND

SHIPMENT FROM NANHAI TO BANGKOK BY VESSEL

NAME OF GOODS	SPECIFICATION	QUANTITY	MARKS & NOS.	N.W./G.W.	UNIT PRICE
BRASS ELECTRODE WIRE TRIANGLE BRAND	CU:90% MIN. SIZE:Φ0.5 MM.	5 000 KGS （100 CARTONS）	XIHANOOK GTHW2012-0331E BANGKOK C/NO.1-100	5 000 KGS 5 300 KGS	USD10.88 RER KG CIF BANGKOK TOTAL: USD54 400.00

SAY：US DOLLARS FIFTY FOUR THOUSAND FOUR HUNDRED ONLY

NO.OF L/C：GTHW2012-0331E

AS PER ORDER NO.：XHB1203008

NO.1 FOSHAN NANHAI NON-FERROUS METAL MANUFACTURER

雷楚君

PACKING　LIST

DATE：MAY 5,2021

NO.：20211011

TO：XIHANOOK INTERNATIONAL CO.，LTD.，136# BRIGHT STREET，BANGK THAILAND

SHIPMENT FROM NANHAI TO BANGKOK BY VESSEL

MARK & NOS.	NAME OF GOODS	WAY OF PACKING	QUANTITY	N.W./G.W.	MEASUREMENT
XIHANOOK GTHW2012-0331E BANGKOK C/NO.1-100	BRASS ELECTRODE WIRE TRIANGLE BRAND	PACKED IN STRONG EXPORT CARTONS OF ABOUT 50 KGS NET EACH.	100 CARTONS	5 000 KGS 5 300 KGS	$15M^3$

SAY：ONE HUNDRED CARTONS ONLY

NO.OF L/C：GTHW2012-0331E

NO.1 FOSHAN NANHAI NON-FERROUS METAL MANUFACTURER

雷楚君

综合训练

请根据给出的信用证审查下面的全套议付单据

27 SEQUENCE OF TOTAL

1/1

40A FROM OF L/C

IRREVOCABLE

20 DOCUMENT CREDIT NO.

00175427KZ133511

31C DATE OF ISSUE（Y/N/T）

20-11-01

40E APPLICABLE RULES

UCP LATEST VERSION

31D DATE AND PLACE OF EXPIRE

21-01-15，CHINA

50 APPLICANT

TIVOL PRODUCTS PL INC.

BERST OFSGADE 48，ROTTERDAM，THE NETHERLANDS

59 BENEFICIARY

GUANGZHOU XINGSHENG TOY TRADING CO.，LTD

RM.3010-3011 ON THE FIRST FLOOR

INTERNATIONAL TOY CITY. YIDE WEST

RD.，GUANGZHOU，CHINA

随堂测 4

32B CURRENCY CODE，AMOUNT
USD13 750.00

39A PERCENTAGE CREDIT AMOUNT
05/05

41D AVAILABLE WITH... BY...
ANY BANK IN CHINA
BY NEGOTIATION

42C DRAFTS AT
SIGHT

42A DRAWEE
BANK OF ABN AMRO

43P PARTIAL SHIPMENT
NOT ALLOWED

43T TRANSSHIPMENT
ALLOWED

44E PORT OF LOADING
GUANGZHOU

44F PORT OF DISCHARGE
ROTTERDAM

44C LATEST DATE OF SHIPMENT
20-12-30

45A DESCRIPTION OF GOODS
ART.NO. KC2048： 300 PIECES LONG HAIR PIG AT USD15 PER PIECE CIFC5% ROTTERDAM
ART.NO.KC2049： 500 PIECES PLUSH BEAR AT USD18.5 PER PIECE CIFC5% ROTTERDAM
ALL GOODS SHOULD BE IN HIGH QUALITY AND GOOD PACKING
PACKED IN PLASTIC BAG OF ONE PIECE EACH， 20 PIECES TO A CARTON

46A DOCUMENTS REQUIRED

+ SIGNED COMMERCIAL INVOICE 3-FOLD.

+ FULL SET OF CLEAN ON BOARD OCEAN BILL OF LADING MAKE OUT TO ORDER AND BLANK ENDORSED,MARKED FREIGHT PREPAID AND NOTIFY APPLICANT.

+ PACKED LIST 3-FOLD.

+ CERTIFICATE OF ORIGIN G.S.P FORM A.

+ INSURANCE POLICY ISSUED TO THE APPLICANT, COVERING RISKS AS PER INSTITUTE CARGO CLAUSE (A) INCLUDING WAREHOUSE TO WAREHOUSE CLAUSE UP TO FINAL DESTINATION AT SCHORNORF, FOR AT LEAST 110 PCT OF THE CIF VALUE, MARKED PREMIUM PAID,SHOWING CLAIM PAYABLE IN GERMANY.

+ BENEFICIARY'S CERTIFICATE EVIDENCING THAT AN ORIGINAL CARTON OF PRODUCTION SAMPLES HAS BEEN SENT TO APPLICANT BY COURIER SERVICE AT LEAST ONE WEEK PRIOR TO SHIPMENT OF GOODS.

47A ADDITONAL CONDITIONS

+ALL DOCUMENTS MUST BEAR THE L/C NO.

+DOCUMENTS MUST HAVE TO BE SENT TO US BY COURIER.

+ALL DOCUMENTS MUST BE ISSUED IN ENGLISH LANGUAGE.

+A DISCREPANCY FEE OF EUR 75.00 OR EQUIVALENT TO BE DECUCTED FROM PROCEEDS OF DOCUMENTS PRESENTED WITH DISCREPANCY (IES). ALL ADDITIONAL EXPENSES OF RESULTINGE THER OF WILL ALSO BE FOR BENEFICIARY'S ACCOUNT.

71B CHARGES

+ALL CHARGES OUTSIDE GERMANY ARE ON BENEFICIARY'S ACCOUNT.

48 PERIOD FOR PRESENTATION

DOCUMENTS TO BE PRESENTED WITHIN 14 DAYS AFTER THE DATE OF SHIPMENT BUT WITHIN THE VALIDITY OF THE CREDT.

49 CONFIRMATION INSTRUCTION

WITHOUT

78 INSTR TO PAY/ACCEP/NEG

+ UPON RECEIPT OF CREDIT CONFORM DOCUMENTS AT OUR COUNTERS WE SHALL REMIT PROCEEDS AT MATURITY, AS PER PRESENTING BANK'S INSTRUCTIONS LESS USD35.00 SWIFT CHARGES, VALUE TWO USA/GERMANY BUSINESS DAYS.

OUR ADDRESS READS AS FOLLOWS:

补充信息：实际装40箱（800个）；净重530千克；毛重570千克；体积12立方米；船期2020-12-20；发票号码和日期自定，自行设计唛头。

COMMERCIAL INVOICE

DATE: DEC. 9,2020

NO.: GBL2020

TO: TIVOL PRODUCTS PL INC.

BERST OFSGADE 48, ROTTERDAM, THE NETHERLANDS

SHIPMENT FROM GUANGZHOU TO ROTTERDAM BY VESSEL

NAME OF GOODS	SPECIFICATION	QUANTITY	MARKS & NOS.	N.W./G.W.	UNIT PRICE
LONG HAIR PIG	ART.NO. KC2048	300 PIECES (15CARTONS)	TIVOL 00175427KZ133511	N.W. 530 KGS	USD15 PER PIECE CIFC5% ROTTERDAM
PLUSH BEAR	ART.NO.KC2049	500 PIECES (25 CARTONS)	ROTTERDAM C/NO.1-40		USD18.5 PER PIECE CIFC5% ROTTERDAM TOTAL: USD 13 750.00

SAY: US DOLLARS THIRTEEN THOUSAND SEVEN HUNDRED AND FIFTY ONLY

NO.OF L/C: 00175427KZ133511

GUANGZHOU XINGSHENG TOY TRADING CO., LTD

罗新雄

BILL OF LADING

<table>
<tr><td colspan="3">Shipper
GUANGZHOU XINGSHENG TOY TRADING CO., LTD
RM.3010-3011 ON THE FIRST FLOOR INTERNATIONAL
TOY CITY. YIDE WEST RD., GUANGZHOU, CHINA</td><td colspan="3">B/L NO.</td></tr>
<tr><td colspan="3">Consignee
TO ODER</td><td colspan="3">Combined transport BILL OF LADING</td></tr>
<tr><td colspan="3">Notify Party
TIVOL PRODUCTS PL INC.
BERST OFSGADE 48, ROTTERDAM, THE NETHERLANDS</td><td colspan="3" rowspan="3">For delivery of goods please apply to:</td></tr>
<tr><td>Pre-carriage by</td><td colspan="2">Place of Receipt</td></tr>
<tr><td>Ocean Vessel Voy. No.
YC LAKE 001</td><td colspan="2">Port of Loading
GUANGZHOU</td></tr>
<tr><td>Port of Discharge
ROTTERDAM</td><td colspan="3">Place of Delivery</td><td colspan="2">Final Destination for the Merchant's Reference only</td></tr>
<tr><td>Container, Seal No.& Marks &Nos.
TIVOL
00175427KZ133511
ROTTERDAM
C/NO.1-40</td><td colspan="3">No. of Package & Description of Goods
FOURTY (40) CARTONS
LONG HAIR PIG,
PLUSH BEAR
NO. OF L/C: 00175427KZ133511</td><td>Gross Weight(Kgs)
570</td><td>Measurement(m^3)
12</td></tr>
<tr><td>FREIGHT & CHARGES</td><td>Revenue Tons</td><td colspan="2">Rate Per</td><td>Prepaid ✓</td><td>Collect</td></tr>
<tr><td rowspan="2">Ex. Rate:</td><td>Prepaid at
GUANGZHOU</td><td colspan="2">Payable at
GUANGZHOU</td><td colspan="2">Place and Date of Issue
GUANGZHOU, DCE. 20, 2020</td></tr>
<tr><td>Total prepaid</td><td colspan="2">No. of Original B(s)/L
TWO (2)</td><td colspan="2">Stamp & Signature</td></tr>
</table>

PACKING LIST

DATE: DEC.10, 2020

NO.: GBL2020

TO: TIVOL PRODUCTS PL INC.

BERST OFSGADE 48, ROTTERDAM, THE NETHERLANDS

SHIPMENT FROM GUANGZHOU TO ROTTERDAM BY VESSEL

MARK & NOS.	NAME OF GOODS	WAY OF PACKING	QUANTITY	N.W./G.W.	MEASUREMENT
TIVOL 00175427KZ133511 ROTTERDAM C/NO.1-40	LONG HAIR PIG, PLUSH BEAR	PACKED IN PLASTIC BAG OF ONE PIECE EACH, 20 PIECES TO A CARTON	40 CARTONS	N.W: 530 KGS GW: 570 KGS	12 CBM

SAY: FORTY CARTONS ONLY

NO. OF L/C: 00175427KZ133511

GUANGZHOU XINGSHENG TOY TRADING CO., LTD

罗新雄

ORIGINAL

<table>
<tr><td colspan="3">1. Goods consigned from (Exporter's business name, address, country)
GUANGZHOU XINGSHENG TOY TRADING CO., LTD
RM. 3010-3011 ON THE FIRST FLOOR INTERNATIONAL
TOY CITY. YIDE WEST RD., GUANGZHOU, CHINA</td><td colspan="3" rowspan="2">Reference No.4501290/WJG09/099
GENERALIZED SYSTEM OF PREFERENCES
CERTIFICATE OF ORIGIN
(Combined declaration and certificate)
FORM A
Issued in THE PEOPLE'S REPUBLIC OF CHINA
(country)
See notes overleaf</td></tr>
<tr><td colspan="3">2. Goods consigned to (Consignee's name, address, country)
TIVOL PRODUCTS PL INC. BERST OFSGADE 48,
ROTTERDAM, THE NETHERLANDS</td></tr>
<tr><td colspan="3">3. Means of transport and route (as for as known)
FROM GUANGZHOU TO ROTTERDAM BY VESSEL</td><td colspan="3">4. For official use</td></tr>
<tr><td>5. Item number</td><td>6. Marks and numbers of packages</td><td>7. Number and kind of packages; description of goods</td><td>8. Origin criterion (see notes overleaf)</td><td>9. Gross weight or other quantity</td><td>10. Number and date of invoice</td></tr>
<tr><td>01
02</td><td>TIVOL
00175427KZ133511
ROTTERDAM
C/NO.1-40</td><td>FIFTEEN (15) CARTONS OF LONG HAIR PIG
TWENTY-FIVE (25) CARTONS OF PLUSH BEAR
NO.OF L/C: 00175427KZ133511
*** *** ***</td><td>"P"</td><td>570 KGS</td><td>GBL2009
DEC.9, 2020</td></tr>
<tr><td colspan="3">11. Certification
It is hereby certified, on the basis of control carried out, that the declaration by the exporter is correct.

GUANGZHOU: DEC.12, 2020, 郝帅奇
Place and date, signature and stamp of certifying authority</td><td colspan="3">12. Declaration by the exporter
The undersigned hereby declares that the above details and statements are correct; that all the goods were
Produced in CHINA
(country)
And that they comply with the origin requirements specified for those goods in the Generalized System of Preferences for goods exported to
THE NETHERLANDS
(importing country)

GUANGZHOU: DEC.10, 2020, 甄梅里
place and date, signature of authorized signatory</td></tr>
</table>

海洋货物运输保险单

MARINE CARGO TRANSPORTATION INSURANCE POLICY

I/P: TWO

NUMBER OF ORIGINAL

发票号码 GBL2020　　　　保险单号次

Invoice No.　　　　Policy No.

中国人民保险公司（以下简称本公司）根据 广州兴盛玩具贸易公司

（以下简称被保险人）的要求由被保险人向本公司缴付约定的保险费，按照本保险单承担的险别和背后所载条款与下列条款承担下述货物运输保险，特立本保险单。

This Policy of Insurance witnesses that the People's Insurance Company of China（hereinafter called "The Company"）, at the request of GUANGZHOU XINGSHENG TOY TRADING CO., LTD（hereinafter called the "Insured"）and in consideration of the agreed premium being paid to the company by the Insured, undertakes to insure the under-mentioned goods in transportation subject to the conditions of this policy as per the Clauses printed overleaf and other special Clauses attached hereon.

标记 Marks & Nos.	包装及数量 Packing & Quantity	保险货物项目 Description of Goods	保险金额 Amount Insured
TIVOL 00175427KZ133511 ROTTERDAM C/NO.1-40	PACKED IN PLASTIC BAG OF ONE PIECE EACH, 20 PIECES TO A CARTON FOURTY(40) CARTONS	LONG HAIR PIG PLUSH BEAR NO. OF L/C: 00175427KZ133511	USD 13 750.00

总保险金额：

Total Amount Insured: US DOLLARS THIRTEEN THOUSAND SEVEN HUNDRED AND FIFTY ONLY

保费　　　　费率　　　　装载工具

Premium as arranged…… Rate as arranged…… per conveyance S.S. YC LAKE 001

开航日期　　　　自　　　　至

Slg.on or abt DCE. 20, 2020 from GUANGZHOU to ROTTERDAM

承保险别：

Conditions

所保货物，如遇风险，本公司凭本保险单及其有关证件给付赔款。

所保货物，如发生保险单项下负责赔偿的损失或事故，应立即通知本公司下述代理人查勘。

Claims, if any, payable in surrender of this Policy together with other relevant documents. In the event of accident whereby loss or damage may result in a claim under this Policy immediate notice applying for survey must be given to Company's Agent as mentioned hereunder.

中国人民保险公司

THE PEOPLE'S INSURANCE CO.OF CHINA

赔款偿付地点

Claim payable at THE NETHERLANDS

出单公司地址

Address of Issuing Office

日期

Date DEC.20, 2020

BENEFICIARY'S CERTIFICATE

DATE: NOV.20, 2020

TO: TIVOL PRODUCTS PL INC.

BERST OFSGADE 48, ROTTERDAM, THE NETHERLANDS

RE: INVOICE NO.GBL2020, LONG HAIR PIG AND PLUSH BEAR, 40 CARTONS

WE HEREBY CERTIFY THAT AN ORIGINAL CARTON OF PRODCUTION SAMPLES HAS BEEN SENT TO APPLICANT BY COURIER SERVICE AT LEAST ONE WEEK PRIOR TO SHIPMENT OF GOODS.

NO. OF L/C: 00175427KZ133511

GUANGZHOU XINGSHENG TOY TRADING CO., LTD

罗新雄

1

汇　票

凭

Drawn under BANK OF ABN AMRO

信用证　第　号

L/C .NO. 00175427KZ133511

日期　年　月　日

Dated NOV.1,2020

按　息　付 款

Payable with interest @ % per annum

号码　汇票金额　中国，广州　年　月　日

NO. ... GBL2020 ....Exchange for USD 13 750.00 GUANGZHOU, China. DEC. 21, 2020

见票　日后（本汇票之复本未付）付

At ....sight of this FIRST of Exchange (Second of exchange being unpaid)

Pay to the order of BANK OF CHINA GUANGZHOU BRANCH 或其指定人

金 额

The sum of US DOLLARS THIRTEEN THOUSAND SEVEN HUNDRED AND FIFTY ONLY

此致

To: BANK OF ABN AMRO

GUANGZHOU XINGSHENG TOY TRADING CO., LTD

罗新雄

参考文献

［1］章安平. 外贸单证操作［M］. 5版. 北京：高等教育出版社，2020.
［2］莫运襟. 最新出口流程及模拟［M］. 北京：化学工业出版社，2009.
［3］莫运襟. 最新国际贸易实务［M］. 南宁：广西民族出版社，2007.
［4］周文苑. 外贸单证操作与实训指导［M］. 北京：清华大学出版社，2019.
［5］屈大磊. 国际贸易实务［M］. 2版. 北京：北京航空航天大学出版社，2017.
［6］李乐锋. 国际贸易实务［M］. 2版. 南京：南京大学出版社，2015.